# STUDIES IN HOMICIDE

*Readers in Social Problems*

DONALD R. CRESSEY, CONSULTING EDITOR
UNIVERSITY OF CALIFORNIA, SANTA BARBARA

# STUDIES IN HOMICIDE

EDITED BY

## MARVIN E. WOLFGANG

PROFESSOR OF SOCIOLOGY
UNIVERSITY OF PENNSYLVANIA

HARPER & ROW
*Publishers*

NEW YORK, EVANSTON, AND LONDON

# CONTENTS

v

## IV. SOME CROSS-CULTURAL EVIDENCE

## V. SUGGESTED THEORETICAL PROPOSITIONS

# PREFACE

THE INDIVIDUAL who expresses violent aggression in the form of a criminal slaying has long been the object of inquiry, fiction, and fear. Law, psychiatry, sociology, psychology, and anthropology have been the major disciplinary perspectives used to develop theoretical insights and empirical research findings about homicide. Like any complex phenomenon, homicide cannot readily be explained or predicted without attention to subtypes and differences in the links of causal chains. Yet certain regularities or uniformities have emerged from systematic research conducted over time and in different societies. Scholars still have much to learn about this form of human behavior, but the studies included in this volume represent some of the major efforts to apply the rubrics of the scientific method to the collection and interpretation of data.

More professional literature has appeared on homicide than on any other specific criminal offense, perhaps because murder has traditionally been viewed in most cultures as the most serious form of violation of collective life. Any injury short of death renders the victim capable of at least some degree of return to his previctimized status. Neither individual nor societal homeostasis is possible with homicide; a piece of the island of humanity is violently torn away. Often the notions of retribution and compassion mingle in society's reaction both to the offender and to the offended. More attention has been focused on the one who remains after the deadly drama, for he is exposed to the institutional processes of arrest, trial, and punishment, as well as being available for study. But as a few of the selections included in this book reveal, the role of the victim as a contributor to his own victimization is now being analyzed.

It should be noted that in this collection, articles and excerpts from books have been kept intact. All references have been retained. I am grateful to the authors and publishers for permission to include the items that appear here. The omission of important works is due to my efforts to have a broad scope while also being cognizant of constraints on size of the book.

The contributors come from varied disciplines and their writings reflect these differences. I have not sought to integrate their perspectives save through whatever theoretical binding may come from my own reference to a subculture of violence. I should rather hope that the students and other scholars who read these selections will be stimulated to think in creatively analytical ways that will lead to increasingly sophisticated theory and research.

MARVIN E. WOLFGANG

*Philadelphia*

# PART I

# Introduction

# PART I

# Introduction

# Criminal Homicide
# and the
# Subculture of Violence

## MARVIN E. WOLFGANG

THE LEVEL and types of data used in sociological research on homicide and other assaultive crimes vary considerably. Some researchers, like Harlan[1] and myself[2] have used predominantly police statistics, others have used court convictions, and still others, like Gillin,[3] prisoner populations. Rates vary, of course, according to the official level chosen, but for general theorizing purposes these differences are not serious impediments. Moreover, although the level of police efficiency in apprehending offenders and the probability of offense reporting may vary considerably between and within culture areas, homicide anywhere still remains one of the most highly visible crimes. Consistency of social variables over time and space tends to reduce the impact of valid criticisms which these probability functions may have in a detailed critique of international criminal statistics.

## AGE AND SEX

If aggression in general is associated with age and sex, homicide as an explicit behavioral form of aggression is es-

This introduction by the editor is, for the most part, abstracted from Marvin E. Wolfgang and Franco Ferracuti, *The Subculture of Violence —Towards an Integrated Theory in Criminology*, London: Tavistock, chap. V, in press, and from the Italian edition, *Il comportamento violento*, Milan: Giuffre, 1966.

All footnotes appear in the Notes section, grouped by article, at the end of this book.

pecially so. Almost universally it can be asserted that the highest incidence of assaultive crimes like homicide are committed by young offenders, most of whom are in their twenties, many of whom are in their late teens or early thirties.[4] Males predominate everywhere.[5] But as Verkko suggested, when the general criminal homicide rate is low in a given culture, the percentage of female offenders is generally higher than when the homicide rate is high, thus suggesting a greater stability in the amount of female homicide.[6]

In reviewing the literature from various disciplines on the topic of homicide, we are struck with the fact that very violent crimes are rarely committed by children, even males, under fourteen or by persons over forty years of age. When these cases occur, causal agents most frequently concentrate around individualistic pathologies like brain damage, abnormal electroencephalographic patterns, clear-cut and marked psychic disturbance, and often without the usual accompanying social pathologies or immersion in a culture milieu where violence is a more common mode of interpersonal action.[7] The child who kills his playmate or sibling and the middle-aged and middle-class woman who kills her husband are regularly perceived by officialdom as having engaged in behavior alien to their past personality performances and are often excused by reason of insanity or some similar social sinecure of exoneration. The slum delinquent gang member who slays in a fight and the barroom brawler who ends a drunken drama with death are officially indicted for homicides that appear to culminate lives dethroned of propriety and dignity, devoted to destruction of property and person. (We are not here arguing on behalf of the persons from our latter example as also being subjects for social protection, although we would strongly maintain that social determinism needs as much judicial recognition as does psychic determinism relative to the "not-guilty-by-reason-of" plea.)

In general, a review of the statistical and clinical literature from many societies indicates that the age-sex category of youthful males contains the highest association with violent crime and that physically aggressive behavior for this group converges with notions about the masculine ideal.

## SOCIAL CLASS

Social class, whatever the position of a society on a closed-open class continuum, looms large in all studies of violent crime. Although some exceptions may be noted, the finding of higher-class suicide and lower-class homicide have been so widely and firmly documented that Morselli[8] long ago posited a kind of social organic law about it, Verkko[9] and others have speculated about it as two streams of violence stemming from the same river of aggression, and Henry and Short[10] have elaborately discussed social psychological variables of the strength of internal and external restraints in relation to self- and other-directed aggression. Henry and Short review relevant studies and with minor exceptions conclude that the higher the class status, the higher the incidence of suicide, and the lower the class status, the higher the incidence of homicide. In 1958, reporting on my own Philadelphia study of homicide and reviewing previous sociological studies with rates according to social class indicators, I noted that in the five-year Philadelphia study all homicides had been committed by representatives from the blue-collar, lower social and economic class, especially the laboring, unskilled working group.[11]

Studies reported since 1958 and in many other languages consistently report the same observation; namely, that the overwhelming majority of homicides and other assaultive crimes are committed by persons from the lowest stratum of a social organization. Of course, it must be noted that most crimes, except the white-collar variety, are attributed to this same social class. Still, the rate differences between the social classes is significantly greater among physically aggressive than among purely acquisitive crimes. It is highly doubtful that the increasing number of self-reporting studies,[12] even the recent and expertly executed ones by Christie, Andenaes, and Skirbekk[13] in Norway and by Elmhorn[14] in Sweden, will alter this conclusion based upon officially recorded crimes. Homicide has rarely—perhaps because it is not a frequent crime—been included in these studies, the serious transgressions of aggression are not usually listed, and there is considerable doubt that people will report, even anonymously, that they ever committed homicide.

Ferri[15] in Italy, Brearley[16] in the United States, and, more recently, Bensing and Schroeder[17] in Cleveland, Svalastoga[18] in Denmark, Morris and Blom-Cooper[19] in England, Verkko[20] in Finland, Jayewardene[21] and Wood[22] in Ceylon, Bustamante and Bravo[23] in Mexico, Lamont[24] in South Africa, Franchini and Introna[25] in modern Italy, and many other authors in these same and other places, report the same general relationship between economic class and homicide.

This is not to say that upper- and middle-class homicides do not occur, nor that in some societies or subsocieties the rates for these groups may not be singularly higher than in other societies. Whites in Southern United States have homicide rates four to five times higher than whites in New England. Moreover, the percentage participation of middle and upper classes in homicide, relative to the total volume of homicide in a society, may be developed into a valid generalization akin to Verkko's statement about sex and the volume of homicide. We cannot be sure because cross-cultural studies have not examined this topic, but material from England, for example, which has a relatively low rate, suggests that there is a higher proportion of middle- and upper-class offenders than in countries like the United States that has a moderately high rate, or like Mexico and Colombia, which have very high rates.[26]

When homicide is committed by members of the middle and upper social classes, there appears to be a high likelihood of major psychopathology or of planned, more "rational" (or rationalized) behavior. Thus, the fact that they commit an act of willful murder, which is in diametric opposition to the set of values embraced by the dominant social class establishment of which they are a part, often means that these persons are suffering severely from an emotional crisis of profound proportions. Or they have been able, like Cressey's[27] embezzler, to meditate and mediate with their own internalized value system until they can conceive of the murder act without the consequence of an overburdening guilt and thereby justify their performing the deed. This self-justificatory behavior undoubtedly requires of the actor considerable time and much introspective wrestling in order to remain within, yet contradict his supportive value system. The infrequency of middle- and upper-class homicide, even in societies like Colombia, Mexico, and, on a lower level, Sardinia or the Southern part of the United States, must attest to the fact that this kind of rationalization to kill is not only extremely unlikely to occur but is very difficult to promote.

In preparing for the rational, premeditated murder, the middle- or upper-class actor also reasons that he has a considerable portion of his ego-involvement and investment in social life to lose should his blatant, legally antithetic act become detected. In a ponderous weighing of the probabilities of apprehension, this "prudent" and "rational" man is surely more likely than the explosive knife-carrier, prepared for battle, to be inhibited even by the highest of statistical odds against apprehension. We are not suggesting that the "average" middle-class man is primarily deterred from committing homicide by reason of the threat of severe penalty, but neither can we deny such threats some power to restrict and to prevent the commission of these criminal acts. However, our thesis contains principally the notion that the man from a culture value system that denounces the use of interpersonal violence will be restrained from using violence because of his positive perspective that conforms to his value system, not because of a negation of it.

The absence of that kind of value system is hardly likely to be a vacuous neutrality regarding violence. Instead, it is replaced by a value system that views violence as tolerable, expected, or required. As we approach that part of the cultural continuum where violence is a requisite response, we also enter a subculture where physically aggressive action quickly and readily can bleed into aggressive crime. The man from this culture area is more likely to use violence, similarly because of a positive perspective that requires conforming to his value system. Restraint from using violence may be a frustrating, ego-deflating, even guilt-ridden experience. Questions of the risks of being apprehended and the distant, abstract notion of the threat of punishment are almost irrelevant to one who acts with quick, yet socially ingrained aggressivity. Neither reasoning nor time for it are at his disposal.

The rarity and complexity of middle- and upper-class criminal homicide are eloquent reasons for its prominence as a literary theme and for the criminologists' primary concern with the frequent type of homicide that is more "normal," i.e., statistically more common and reflective of the learned, habituated aggressive reaction to sets of stimuli perceived as noxious.

## RACE

Whenever a culture is racially heterogeneous, with a minority that is subservient, suppressed, or in some other manner superordinated by a ruling majority, the minority group is likely to be viewed as socially inferior and to have high proportions of its people in the lower social and economic class. The Negro protest that burst into the history of the United States is still so recent that for a long time validity will be retained in economic statistics which indicate the prevalence of Negroes in the lower-class structure of that country. Restricted and isolated from the institutionalized means to achieve the goals of the dominant culture, many more Negroes than whites are caught in what Merton,[28] Cloward and Ohlin,[29] and others refer to as the differential opportunity structure, and are more likely to commit crime. The massive mobilization of federal and other public monies to provide new economic opportunities is partially an official testimony to this thesis. And as I have recently remarked in a review of the literature on crime and race:

. . . if a careful, detached scholar knew nothing about crime rates but was aware of the social, economic and political disparities between whites and Negroes in the United States, and if this diligent researcher had prior knowledge of the historical status of the American Negro, what would be the most plausible hypothesis our scholar could make about the crime rate of Negroes? Even this small amount of relevant knowledge would justify the expectation that Negroes would be found to have a higher crime rate than whites.[30]

Statistics on homicide and other assaultive crimes in the United States consistently show that Negroes have rates between four and ten times higher than whites. Aside from a critique of official arrest statistics that raises serious questions about the amount of Negro crime,[31] there is no real evidence to deny the greater involvement that Negroes have in assaultive crimes. What *is* forcefully denied is any genetic specificity for committing crime and any biological proclivity peculiar to Negroes or any other racial group for engaging in criminal behavior. There is reason to agree, however, that whatever may be the learned responses and social conditions contributing to criminality, persons visibly identified and socially labeled as Negroes in the United States appear to possess them in considerably higher proportions than do persons labeled white. Our subculture of violence thesis would, therefore, expect to find a large spread to the learning, resort to, and criminal display of the violence value among minority groups like Negroes.

## OTHER VARIABLES

A bundle of other variables is commonly collected in homicide studies, including references to marital status, broken homes, level of intelligence, police-recorded motives, methods and weapons used, the presence of alcohol, previous criminal record, census tract or other ecological data, patterns of social disorganization and anomie.[32] When these types of information have been available to the researchers, they generally have been included as part of the internal analysis of the data on homicide offenders, and sometimes, but rarely, on homicide victims. Although these items make for interesting descriptive analysis in a comparison of homicide offenders and victims with other types of offenders, or even with other cultures, they have contributed little to a higher order of abstraction and general theory construction.[33] Perhaps the item of I.Q. is a mild exception, for most assaultive offenders have been shown to have significantly lower mean I.Q.'s than property offenders, and certainly lower than the general population.

But this last point, i.e., comparison with the population at large, is an important one generally overlooked or unavailable to the investigators. Groups of non-homicide subjects matched with homicide offenders are almost never obtained. Random representatives from the general non-criminal population are not compared with assaultive offenders, and base-line statistics from the population at large are commonly not mentioned. For example, the presence of alcohol in two-thirds of the homicide situations, where alcohol had been ingested just prior to the homicide by the offender, the victim, or both, is a statistic that has not been (and perhaps cannot be) stated in relation to the abundance of many other occasions of social intercourse in which alcohol was an ingredient.[34] Almost trite questions arise: Although alcohol may be an inhibition-reducing agent, on how many other occasions did the homicide offenders imbibe? If we knew the incidence of alcohol-related

homicide among all alcohol-related social interactions, would
we be at all impressed by the coefficient? Among persons from
broken homes, working mothers, inadequate fathers, low educational levels, and an ecological residence characterized by
poverty, general physical deterioration, transiency, and density, very few persons commit homicide or other aggressive
crimes. Neither the *length of exposure* to many of these conditions (How long was the father absent or "inadequate"?
When was the home broken? When did the mother start working? Have poverty and density always been present?), nor
the *quality* of them (How was the home broken? Would it
have been better unbroken? Did the mother provide supervision, even though she worked? Was it a poor but wholesome
family? Just what does "density" mean?) is generally accounted for in the references.

Motives for homicide, as described by the police or court
records, are not widely different among the many studies, although frequency distributions sometimes vary, as might be
expected, from tribes in Africa to cities in Western countries.[35] "Jealousy," "domestic quarrels," "altercations" and so
forth, are terms that are commonly used by researchers because they rely upon officially recorded items. Obviously, these
are "motives" only as used in the vernacular; they are not
finely differentiated, and they convey little of the dynamics of
personal interaction that lead to homicide. Still, the terms
used almost universally express the recognized generalization
that most homicides represent a form of behavior from a wider
pool of aggression that is in a ready state for use. Again we
would ask, if the data were available, how many domestic
quarrels end in homicide? Why do *some* domestic quarrels,
why do *some* jealousies, why do *some* arguments over dice in
a back alley game in New York, over property boundaries in
Ceylon, or over family honor in Sicily, end in criminal slayings? Neither the incidence information nor the explanations
for these topics seem to be readily available without reference
to cultural and subcultural variations on the theme of violence; or without resort to a psychopathologic condition, which
in the ultimate analysis begs the question and succeeds only
in removing the case from the field of criminology to that of
forensic psychiatry. The need remains for a "differential social psychology" which must be theoretically constructed
within an integrated frame of reference. As we have men-

tioned, the concept of a subculture of violence may provide these requisites.

There is another pattern of homicide that is almost universal; namely, its intragroup character and the small proportion of cases with a stranger relationship between victims and offenders. Relatives, close friends of both sexes, acquaintances with residential proximity, members of the same ethnic, tribal, or other similarly denoted social group constitute the main targets of aggression. The voluminous number of vis-à-vis relationships experienced by all members of society makes the number of intragroup homicide appear high, although if it were possible to count the number of fleeting, impersonal, secondary types of contacts an individual has in a lifetime, a year, or a day, this number would also be enormous and increase with the complexity and population of the society. Clearly it is more than the number of exposures to primary or secondary relationships that results in high rates of intragroup targets and agents of assault. And it is more than the fact that primary, vis-à-vis relationships are charged with high emotional content, for there is no reason to believe that intensity of personal interaction is greater in number or degree among specific social groups, among lower classes, minority groups, the unskilled, the young adult, or the male population. The sentiments of attraction and hostility are widely and probably randomly distributed. Professional and managerial occupational groups, the better educated and higher income families also have arguments, domestic quarrels, and love triangles. But within a portion of the lower class, especially, there is a "life style," a culturally transmitted and shared willingness to express disdain, disgruntlement, and other hostile feelings in personal interaction by using physical force. The repertoire of response to unpleasant stimuli is delimited for them; it is not simply that more stimuli are displeasing. And in this limited repertoire of alternatives, the ultimate weapon of efforts to control others, violence, not only is available but has been incorporated into the personality structure through childhood discipline, reinforced in juvenile peer groups, confirmed in the strategies of the street. The aggressive male is socially "castrated" only for short periods of time in school, at work, and in other encounters with external controls. But the fighting routine in his personal milieu is continued, for his subcultural group is prepared to use the same violence as he, to respond in similar fashion to his attack, to be governed by the same norms containing the same values. Within this value set, the external expectations of aggression more readily activate the internal physiological responses of excitation, and the circle of violence circumscribes a situation containing the essential ingredients for assaultive crime.

# PART II

# The Sociology of
# Homicide

# A Sociological Analysis of Criminal Homicide

## MARVIN E. WOLFGANG

MURDER and other types of criminal homicide are deviations of the most serious and visible kind in our society. Public concern, the amount of time the police spend in detection and investigation, the ratio of the number of police to the number of these crimes, and the quantity of stories in literature and the drama that use murder as a central theme all attest to the interest we have in homicide. However, the television or literary mystery usually is concerned with the relatively rare premeditated type of killing. Most homicides have typical forms and are crimes of passion that arise from a world of violence.

The typical criminal slayer is a young man in his twenties who kills another man only slightly older. Both are of the same race; if Negro, the slaying is commonly with a knife, if white, it is a beating with fists and feet on a public street. Men kill and are killed between four and five times more frequently than women, but when a woman kills she most likely has a man as her victim and does it with a butcher knife in the kitchen. A woman killing a woman is extremely rare, for she is most commonly slain by her husband or other close friend by a beating in the bedroom.

These are some of the findings of a study more fully described in *Patterns in Criminal Homicide*.[1] Since publication of this book, a variety of requests for a summary discussion have come to my desk, partly, I imagine, because of the re-

REPRINTED with the permission of the author and the publisher from Marvin E. Wolfgang, "A Sociological Analysis of Criminal Homicide," *Federal Probation* (March, 1961) 23:1:48-55.

cent renewed interest in the sociopsychological aspects of criminal homicide reflected in Guttmacher's *The Mind of the Murderer*,[2] Palmer's *A Study of Murder*,[3] and in Bohannan's *African Homicide and Suicide*.[4] What follows, therefore, is an abbreviated analysis of my own sociological study with suggestive theoretical points of departure for additional research. For detailed information of the research methods and interpretive analysis of criminal homicide, the reader is referred to the present author's book.

## WHAT IS CRIMINAL HOMICIDE?

The popular press and even some of our national, state, and municipal police officials sometimes confuse murder with other types of criminal homicide. As every capable policeman should know, homicide is the killing of another person and is divided into criminal and noncriminal homicide. The former category comprises murder (commonly in the first and second degree) as well as voluntary (nonnegligent) and involuntary (negligent) manslaughter. Noncriminal homicide is excusable, or a killing in self-defense, and justifiable homicide, or homicide performed as a legal duty by a peace officer or executioner. Confusion of these terms, mixing criminal with noncriminal cases, and mislabeling murder for other types of criminal homicides, has occurred in both professional and popular studies.

In order to produce some clarity among these terms and to provide a sociological and statistical analysis of criminal homicide, research was conducted in Philadelphia, using all criminal homicides recorded by the Philadelphia Homicide Squad from January 1, 1948 through December 31, 1952. Excusable and justifiable homicides were excluded from the study and concentration was only on criminal cases listed by the police. I spent many long hours over several years collecting the data and participating in arrest and interrogation of offenders, and I have the highest respect for the police officers with whom I came into contact during that period. The homicide detectives consistently showed due respect for the constitutional rights of persons they arrested as well as an attitude of understanding rather than that of vengeance and retribution. These are, of course, qualities desirable in all police officers, for their function is to protect as well as to apprehend, to make suspects available for prosecution, but not to judge guilty.

It is almost axiomatic in criminal statistics that for purposes of determining the amount and type of crime committed in a community, police statistics yield the most valid data.[5] Too many cases are lost through court trials to use court statistics, and to use prison data means a still further reduction of cases that are highly selected to result in incarceration instead of probation or some other form of disposition. For this reason, police statistics were used to obtain the most valid picture of criminal homicides over this 5-year period.

Another important aspect of the research design was to distinguish between victims and offenders in terms of their major social characteristics. Usually this distinction is not maintained in studies of homicide, especially in those that rely only on mortality statistics published by the Office of Vital Statistics from death certifications. The Philadelphia study and review of the literature on criminal homicide reveal that much confusion of terminology pervades the field; that data about victims often are confused with data about offenders; rates per population unit are sometimes confused with reports about proportionate distributions or percentages of criminal slayings. We have emphasized constantly the invalidity of inferring characteristics about victims from criminal statistics, some of which supply data only for offenders; or of inferring characteristics about offenders from mortality statistics, which supply data only for victims.

Most previous research has examined *either* the victim *or* the offender. In the present work, analysis has been made of *both* victims and offenders, separately, as distinct units, but also as mutual participants in the homicide. A broad social approach is interested both in the active, "to kill," and in the passive, "to be killed." It is one type of analysis to consider victims as a social group and offenders as another social group; it is quite a different and more refined type of analysis to consider specific victim-offender relationships, and to find race, sex, age, and other patterns among them.

During the period from 1948 through 1952 there were 588 cases of criminal homicide in Philadelphia; i.e., there were 588 victims. Because several people were sometimes involved in killing one person, there were 621 offenders arrested by the police and taken into custody. In terms of a mean annual rate per 100,000 population in the city, the victim rate was 5.7 and the offender rate 6.0. This is neither · high nor low. Compared with 18 other cities across the country, each of which had a population of a quarter of a million or more in 1950, Philadelphia ranks ninth, with a range between Miami having a victim rate of 15.1 and Milwaukee having a low of 2.3. New York's rate was only 3.7, Los Angeles 4.0, and Chicago 7.8. The rate for Pennsylvania as a whole for 1950 was only 3.5, but the most fair comparison is between cities of comparable size.[6]

The years 1948–52 were advantageous years for research purposes because the census fell exactly in the middle of this period so that the population statistics for 1950 could be used for computing a rate for any of the single 5 years or for all of them together. Moreover, it should be noted that the data collected from police files and used to analyze suggested associations and questions are expressed in numerical and percentage frequency distributions, in rates per 100,000 population in some cases, and in ratios. In order to safeguard against loose generalizations, several tests of statistical significance were employed.[7]

## SOME BASIC FINDINGS:
## RACE, SEX, AND AGE

Research has shown that although criminal homicide is largely an unplanned act, there are nonetheless in the act regular uniformities and patterns. We have found, as previous research has noted, that there is a statistically significant association between criminal homicide and the race and sex of both victim and offender. Negroes and males involved in homicide far exceed their proportions in the general population and rates for these two groups are many times greater than for whites and females. The rate per 100,000 by race and sex of offenders reveals the following rank order of magnitude: Negro males (41.7), Negro females (9.3), white males (3.4), and white females (.4). Although Negroes of either sex, and males of either race, are positively related to criminal slayings, the association between race and homicide is statistically more significant than that between sex and homicide. This relationship of Negroes and males to criminal homicide confirms reports and studies made elsewhere in this country, although the proportion of female offenders is reportedly much higher in England. It should be noted, however, that the whole of the British Isles has no more criminal homicides in a year than the city of Philadelphia alone (or about 125 annually).

Among offenders, the age group 20–24 predominates with a rate of 12.6 per 100,000, while the highest rate for victims is in the age group 25–34. In short, victims are generally older than their offenders; the median age of the former being 35.1 years and of the latter, 31.9 years. The importance of the race factor here is striking in view of the fact that the *lowest* 5-year age-specific rates for Negro males and females are similar to, or higher than the *highest* of such rates for white males and females, respectively. Although males of both races more frequently commit criminal homicide during their twenties than during any other period of life, Negro males in their early sixties kill as frequently as do white males in their early twenties.

The race factor in criminal homicide is alarming and should be the cause of both Negro and white community leaders to examine more closely the reasons for this differential. The child is not born with homicide tendencies in his genes, so that in no way can we infer a biological explanation for this difference. Negroes are a minority group that still suffer from residential and general cultural isolation from the rest of the community, despite recent advances in integration. So long as this ethnic group is socially isolated and required to live in restricted residential areas they will continue to constitute a "subcultural" area. This subculture is characterized by poor housing, high density of population, overcrowded home conditions, and by a system of values that often condones violence and physical aggression from child-rearing processes to adult interpersonal relationships that sometimes end in criminal slayings. To a lesser degree, whites in the lower socioeconomic classes as well as Negroes become part of this *subculture of violence* and participate in criminal homicide. Only by breaking up this culturally isolated group and by integrating them into the general community of morality and values can society hope to reduce violence that results in homicide.

## METHODS AND TIME OF ASSAULT

We have also noted significant associations between
methods of inflicting death and the race and sex of both
victims and offenders. In Philadelphia 39 percent of all homicides were due to stabbings, 33 percent to shooting, 22 percent
to beatings, and 6 percent to other and miscellaneous methods. There appears to be a cultural preference for particular
types of methods and weapons. Males, if Negro, usually stab
and are stabbed to death; and if white, beat and are beaten
to death. Females generally stab their victims with a butcher
knife, but are very often beaten to death.

Although homicides tend to increase during the hot summer months, there is no significant association by seasons or
months of the year. But homicide is significantly associated
with days of the week and hours of the day. The weekend in
general, and Saturday night in particular, are related to homicide, as are the hours between 8:00 p.m. and 2:00 a.m.
Between 8:00 p.m. Friday and midnight Sunday there were,
during the 5 years under review, 380 criminal homicides; but
from the beginning of Monday morning to 8:00 p.m. Friday,
there were only 208. Thus, on the average, 65 percent of all
homicides occurred during the shorter time span of 52 hours,
while only 35 percent occurred during the longer time span
of 116 hours.

The time between assault and death of the victim varies
according to the method employed by the offender. Relatively
quick death (within 10 minutes after assault) occurred for
half of the victims in a shooting, for less than three-tenths in
a stabbing, and for only one-sixteenth in a beating. About a
third of the victims were dead within 10 minutes after assault,
slightly less than three-fifths after the first hour had passed,
and four-fifths within a day. Only 5 percent lived more than
10 days after being assaulted. Probably fewer persons today
die from aggravated assault wounds than was true a generation ago, for data suggest that (1) improved communication
with the police, (2) more rapid transportation to a hospital
(usually by the police), and (3) advanced medical technology
have contributed to the decreasing homicide rates in this
country during the last 25 years.

We do not know, of course, just how many aggravated
assaults, assaults with intent to kill, and other violent assaults

are today prevented from becoming classified as criminal homicides because of these three factors, but the steady increases of other crimes of personal violence, such as aggravated assaults and rapes, regularly reported in the Uniform Crime Reports lead us to suggest that something other than a greater repugnance to commit crimes of personal violence has entered our mores. Many factors are involved in changing rates of homicide, such as the age composition, business cycles, etc. But because crimes of violence against the person, excluding homicide, appear to have increased during the past two decades, it is logical to assume that if these gross social factors affect homicide, they should affect other crimes of violence in the same way.

Research testing the hypothesis suggested by the three factors mentioned above might be useful in explaining the general decrease in criminal homicide over the past 25 years.[8] It would be valuable, for example, to know the recovery rate for those who are today grievously assaulted but who would have probably died under medical and other conditions of a generation ago. Although this type of analysis fails to account for any psychological dimensions in the phenomenon of homicide, the approach nonetheless has the virtue of mensurability in testing the validity of the explanation.

## PLACE WHERE CRIMES OCCUR

The place where the crime occurred is also important. The most dangerous single place is the highway (public street, alley, or field), although more slayings occur in the home than outside the home. Men kill and are killed most frequently in the street, while women kill most often in the kitchen but are killed in the bedroom. For victims and offenders of each race and sex group significant differences have been noted. Most cases of Negro males who kill Negro males involve a stabbing in a public street; most cases of white males who kill white males involve a beating in a public street. However, the high proportion of females who kill with a butcher knife in a kitchen, and of those who are killed in a bedroom by being beaten is associated with the fact that 84 percent of all female offenders slay males and 87 percent of all female victims are slain by males.

## PRESENCE OF ALCOHOL

Either or both the victim and offender had been drinking immediately prior to the slaying in nearly two-thirds of the cases. The presence of alcohol in the homicide situation appears to be significantly associated with Negroes—either as victims or as offenders—and, separately, with Negro male and female victims. Particular caution[9] must be exercised in evaluating the presence of alcohol in these homicides, since drinking—particularly on Saturday night, the time of highest incidence of homicide—is an integral part of the mores of most groups involved in this crime. A significantly higher proportion of weekend homicides than of homicides occurring during the remainder of the week had alcohol present (in either the victim, the offender, or both). An association between alcohol, weekend slayings, and the payment of wages on Friday was indicated and crudely confirmed by the available data. We have, therefore, suggested that when the socioeconomic group most likely to commit homicide almost simultaneously receives its weekly wages, purchases alcohol, and meets together socially, it is not unlikely that the incidence of homicide should also rise.

## PREVIOUS POLICE RECORD AND
## VICTIM-OFFENDER RELATIONSHIPS

Contrary to many past impressions, an analysis of offenders in criminal homicide reveals a relatively high proportion who have a previous police or arrest record. Of total offenders, nearly two-thirds have a previous arrest record, and of total victims, almost half have such a record. Having a previous record is also associated with males both among victims and offenders, and is obvious from the fact that more *male victims* have such a record than do *female offenders*. Moreover, when an offender has a previous record, he is more likely to have a record of offenses against the person than against property; and when he has a record of offenses against the person, he is more likely than not to have a record of having committed a serious assault offense, such as aggravated assault or assault with intent to kill. A greater proportion of Negro male and female victims have a previous arrest record than do white male and female offenders, respectively. In view of

these facts, it is of interest to future attempts at prevention and control of potential offenders in criminal homicide that *a larger proportion of offenders with an arrest record have a record of aggravated assault than of all types of property offenses combined.* The courts should take special care no to release too hastily and without proper individualized trea' ment those persons arrested on charges of personal assau' in order to prevent later homicides.

Criminal homicide usually results from a vaguely defin altercation, domestic quarrel, jealousy, argument over mon and robbery. These five police-recorded "motives" are involv in 8 out of 10 cases. Most of the identified victim-offen relationships may be classified as "primary group" relatic or those that include intimate, close, frequent contacts. C' friends and relatives accounted for over half of the conta and the combined categories which involve primary g' contacts constitute 59 percent of all victim-offender rela' ships among males, but significantly as much as 84 pe among females. Because white males were killed more quently than Negro males during the commission of a rol the former were also more frequently strangers to their s' than the latter.

Mate slayings have been given special attention.[10] ( 100 husband-wife homicides, 53 victims were wives a were husbands. The number of wives killed by their hu constitutes 41 percent of all women killed, whereas hu slain by their wives make up only 11 percent of a killed. Thus, when a woman commits homicide, she likely than a man to kill her mate; and when a man by a woman, he is most likely to be killed by his wi bands are often killed by their wives in the kitche' butcher knife, but nearly half of the wives are sla' bedroom. More male than female offenders in thes slayings were found guilty, were convicted of mo' degrees of homicide, and committed suicide.

In 94 percent of the cases, the victim and offe' members of the same race, but in only 64 percent of the same sex. Thus, the ratio of intra- to interacia is 15.2 to 1; but the ratio of intra- to intersex ' only 1.8 to 1. In general, it may be said that vi homicidally assaulted most frequently by males o' race, and least frequently by females of another r'

In 32 cases involving 57 offenders and 6 victims, a felony, in addition to the killing, was perpetrated at the time of the slaying. In most cases the other felony was robbery, and white males accounted for a larger proportion of these felony-murders than they did among all homicides in general.

## VICTIM-PRECIPITATED HOMICIDE

The term *victim-precipitated* homicide has been introduced to refer to those cases in which the victim is a direct, positive precipitator in the crime—the first to use physical force in the homicide drama. After establishing a theoretical and legal basis for analysis, the Philadelphia data reveal several factors significantly associated with the 150 victim-precipitated homicides, which is 26 percent of all homicides. These factors are: Negro victims and offenders, male victims, female offenders, stabbings, victim-offender relationships involving male victims and female offenders, mate slayings, husbands who were victims in mate slayings, alcohol, victims with a previous arrest record, particularly an arrest record of assault. Thus, in most of these cases, the role and characteristics of the victim and offender are reversed, the victim assumes the role of determinant, and the victim makes a definite contribution to the genesis of his own victimization.[11]

Recently, I have extended the meaning of victim-precipitated homicide to include a sociological and psychoanalytic discussion of these 150 victims as being bent on suicide.[12] Although it is impossible to verify an assumption of subconscious suicide wishes among these victims, empirical data from broad social factors combine with psychological and sociological data suggesting that victims in many cases present themselves as willing targets for violent aggression leading to homicide. The material collected by John M. Macdonald at the Colorado Psychopathic Hospital on "The Murderer and His Victim"[13] sheds additional light on this area of analysis.

## SUICIDE AFTER PERFORMING HOMICIDE

In 24 cases the offenders committed suicide after performing the homicide.[14] Of these, 22 were males, nearly half of whom were men who had killed their wives. Analysis and

evaluation of these homicide-suicides indicate that half of the homicides would have been classified as first-degree murder had the offender experienced a court trial. As a result, even with the low amount of suicide after homicide in this country, more offenders inflict death upon themselves than are put to death by the social sanction of legal execution. Twelve persons who committed suicide appear to have committed first-degree murder. Thus the number of self-inflicted "executions" is greater than the 7 offenders who were sentenced to death by a court of record. However, suicide following homicide is 5 to 6 times more frequent in England than in the United States.

## UNSOLVED HOMICIDES

Of particular importance to the police are unsolved homicides. The definition used in this study was not exactly like that of offenses not cleared by arrest, which is used for uniform crime reporting purposes, but there were similarities. Comparisons of the unsolved with solved cases reveal that the former have higher proportions of: white male and female victims, victims 65 years of age and over, robbery as a prelude to the slayings, victims who were strangers to their assailants, beatings, weekend slayings, and assaults that occurred in the public street.

## COURT DISPOSITIONS

Finally, analysis has been made of the tempo of legal procedures, of court disposition, designation of the degree of homicide, insanity, and sentences imposed by the court. Two-thirds of the offenders were arrested on the same day that the crime was committed, and over half appeared in court for trial within 6 months after the crime. Two-thirds of those taken into police custody, and over three-quarters of those who experienced a court trial were declared guilty. Proportionately, Negroes and males were convicted more frequently than whites and females; but previous analysis of the nature of these cases reveals that Negroes and males had in fact committed more serious offenses, and that a charge of unjust race and sex discrimination in court would not necessarily be correct.[15] Of the 387 offenders convicted and sentenced, 30 percent were guilty of murder in the first degree, 29 percent of murder in the second degree, 36 percent of voluntary manslaughter, and 15 percent of involuntary manslaughter. Less than 3 percent of the offenders were declared insane by the courts, which is a proportion similar to that reported in other studies in this country, but considerably smaller than the 30 percent or more reported insane in England.

## FURTHER RESEARCH

We have only touched on some of the highlights of this analysis of criminal homicide. There are many aspects of special importance to the police that can aid them in making investigations and particularly in working on cases in which it is difficult to determine suspects, or that are listed as unsolved cases. Each city and each police department has its own peculiar problems, of course, but studies of this sort can easily be made if proper records are kept. Other types of crime need the same kind of research attention, but ultimately all such research depends on the veracity and efficiency of the police in recording and reporting their information. The greatest service the police can make to scientific research is their cooperation with the social scientist and the maintenance of valid, efficient records of their cases.

The Baltimore Criminal Justice Commission, under the direction of Ralph Murdy, former agent of the Federal Bureau of Investigation, is presently engaged in a 5-year study (1960–1965) of criminal homicides in Baltimore—a study modeled on the kind of analysis made in Philadelphia. Dr. John Macdonald, Assistant Director of the Colorado Psychopathic Hospital, intends to collect similar data for Denver over a 5-year period. Professor Franco Ferracuti, from the Institute of Criminal Anthropology at the University of Rome, has proposed simultaneous analyses of criminal homicide in San Juan, Puerto Rico, and in Rome, Italy. On-going research like these that seek to duplicate and to expand on the Philadelphia study will confirm, reject, or modify the patterns in criminal homicide that have thus far been described and analyzed. Only in this way, as Albert Morris[16] has suggested, can science produce meaningful understanding of this delimited phenomenon, leading from empirical data to a meaningful sociopsychological theory of crimes of violence.[17]

## CONCLUSION

On the basis of these findings thus far, it is obvious that homicides are principally crimes of passion, or violent slayings that are not premeditated or psychotic manifestations. Emerging out of the data is a theory that suggests a conflict between the prevailing middle class values of our society and the values of a subsocial or subcultural group. Previously we have referred to this group as constituting a "subculture of violence." If there exists a subculture of violence, then we must further propose that the greater the degree of integration of the individual into this subculture the higher the likelihood that his behavior will often be violent; or, we may assert that there is a direct relationship between rates of homicide and the degree of integration of the subculture of violence to which the individual belongs. The importance of human life in the scale of values, the kinds of expected reactions to certain types of stimuli, the perceptual differences in the evaluation of the stimuli, and the general personality structure are all factors of importance in this theory.

Highest rates of rape, aggravated assaults, persistency in arrests for assaults (recidivism) among these same groups with high rates of homicide are additional confirmations of the contention of a subculture of violence. Ready access to weapons may become essential for protection against others in this millieu who respond in similarly violent ways, and the carrying of knives or other protective devices becomes a common symbol of willingness to participate in and to expect violence, and to be ready for its retaliation. As in combat on the front lines during wartime where the "it-was-either-him-or-me" situation arises, there are similar attitudes and reactions among participants in homicide. The Philadelphia study shows that 65 percent of the offenders and 47 percent of the victims had a previous police record of arrests. Here, then, is a situation often not unlike that of combat in which two persons committed to the value of violence come together, and in which chance often dictates the identity of the slayer and of the slain.

We have not tried to explain the causes of this subculture of violence, but such an endeavor would involve analysis of social class and race relations that would include residential, occupational, and other forms of discrimination and social isolation as important factors. Some consideration of the groups from which the individual obtains a conception of himself and an analysis of child-rearing practices that employ punishment and promote early patterns of physical aggression would aid the search for causal factors and methods of treatment.

As we have indicated, dispersing the group that shares the subculture of violence should weaken the value. Through wider economic opportunities, freedom of residential mobility, etc., integration of the group members into the larger society and its predominant value system should function to destroy or at least to reduce the subculture of violence. The work done in New York City in breaking up delinquent gangs has demonstrated the effectiveness of this approach. Similarly in correctional institutions, the treatment program, especially when using individual or group psychotherapy, should try to counterbalance or to eliminate the allegiance of the individual to the subculture of violence and his violent perception of the world.

# Homicide in England

## TERENCE MORRIS and
## LOUIS BLOM-COOPER

ALTHOUGH murder is regarded as a serious crime in this country [England], it can hardly be said to be a serious social problem. As a form of violent death it is a comparative rarity; between 1900 and 1949 there were just under 7,500 murders "known to the police" in England and Wales—only about 2,500 more than the average number of suicides and about 1,500 more than the average number of persons killed on the roads *in a single year*. And every year about three times as many people are killed by drunken drivers as are murdered. As a form of violent crime it is also rare, accounting for no more than 136 of the 11,519 crimes of violence against the person, and the 806,900 indictable crimes of all types committed in 1961. And of the 182,217 persons found guilty of indictable offenses in that year only 56 (of the 124 persons who stood trial for murder)[1] had a verdict of guilty brought in against them. That a crime, which occupies such an insignificant part of the time of the police, the courts and the penal system, should nevertheless be regarded as the most serious of crimes would be absurd were it not for the special quality of murder and the character of the social reaction that criminal homicide provokes. It is noteworthy that since the passing of the Homicide Act and the limitation of the death sentence to special categories of killing, there is a

---

REPRINTED with the permission of the authors and the publisher from Terence Morris and Louis Blom-Cooper, "Homicide—The Statistical Picture," *A Calendar of Murder: Criminal Homicide in England since 1957*, London: Michael Joseph, Ltd., 1964, Chap. III, pp. 277-282.

general impression that public attendance at murder trials has fallen off appreciably and press coverage has become much more selective. The fact that the commonest punishment for murder is now life imprisonment has in one respect reduced the status of murder to that of other crimes punished by imprisonment. By and large, the community is not nearly so interested in murder trials which are no longer dramatised by the shadow of the gallows.

Murder in England and Wales is not only a rare phenomenon but one characterized by a stability which is most marked when comparisons are made with other types of serious crimes, especially violent crime.

Although the actual number of murders fluctuates from year to year, the oscillations of the murder pendulum are

TABLE 1.  *Murders Known to the Police per Million of Population*

| ANNUAL | AVERAGES |
|--------|----------|
| 1900–09 | 4.4 |
| 1910–19 | 4.0 |
| 1920–29 | 3.8 |
| 1930–39 | 3.6 |
| 1940–49 | 4.4 |
| 1950–56 | 3.7 |
| 1957–60 | 4.1 |

SOURCES:  *Annual Criminal Statistics* (England and Wales)

remarkably regular, even under the stress of wartime conditions. In 1931 there were 138 murders known to the police: in 1961 the corresponding figure was 136. In the intervening years the highest figure occurred in 1942 with 192 murders and the lowest in 1937 with 111 murders. When expressed as a *murder rate,* i.e. as related to the number of persons at risk in the population, the fluctuations appear as much less marked even than those of the crude figures. For the period 1900–49 the murder rate was 3.9 per million,[2] with a standard deviation[3] of 0.45; in the sixty odd years since the beginning of the century the total volume of recorded crime of all types has increased enormously, and by over 300 per cent since

1930. Wounding, a serious crime of violence, had an average rate of 46.1 per million in the decade 1930–39, but by 1961 the rate had risen to 391.9 per million. That the incidence of murder should be so remarkably consistent while all other recorded crime, both serious and not so serious, has continuously and substantially increased, suggests that the aetiology of murder must be quite distinct from that of other crimes.

One factor which immediately suggests itself is the state of mind of the murderer. In no other crime is there such an incidence of suicide by the offender before he can be brought to trial. The Royal Commission on Capital Punishment[4] found that between 1900 and 1949 no fewer than 29.1 per cent of murder suspects committed suicide. For the period 1950–59 the corresponding figure is 33 per cent. While some people may argue that suicide on the part of a murderer is not necessarily proof of his mental illness or abnormality, the weight of clinical evidence about suicide in general suggests that a dramatic change in an individual's normal instinctual drives is a pre-condition of self-destruction.

Before the Homicide Act it might be argued that a man would prefer to kill himself rather than be hanged; suicide on the part of a non-capital murderer must, if this line of reasoning is to be pursued, be based on a preference for death rather than life imprisonment, a much less plausible explanation. Rather, from what we know of those offenders who do stand trial, morbid depression which can be simultaneously associated with both homicide and suicide is a recurrent feature. Bearing in mind the stringent tests of mental abnormality necessitated by the M'Naghten Rules (which were employed in forensic work before the Homicide Act 1957 and the Mental Health Act 1959), it is all the more remarkable that over the period 1900–49 as many as 21.4 per cent of persons brought to trial were found either unfit to plead or guilty but insane. Since 1957 the percentage of apprehended killers found unfit to plead or guilty but insane fell to 13 per cent. Those successfully pleading diminished responsibility formed an additional 14 per cent of the total number indicted for capital or non-capital murder. And by no means all of those who were unable to plead "M'Naghten-madness" were executed; by the exercise of the Prerogative of Mercy some, though by no means all, of the mentally abnormal killers were reprieved after having been sentenced

to death—principally to penal servitude for life, though in a
few instances specifically to Broadmoor. During the decade
1950–59, 26.5 per cent of apprehended killers were found
unfit to plead or guilty but insane. The introduction by the
Homicide Act of the plea of diminished responsibility has
made it more difficult to compare the incidence of mental
abnormality and mental illness in the periods before and
after 1957. The Home Office Research Unit found[5] that most
of the cases of manslaughter on grounds of diminished responsibility would previously have resulted in verdicts either
of murder (carrying the death penalty) or guilty but insane,
and suggest that although now classified as manslaughter they
should be treated for comparative purposes as murder.

A second factor which distinguishes murder from other
crimes is the extent to which the killer and victim are related,
or known to each other, in contrast to the situation in most
other offenses.

TABLE 2.   *Murder-Victim Relationships, 1957–60*

|  | CAPITAL MURDER | NON-CAPITAL MURDER | ALL MURDERS |
|---|---|---|---|
| Per cent related | 22.5 | 59.5 | 53.0 |
| Per cent known | 37.5 | 25.5 | 27.9 |
| Per cent strangers | 40.0 | 14.9 | 19.0 |
| Relationship unknown | 1 | 6 | 7 |
| Number | 81 | 385 | 456 |

SOURCE: Press reports of trials, 1957–60.

These data, those collected by the Home Office Research
Unit and the study of Wolfgang in Philadelphia,[6] all indicate
that homicidal violence is associated with close inter-personal
ties. In this country murder is overwhelmingly a domestic
crime in which men kill their wives, mistresses and children,
and women kill their children. Of the murder victims over
the age of 16, 70 per cent are female, and of those females
nearly half are killed by their legal hubsands and a quarter
by other relatives or lovers.[7] When considering victims under
16, again, about three quarters are killed by their parents
or other relatives.[8] Our own analysis, as does the analysis
made by the Gowers Commission, confirms that the commonest murder is that of a wife by her husband, a child by one

of its parents or a woman by her lover. Between 1900 and 1949 of the 1,210 persons convicted, 224 had killed a wife or husband, lover or sweetheart, compared with only 161 who had killed in the course of robbery and 19 who had killed police or prison officers. Sir John Macdonnell, commenting on an analysis (given in the Criminal Statistics for 1905) of the motives of murderers convicted between 1885 and 1905, said:

I am inclined to think that this crime is not generally the crime of the so-called criminal classes, but in most cases rather an incident in miserable lives in which disputes, quarrels, angry words and blows are common. The short history of a large number of cases which have been examined might be summed up thus: —
   Domestic quarrels and brawls; much previous ill treatment, drinking, fighting, blows; a long course of brutality and continued absence of self-restraint. There is, however, a clearly marked class of murders, of *rare occurrence* [our italics] the motive of which is robbery, committed by habitual criminals and forming the climax, and usually the termination, of a career of crime.[9]

Bearing in mind that the physical violence to wives and children associated with drunkenness, which was characteristic of life among the poorer sections of society at the turn of the century, is now a mere shadow of its former self, and that in any case these "miserable lives" which resulted in domestic quarrels probably had a considerable element of mental illness behind them, there is little in Sir John Macdonnell's view with which our own evidence collected since 1957 would lead us to disagree. Moreover, the "clearly marked class" of murders committed by habitual criminals is still very much with us in a form so neatly delineated by the Homicide Act of 1957—those who murder in the course or furtherance of theft.

The Home Office Research Unit Report on Murder, published in 1961, cast some doubts, nevertheless, on the view, widely held by opponents of capital punishment, that murder is for the most part a solitary blot on a hitherto unblemished character. The Research Unit study found that the proportion of convicted murderers with criminal records has steadily increased, from 26 per cent in the period from 1 January 1955 to the enactment of the Homicide Act on 20 March 1957, to 36 per cent in the period from then until 31 December 1960. In both periods previous convictions were primarily for property offenses and secondarily for offenses of violence. But in the lower class milieu, from which such a large proportion of murderers are drawn, convictions for property offenses are by no means uncommon, and violence in words and deeds is a commonplace expression of feeling. The increase in the proportion with previous convictions is probably associated closely with the increase in property crimes in general, of which the increase in capital murder is itself certainly a reflection.[10]

Seventy-nine per cent of the men convicted of capital murder until the end of 1960 (and 84 per cent of those executed) had previous convictions, while among those convicted of non-capital murder the proportion was 55 per cent.[11] It is vital, however, to consider the proportions of capital and non-capital murder. Among the 762 indictments from 21 March 1957 to 31 December 1962, 640 were for non-capital and only 122 for capital murder. Nearly all those convicted in capital cases with previous convictions had more than one conviction, usually for larceny and breaking and entering. In the non-capital category the proportion of offenders with records of violence and sex offenses was somewhat higher than in the capital category. Vickers (1957) and Riley (1960) were typical of the capital murderer; Jones (1961) a fair example of a non-capital murderer with a record of violence and a sexual offense.

The proposition put forward half a century ago by Macdonnell, that murder is not a crime of the so-called "criminal classes," may need some modification both in the light of modern knowledge about mental illness and the fact that the lower a person's status in the social hierarchy, the more likely he is to have a previous conviction for crime, generally property crime. On the other hand it is not clear whether the incidence of psychopathology as evidenced in sexual offenses and violence against the person is increasing; statistically it would appear to be so. But even if there are among us more aggressive psychopaths (some of them manifesting their disorders in sexual offenses) as well as more panic-stricken housebreakers (to swell the category of capital murder) none of these groups significantly alters the picture of murder as an act committed largely under the stress of emotion, or in consequence of mental illness, by those who are closely related to their victims. The increases in property and violent crime are, as it were, no more tributaries to swell the mainstream of murder whose waters are clouded by sickness, unhappiness and domestic strife. And so far as the murder rate is concerned, these additions have made little significant increase to the level of murder and only a marginal acceleration in the flow of persons indicted for it through the courts.

# Static and Dynamic
# "Laws" of
# Sex and Homicide

## VELI VERKKO

IN SOCIOLOGY, and especially in that branch of it dealing
with wrongdoing, social pathology, certain regularities can
be ascertained, as, for instance, the contrast prevailing between the trends of development in crimes against life and
suicides and the parallelism observed in the nineteenth century in various countries between the number of larcenies
and burglaries and the fluctuations in the price of grain.[1] But
these phenomena are affected by such a multitude of disturbing factors that no regular sequences are discernible in
them. The regular relationship between larcenies and grain
prices, for instances, is no longer apparent. There is, however,
a remarkable exception. In the previous chapter I showed that
the number of female victims of crimes against life in Finland, through the different centuries and in the most varied
circumstances, independent of the total number of crimes
against life, remained in the main unchanged, and the same
applies to Sweden during the sixty years for which data on
that country are available. The fluctuations in crimes against
life have mainly been in the numbers of male victims only.
In this connection I have noticed a very remarkable fact, viz.
that the phenomenon is by no means limited to Finnish and
Swedish conditions alone, but can be traced in all countries
on which cause-of-death statistics supply information on the

REPRINTED with the permission of the publisher from Veli Verkko,
"Are There Regular Sequences in Crimes Against Life Which Can Be
Formulated as Laws?" *Homicides and Suicides in Finland and Their
Dependence on National Character*, Scandinavian Studies in Sociology,
3, Copenhagen: C. E. S. Gads Forlag, 1951, Chap. V, pp. 50-57.

number of proved crimes against life. My investigation into
the trend of development and level of frequency of crimes
against life and of assault and battery, mentioned previously,
contains information of this kind. In examining this material
I have found regular sequences of circumstances the existence
of which has escaped the notice of earlier researchers. To
start with, the following rule may be formulated: *Distribution
by sexes of victims of crimes against life in any country is
always dependent on the frequency level of the crimes concerned.*

This rule is illustrated in greater detail by two laws, one of
them static and the other dynamic.

*The static law* is as follows:

*In countries of high frequency of crimes against life the
female proportion of those killed is small;* and vice versa: *in
countries of low frequency of crimes against life the percentage of female victims is perceptibly greater than in countries of high frequency of crimes against life.*

Figures 1 and 2 illustrate the percentage of male and female
victims of crime in countries of high and low frequency of
crimes against life, respectively.

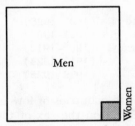

**FIGURE 1.** *Schematic illustration of the proportion
by sexes in countries of high frequency of crimes
against life.*

To prove the validity of this law, I shall first, on the basis
of my afore-mentioned investigation, provide data on countries of high frequency of crimes against life. This information can be divided into two groups: 1) such information as
concerns all known victims of crimes against life, and 2)
information permitting of the conclusion that a part only of
the total number of victims of crimes is covered. In my investigation into crimes against life, and assault and battery,
I have found that, in addition to Finland, Serbia, Bulgaria,

Italy and Chile come in the former group, whereas Roumania, Greece, Spain and the United States obviously have to be counted among the latter. As the latter may provide an errone-

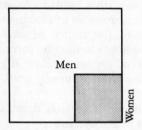

FIGURE 2. *Schematic illustration of the proportion by sexes in countries of low frequency of crimes against life.*

ous picture of the distribution of the victims of crimes by sexes, they, have to be excluded. The following list gives the percentages of female victims of crimes in the first-mentioned countries of high frequency of crimes against life. The years in brackets show the periods of time used as the basis of calculations.

| Finland | (1921–1926) | 4% |
| Serbia | (1901–1908) | 8% |
| Bulgaria | (1903–1912) | 5% |
| Italy | (1913–1924) | 9% |
| Chile | (1922–1925) | 9% |

Next, let us deal with countries of low frequency of crimes against life. Information on the sex of the victims of crime is available for Sweden, Norway, Denmark, Prussia, England and Wales, Switzerland, and Japan. Of these countries, Japan is the only one with incomplete information on the victims of crime and must therefore be excluded.

The list of percentages of female victims in countries of low frequency of fatal crimes against life is:

| Sweden | (1915–1924) | 22% |
| Norway | (1915–1924) | 18% |
| Denmark | (1920–1926) | 38% |
| Prussia | (1920–1923) | 28% |
| England and Wales | (1917–1926) | 48% |
| Switzerland | (1917–1926) | 32% |

On the basis of the above we can state that the percentage of female victims, in countries of high frequency of crimes against life, keeps below 10 per cent, while in countries of low frequency of crimes against life it fluctuates between 18 and 48 per cent.

*The dynamic law* reads:

*If frequency of crimes against life in a country is on the increase, the increase affects mainly the number of male victims of crimes against life; and vice versa: if the statistics of crimes against life in a country reveal a declining trend, the reduction affects primarily the number of men killed.*

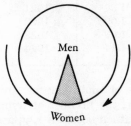

FIGURE 3. *Schematic illustration of the fluctuation in the percentage of female victims in countries in which crimes against life tend to increase.*

Figures 3 and 4 illustrate schematically the proportion of male and female victims of crime, with criminality tending to increase or to decline.

In the period 1878–1898 those killed in Finland totalled 2.80 per 100,000 inhabitants, in 1899–1904 3.14 and in 1905–1913 5.04. The ratios for men were, respectively, 4.87, 5.47, and 8.78, those for women 0.79, 0.85, and 1.34 only, per 100,000 inhabitants. In 1914–1916 the ratio for those killed

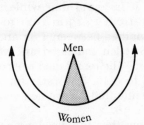

FIGURE 4. *Schematic illustration of the fluctuation in the percentage of female victims in countries in which crimes against life tend to decline.*

was 3.57 and in 1920–1932, 8.43; during the former period
the ratio for men was 5.83 and for women 1.33, during the
latter no less than 15.62 for men, and only 1.42 for women.

From Italy also evidence is available for 1913–1924. The
number of men and women killed, per 100,000 inhabitants,
were as follows:[2]

| YEAR | MEN | WOMEN | YEAR | MEN | WOMEN |
|------|------|-------|------|-------|-------|
| 1913 | 5.95 | 1.05 | 1919 | 7.47 | 1.53 |
| 1914 | 6.50 | 1.27 | 1920 | 12.97 | 1.62 |
| 1915 | 5.99 | 1.32 | 1921 | 13.13 | 1.84 |
| 1916 | 4.23 | 1.09 | 1922 | 11.61 | 1.68 |
| 1917 | 4.92 | 1.00 | 1923 | 8.16 | 1.77 |
| 1918 | 4.31 | 1.14 | 1924 | 7.96 | 1.56 |

While the number of male victims greatly increased between 1919 and 1921, the number of female victims, during
the same period, remained between 1.53 and 1.84.

The second part of the dynamic law is illustrated by the
statistics for Finland and Italy, and also by the statistics for
Sweden. While the ratio for those killed in Finland from the
period 1905–1913 to the period 1914–1916 declined from 5.04
to 3.57, the ratio for men was reduced from 8.78 to 5.83, and
the ratio for women remained practically unchanged (1.34–
1.33). During the period of Prohibition, 1920–1932, the ratio
for those killed was 8.42, but on the introduction of the new
alcohol legislation it was reduced to 4.69. The ratio for men
declined from 15.60 to 7.75, while the ratio for women slightly
increased (1.42–1.73).

As regards Italy, it is found that while the ratio for male
victims was reduced from 13.13 in 1921 to 7.96 in 1924, the
ratio for women remained between 1.84 and 1.56.

The figures for Sweden indicated an even decline during
the period 1881–1940. The total killed per 100,000 inhabitants
declined from 0.90 to 0.49. The ratio for men was reduced
from 1.46 to 0.60, while that for women was at the beginning
0.37 and at the end 0.38.

The examples show that the development in the numbers
of female victims, as a rule, is smooth and uneventful, even
when there are violent fluctuations in the frequency of crimes

against life or when the frequency is on the decline. The fluctuations are reflected quite clearly in the numbers of male victims of crime only.

This phenomenon is due to the fact that the woman lives in a somewhat different and more peaceful atmosphere than the man, and that the factors influencing her, also, are not nearly so subject to changes as those affecting a man.

The laws prove useful whenever information on frequency of crimes against life in a country is defective. We know that Albania and Caucasia are countries of high frequency of crimes against life. But this is all we know. On the basis of the static law, however, we may conclude that a small percentage only of the killed in these countries represents female victims of crimes against life. The reverse is the case in countries of low frequency of crimes against life in which the number of female victims may approach that of male victims.

The dynamic law is of importance as an indicator of the trend of development when distribution by sex of the victims of crimes against life is estimated, with the crimes increasing or declining.

The laws described above do not refer to the victims of crimes against life only. They may also be applied to criminal statistics on men and women accused and convicted of crimes against life. In such circumstances their criminological significance is considerably enhanced. However, it must be borne in mind that the data on homicidal crimes contained in criminal statistics refer to a material of a kind other than the data on those killed contained in the cause-of-death statistics dealt with above. In the latter case, the question concerns victims of crimes against life, i.e. proved and successful crimes against life, in the former again, the question is one of detected committers of crimes against life or those suspected of committing such crimes, insofar as they have been prosecuted at Court or convicted of these crimes. There may be a considerable difference between the number of persons and the number of crimes: several persons may participate in one and the same crime, and one person may be guilty of several crimes. Furthermore, criminal statistics cover, not only committed crimes but attempted crimes as well. It must be noted that those found guilty include, apart from the persons guilty of the crime itself, those punished for instigation of and for connivance in the crime.

Criminal statistics on those prosecuted for and found guilty of crimes against life, by sexes, include a number of disturbing factors. If, however, the absolute numbers examined are big enough, chance factors will be eliminated, and the successions show distinct conformity to the laws, as in the case of the victims.

Much more abundant than the data on the sex of homicidal victims is the information included in the criminal statistics on the numbers of men and women prosecuted for and found guilty of crimes against life, collected for an earlier investigation. In examining this material, too, I have found regular sequences of the character of laws, exactly similar to those described above. These have not been discovered by earlier researchers, nor could they have been, as the frequency relations of crimes of violence have never before been studied methodically and to such an extensive degree. On this point also I have been able to ascertain that the proportion by sexes in the crimes against life in a country is always dependent on the frequency of these crimes.

Two laws, one of them static and the other dynamic, illustrate the contents of this rule, in greater detail.

*The static law* reads as follows: *In countries of high frequency of crimes against life the participation of women in these crimes is small;* and vice versa: *in countries of low freqency of crimes against life the participation of women in these crimes is perceptibly larger than in countries of high frequency of crimes against life.*

To elucidate the conditions in countries of high and low frequency of crimes against life, we may utilize Figures 1 and 2, given above, substituting for male and female victims of crimes, male and female criminals.

The following calculations, indicating the percentage of female participation in crimes against life (excluding negligent manslaughter and infanticide) in the different countries, may suffice to prove the validity of this static law.

*The dynamic law* reads:

*If the frequency of crimes against life in a country tends to increase, the increase primarily affects the number of male criminals;* and vice versa: *if the frequency of crimes against life in a certain country is on the decline, the decline primarily affects the number of male criminals.*

Figures 3 and 4 above illustrate the changes in the per-

centages of male and female criminals where the frequency
of crimes against life is increasing or decreasing.

### Countries of high frequency of crimes against life

| | | | |
|---|---|---|---|
| Finland | prosecuted 1921–1926 | | 4.0% |
| | convicted " " | | 3.1% |
| Bulgaria | convicted 1910–1912 | | 1.3% |
| Greece | convicted 1911–1913 | | 2.4% |
| Spain | held pending investigation or confined | | |
| | in convict prisons 1921–1924 | | 4.6% |

### Countries of low frequency of crimes against life

| | | | |
|---|---|---|---|
| Sweden | prosecuted 1921–1926 | | 17.9% |
| | convicted " " | | 10.3% |
| Norway | convicted " " | | 30.8% |
| Denmark | convicted " " | | 25.0% |
| Germany | convicted " " | | 11.5% |
| England and Wales | prosecuted " " | | 30.8% |
| France | prosecuted 1921–1923 | | 10.3% |

This law may be derived from the static law. Excellent evidence is obtainable from Finland.

Let us examine the group of crimes covering murder, intentional manslaughter with fatal results, including also that resulting from battery or a fight (Criminal Law, Chapter 21, Secs. 1–4 and 6–9).

If we start from the initial years of the present Criminal Law, 1895 and 1896, and check the situation at ten-yearly intervals, we find that the numbers of men and women found guilty, per one million inhabitants, are:

| YEAR | MEN | WOMEN |
|---|---|---|
| 1895 | 28.9 | 4.7 |
| 1896 | 49.0 | 4.6 |
| 1905 | 71.0 | 4.1 |
| 1906 | 93.9 | 5.4 |
| 1915 | 35.4 | 3.0 |
| 1916 | 44.7 | 5.4 |
| 1925 | 182.6 | 4.5 |
| 1926 | 160.5 | 3.9 |
| 1935 | 95.8 | 2.6 |
| 1936 | 93.7 | 3.6 |

It is obvious from the above that the number of women, whether the number of men increases or decreases, shows no tendency to follow suit.[3]

The benefit of the regularities hereby established is obvious in the numerous cases in which there are gaps in statistical data concerning frequency of crimes against life in the different countries. These may be bridged with the aid of the regular successions. If, for instance, we know that frequency of crimes against life in a certain country, e.g. in Chile or Albania, is very high, we may draw the conclusion that the percentage of women concerned is negligible.

The static law is applicable in the above cases. On the strength of the dynamic law, again, advance conclusions can be drawn as to how the proportion by sexes will develop if frequency of crimes against life in a country reveals a permanent tendency to increase or to decrease. In 1933 I pointed out that if the high figures of crimes against life in Finland, for one reason or another, should start indicating a permanently decreasing trend, we could tell in advance what effect this change would have on the percentages of men and women prosecuted and found guilty.[4] Due to the improvement in the alcohol situation the number of crimes against life, in fact, started decreasing in Finland from 1934 onwards. At the same time it could be ascertained that the percentage of women participating in crimes against life had considerably increased.

The regularities dealt with are based on the fact that female criminality against life is, figuratively speaking, a constant, which, as a rule, remains at the same level even if male criminality fluctuates strongly in either direction. It is obvious that the different biological qualities of men and women are the fundamental cause of this phenomenon.

# Inter- and Intra-racial
# Homicides

## HAROLD GARFINKEL

THE PURPOSES of this paper are first, to furnish materials
dealing with the treatment afforded white and colored offenders involved in inter- and intra-racial homicides, and second,
to submit a hypothesis to account for the peculiarities of the
data that emerge when the various indices of treatment, i.e.,
types of trials, indictments, convictions, sentences, are categorized by race of offender and victim.

The data cover the eleven year period, January 1, 1930 to
December 31, 1940. The data were collected from the death
certificates and Superior Court records of ten counties in
North Carolina: Alamance, Caswell, Chatham, Durham,
Granville, Guilford, Orange, Person, Rockingham, and Wake.
Three cities, Raleigh, Durham, and Greensboro are located in
this area.

The discussion that follows is based on 673 instances of
homicide which involved 821 offenders.[1] Of 689 instances
that were found, 16 were rejected for lack of information regarding race and sex of offender and/or victim; of 839 cases,
18 were rejected because of a similar lack of information.

## FINDINGS

### Number of Cases (Table 1)

Generally speaking, the men and women of this region
killed their own kind; Negroes killed Negroes and whites
killed whites. Intra-racial homicides made up 90 percent of

REPRINTED with the permission of the author and the publisher from
Harold Garfinkel, "Research Note in Inter- and Intra-racial Homicides,"
*Social Forces* (May, 1949), 27: 4: 370-381.

TABLE 1. *Percentage Distribution of Cases by Race, and Race and Sex of Offenders and Victims*[a]

| | N-W No. | Percent | | W-W No. | Percent | | N-N No. | Percent | | W-N No. | Percent |
|---|---|---|---|---|---|---|---|---|---|---|---|
| MN-MW | 42 | 5.1 | MW-MW | 134 | 16.3 | MN-MN | 403 | 49.1 | MW-MN | 24 | 2.9 |
| MN-FW | 7 | .9 | MW-FW | 12 | 1.5 | MN-FN | 101 | 12.2 | MW-FN | 0 | .0 |
| FN-MW | 2 | .2 | FW-MW | 12 | 1.5 | FN-MN | 56 | 6.8 | FW-MN | 0 | .0 |
| FN-FW | 0 | .0 | FW-FW | 7 | .9 | FN-FN | 21 | 2.6 | FW-FN | 0 | .0 |
| | 51 | 6.2 | | 165 | 20.2 | | 581 | 70.7 | | 24 | 2.9 |

821 = 100 percent

M = male; F = female; W = white; N = Negro; - = "versus"

[a] The data in this and succeeding tables cover the period January 1, 1930 to December 31, 1940 for the following ten North Carolina counties: Alamance, Caswell, Chatham, Durham, Granville, Guilford, Orange, Person, Rockingham, Wake.

the 821 cases; inter-racial homicides, barely 10 percent. Of the 821 cases, almost 71 percent involved Negroes against Negroes and 20 percent involved whites against whites. Of the remaining 9 percent, which represented out-group offenses, Negroes and whites were involved in 6 percent of the cases, and whites against Negroes were involved in the remaining 3 percent.

Two-thirds of all the cases involved males of the same race as offenders and victims. Almost half of all the reported cases involved male Negro slayers and victims. The next largest category, representing one-sixth of all the cases, involved male white slayers and victims. Female slayers were for the most part involved with male victims, and then almost entirely with male victims of their own race.

Where male slayers were involved with female victims, the two races differed markedly. While 12 percent of all the cases involved male Negro slayers and female Negro victims, only 1.5 percent of the cases involved male white slayers and female white victims.

There were no inter-racial–inter-sexual homicides which involved white offenders. Negro males, however, were tried in the courts as slayers of both sexes of whites, while female Negro offenders were involved with male whites but not with female whites.

In absolute numbers there were more cases of Negroes than whites involved in inter-racial homicides. In percentage terms, however, whites were somewhat more frequently involved with members of the other race than were Negroes. Thirteen percent of all white slayers were involved in inter-racial homicides while 8 percent of Negro offenders were so involved. No cases were found for MW-FN, FW-MN, FW-FN, and FN-FW.[2]

## *Trial Experience (Tables 2, 3)*

We shall speak of three stages of trial: indictment, charge, and conviction.[3] The percentages of all the cases in each of the four classes of offenders remaining at the three stages of the definition of the offense is shown in Table. 2.

*Indictments, charges, and convictions of Negroes versus whites.* N-W were indicted for 1°[4] murder and convicted of 1° and 2°. This category showed fewer changes of indictment than did any of the other three categories. Particularly is this true of changes from an indictment of 1° to a charge of "2°-or-

TABLE 2. *Percentage Distribution of All Offenders Remaining at Indictment, Charge, and Conviction*

|  | N-W | W-W | N-N | W-N |
|---|---|---|---|---|
| All cases | 100.0 | 100.0 | 100.0 | 100.0 |
| Indictment: |  |  |  |  |
| First degree murder | 94.0 | 83.6 | 91.3 | 70.9 |
| Second degree murder | 2.0 | 3.0 | 3.8 | 8.3 |
| Manslaughter | 2.0 | 7.9 | 3.4 | 20.8 |
| Other | 2.0 | 5.5 | 1.5 | 0.0 |
| Charge: |  |  |  |  |
| First degree murder | 68.6 | 44.2 | 52.9 | 41.6 |
| Second degree murder | 1.9 | 6.6 | 7.9 | 8.3 |
| Manslaughter | 3.8 | 8.5 | 4.5 | 25.0 |
| Second degree-or-manslaughter | 13.7 | 17.0 | 21.4 | 20.8 |
| Lesser charges and nol pros | 22.0 | 23.7 | 13.3 | 4.3 |
| Conviction: |  |  |  |  |
| First degree murder | 29.4 | 6.7 | 2.6 | 0.0 |
| Second degree murder | 31.4 | 27.3 | 35.4 | 34.2 |
| Manslaughter | 9.8 | 20.0 | 35.6 | 16.7 |
| Other | 9.8 | 6.6 | 3.1 | 12.5 |
| Acquittal and dismissal | 19.6 | 38.4 | 23.3 | 36.6 |

Percentages are based on the following figures: N-W 51; W-W 165; N-N 581; W-N 24, the over-all total being 821. Each of these totals represents all the cases in each of the offender-victim categories.

TABLE 3. *Convictions for Offenders Charged with First Degree Murder*

|  | N-W | | W-W | | N-N | | W-N |
|---|---|---|---|---|---|---|---|
|  | No. | Percent | No. | Percent | No. | Percent | No. |
| All convictions | 35 | 100.0 | 73 | 100.0 | 307 | 100.0 | 8 |
| First degree murder | 15 | 42.9 | 11 | 15.1 | 15 | 4.9 | 0 |
| Second degree murder | 14 | 40.0 | 40 | 54.8 | 162 | 52.8 | 5 |
| Manslaughter | 1 | 2.0 | 12 | 16.4 | 119 | 38.8 | 2 |
| Other | 5 | 14.2 | 10 | 13.7 | 11 | 3.5 | 1 |

manslaughter-as-the-evidence-permits."[5] While this would tend to bear out ordinary expectations, there is an accompanying anomaly. Changes from indictments of 1° to nol pros and to charges less than manslaughter were fully as large in relative percentages for N-W as changes for the other three categories of offenders. This can be seen in Table 2. Peculiarly enough, the largest number of changes of indictment for N-W were changes from 1° to nol pros or to charges less than manslaughter.

*Indictments, charges, and convictions of whites versus whites.* Although they were principally indicted for 1°, W-W were indicted to some extent for lesser offenses. The changes of indictment for the W-W group were similar in pattern to the changes for N-W although the changes were spread over a greater number of categories for W-W than for N-W. As the definition of the offense changed for W-W it changed from an indictment of 1° to (a) 2°-or-manslaughter, or (b) to lesser charges than manslaughter, or (c) to judgments of nol pros. W-W were disposed of through acquittal, or conviction of either 2° or manslaughter.

*Indictments, charges, and convictions of Negroes versus Negroes.* N-N were overwhelmingly indicted for 1°. The percentage of change between indictment and the offense as it was defined for the jury was as great for N-N as it was for W-W. The distribution of changes in the N-N group, however, showed a concentration in the ambiguous class of 2°-or-manslaughter-as-the-evidence-permits. Comparatively fewer cases of N-N than W-W were nol prossed or defined as lesser crimes than manslaughter. As they were finally disposed of, cases were concentrated in convictions for 2°, manslaughter, and to a lesser extent, in acquittal or dismissal.

*Indictments, charges, and convictions of whites versus Negroes.* W-N were indicted for 1° and manslaughter. There was as much percentage change of indictment for W-N as there was for N-N, both categories showing less change than N-W and more change than W-W. Most of the change of definition of the offense involved a change from an indictment of 1° to a charge of 2°-or-manslaughter-as-the-evidence-permits. Compared with the other categories, fewer cases of W-N were changed to lesser charges than manslaughter or nol pros. The cases were disposed of by acquittal, and convictions of 2° murder, with a considerable percentage of cases convicted of manslaughter and lesser offenses. No cases of W-N were convicted of 1°. This is to be compared with almost 30 percent of N-W that were convicted of 1°

Two types of patterns can be seen at indictment: (a) the pattern for N-W, W-W, and N-N, which shows a concentration of indictments for 1°, with the other indictments being more or less evenly distributed among indictments for 2°, manslaughter, and lesser offenses, and (b) the pattern for W-N, which shows two points of concentration, 1° and manslaughter, with no indictments for less than manslaughter.

Two types of patterns emerge again at the point where the solicitor entered the charge for which the defendant was tried. First, there is the same similarity noted before between the distributions for N-W, W-W, and N-N. For all three there is a concentration of offenses defined as 1°, with another though lesser concentration for 2°-or-manslaughter-as-the-evidence-permits. The second pattern type, that for W-N, shows a concentration in the three categories of 1°, manslaughter, and 2°-or-manslaughter.

Three patterns, each quite different from the others, emerged after judgment. The first pattern, that for N-W, showed strong and almost equal concentration of convictions for 1° and 2° murder. The pattern that describes the distribution of convictions for W-W and N-N showed a concentration of convictions for 2° and manslaughter, although a greater percentage of W-W than N-N were finally dismissed. The third pattern is that of W-N with its heaviest concentration of convictions for 2°, with similar though lesser percentages of convictions for manslaughter and lesser offenses. There were no convictions for 1° murder.

Table 3, which shows how offenders charged with 1° murder were convicted, bears out in finer detail the different patterns of convictions for the three offender-victim categories.

### Solicitor's Demand (Table 4)

While changes of indictment were asked for all of the four categories of offenders, there were marked discrepancies in the frequency with which changes were requested for the various classes of offenders. Changes were least frequently asked for N-W and most frequently asked for W-N. Changes were asked in approximately 15 percent of the cases for N-W and in 6 out of 13 cases of W-N. Changes were requested for

TABLE 4.  *Indictments for First and Second Degree Murder by Solicitor's Demand*

| | N-W | | W-W | | N-N | | W-N |
|---|---|---|---|---|---|---|---|
| | No. | Percent | No. | Percent | No. | Percent | No. |
| All indictments for first and second degree murder | 48 | 100.0 | 144 | 100.0 | 552 | 100.0 | 19 |
| No change asked | 41 | 85.4 | 106 | 73.6 | 387 | 70.1 | 13 |
| Change asked | 7 | 14.6 | 38 | 26.4 | 165 | 29.9 | 6 |
| Change asked to: | | | | | | | |
|   Second degree | 0 | | 6 | 15.8 | 26 | 15.8 | 0 |
|   Manslaughter | 0 | | 3 | 7.9 | 7 | 4.2 | 1 |
|   Second-degree-or-Manslaughter | 7 | | 29 | 76.3 | 126 | 76.4 | 5 |
|   Other | 0 | | 0 | 0.0 | 6 | 3.6 | 0 |

W-W in 26 percent of the cases and for N-N in 30 percent of the cases. In all four categories the principal changes were from 1° and 2° to 2°-or-manslaughter-as-the-evidence-permits.

## Types of Trials (Table 5)

Most of the cases of N-W and W-W charged with first degree murder were tried by jury. The few cases of W-N similarly charged, were tried in equal numbers by judge and

TABLE 5.  *Types of Trials of Offenders Charged with First Degree Murder*

| | N-W | | W-W | | N-N | | W-N |
|---|---|---|---|---|---|---|---|
| | No. | Percent | No. | Percent | No. | Percent | No. |
| All trials | 38 | 100.0 | 85 | 100.0 | 332 | 100.0 | 11 |
| Trial by judge | 8 | 23.7 | 20 | 23.5 | 223 | 67.1 | 5 |
| Trial by jury[a] | 29 | 76.3 | 53 | 62.4 | 84 | 25.3 | 6 |
| Trial by jury from another county | (3) | (7.9) | (3) | (3.5) | 0 | 0.0 | 0 |
| Change from trial by jury to trial by judge | 0 | 0.0 | 12 | 14.1 | 25 | 7.5 | 0 |

[a] Includes items in row entitled, "Trial by jury from another county."

jury, while most of the cases of N-N were tried by judge.
Under the rules of trial procedure in North Carolina, trial by
judge is possible only if the defendant enters a plea of guilty
to some degree of crime which is less than 1° and which is
acceptable as a plea to the court. If the plea is accepted by
the court, the trial is held by the judge to determine the appropriate punishment. This plea may be entered before the
trial begins or during the course of the trial.

Only cases of W-W and N-N entered such pleas of guilty
during the trial so that a change of trial took place for them.
No such changes of trial were found for W-N and N-W. A
little less than half of all the W-W who were tried by judge
entered pleas of guilty prior to trial, while something around
90 percent of N-N who were tried by judge entered pleas of
guilty before trial. Finally, it might be noted that only for
cases of N-W and W-W were requests made and granted for
trial by jury selected from a county other than the one in
which the crime had been committed.

### Disposition of Offenders (Tables 6, 7, 8, 9)

Table 6 shows how offenders charged with first degree murder were finally disposed of. The sentences are those given for
convictions ranging from 1° and accessory before the fact,
which carry the mandatory sentences of death and life imprisonment, respectively, to assault with a deadly weapon,
abortion, and aiding and abetting a felony.

A distinctive pattern of sentences can be observed for each

TABLE 6.    *Disposition of Offenders Charged with First Degree*
*Murder*

|  | N-W | | W-W | | N-N | | W-N |
|---|---|---|---|---|---|---|---|
|  | No. | Percent | No. | Percent | No. | Percent | No. |
| All | 41 | 100.0 | 101 | 100.0 | 372 | 100.0 | 11 |
| Acquitted | 6 | 14.6 | 28 | 27.7 | 65 | 17.5 | 3 |
| 0–9 years | 2 | 4.9 | 16 | 15.8 | 137 | 36.8 | 2 |
| 10–19 years | 1 | 2.4 | 12 | 11.9 | 77 | 20.7 | 2 |
| 20–29 years | 4 | 9.7 | 22 | 21.8 | 59 | 15.9 | 3 |
| 30 years | 9 | 22.0 | 9 | 8.9 | 18 | 4.8 | 1 |
| Life imprisonment | 4 | 9.7 | 3 | 3.0 | 1 | .3 | 0 |
| Death | 15 | 36.6 | 11 | 10.9 | 15 | 4.0 | 0 |

TABLE 7. *Sentences Given to Offenders Convicted of First and Second Degree Murder*

| | N-W | | W-W | | N-N | | W-N |
|---|---|---|---|---|---|---|---|
| | No. | Percent | No. | Percent | No. | Percent | No. |
| All sentences | 35 | 100.0 | 59 | 100.0 | 223 | 100.0 | 7 |
| 0–9 years | 1 | 2.8 | 3 | 5.1 | 44 | 19.7 | 0 |
| 10–19 years | 1 | 2.8 | 10 | 16.9 | 71 | 31.8 | 1 |
| 20–29 years | 5 | 14.3 | 23 | 39.0 | 73 | 32.7 | 3 |
| 30 years | 9 | 25.7 | 9 | 15.3 | 19 | 8.5 | 3 |
| Life imprisonment | 4 | 11.4 | 3 | 5.1 | 1 | .4 | 0 |
| Death | 15 | 42.9 | 11 | 18.6 | 15 | 6.7 | 0 |

of the three offender-victim categories, N-W, N-N, and W-W. An insufficient number of cases of W-N made percentage expressions impractical for this category. The cases of N-W fall into a U-shaped distribution with the heaviest concentration found at extreme severity of punishment, while another, but milder concentration is found at acquittal.[6]

TABLE 8. *Disposition of Offenders Charged with Second Degree Murder, Manslaughter, and "Second-Degree-or-Manslaughter"*

| | N-W | W-W | | N-N | | W-N |
|---|---|---|---|---|---|---|
| | No. | No. | Percent | No. | Percent | No. |
| All | 9 | 55 | 100.0 | 200 | 100.0 | 13 |
| Acquitted | 3 | 29 | 52.7 | 61 | 30.5 | 8 |
| 0–9 years | 4 | 20 | 36.3 | 103 | 51.5 | 3 |
| 10–19 years | 1 | 3 | 5.5 | 22 | 11.0 | 0 |
| 20–29 years | 1 | 3 | 5.5 | 13 | 6.5 | 0 |
| 30 years | 0 | 0 | 0.0 | 1 | .5 | 2 |

The pattern for N-N might almost be described as the converse of the N-W distribution. Unimodal in character, it is heavily weighted by the lighter punishments, with the convictions for manslaughter being reflected in the heavy concentration in sentences of 10 years or less.

Unlike either of the other two, the pattern for W-W suggests a comb, with concentrations at acquittal, moderately severe sentences, and extreme punishment.

When the effect of acquittals and sentences given for lesser crimes is removed, the patterns of sentences given for convictions of first and second degree murder are almost exaggeratedly different from each other. The same three types of patterns are found in the essential forms noted previously, although now there is no question of the severity of punishment given to Negroes who were convicted of second degree murder of whites.

If sentences for N-W pushed the limits of severity of punishment, the sentences for N-N, in their concentration within a sentence range of 10 to 29 years, with comparatively fewer cases found in the extremes of punishment, bespoke a more "moderate" regard.

The pattern of sentences for W-W is rather complex. The comb effect is very clear. Concentration occurs at the moderate range of 20 to 29 years and at the extreme penalties. Only 5 percent of the cases of W-W received less than 10 years, compared with 20 percent of the N-N who were so punished.

Of the seven cases of W-N who were convicted of second degree murder, six received sentences of 20 years or more.

TABLE 9.   *Sentences Given for Convictions of Manslaughter*

|  | N-W | W-W | | N-N | | W-N |
|---|---|---|---|---|---|---|
|  | No. | No. | Percent | No. | Percent | No. |
| All sentences | 7 | 32 | 100.0 | 211 | 100.0 | 4 |
| 0–4 years | 3 | 17 | 53.1 | 107 | 50.7 | 3 |
| 5–9 years | 2 | 12 | 37.5 | 74 | 35.1 | 0 |
| 10–14 years | 1 | 3 | 9.4 | 17 | 8.1 | 1 |
| 15–19 years | 1 | 0 | 0.0 | 12 | 5.7 | 0 |
| 20 years (max) | 0 | 0 | 0.0 | 1 | .5 | 0 |

Table 8 shows the disposition of offenders charged with 2°, manslaughter, and "2°-or-manslaughter." Peculiarly enough, of the 9 cases of N-W so charged, 3 were acquitted, and 4 received sentences of less than 10 years. A striking difference as far as interpretation is concerned, is found between the disposition of N-N and W-W. For the two modes of disposition, acquittal and less than 10 years, the two types of cases are the converse of each other. In the cases of N-N, 30 percent were acquitted and 50 percent were given something less than 10 years, while W-W were acquitted in 53 percent of the cases and were given less than 10 years in 36 percent of the cases. N-N showed a heavier concentration than did W-W in the heavier sentences for crimes defined out of the charges of 2°, manslaughter, and "2°-or-manslaughter."

The actual sentences given for convictions of manslaughter are almost identical in the relative numbers of W-W and N-N who were given less than 15 years. N-N alone received sentences of 15 years or more for convictions of manslaughter.

## DISCUSSION

The indices of treatment for each of the four offender-victim categories will be interpreted with the use of four types of social definitions of the situation of trial which were employed by participants making up the white court. These definitions are rather tentative. They are offered not only in the sense of their possible accuracy, but in the sense of the implied method of effecting comparisons of treatment. The attention of the reader is called to the fact, for example, that within the interpretive contexts employed here, differentials of treatment may exist even in the face of numerically equivalent indices of treatment.

The interpretations are based on the view that the processes of trial consist of activities oriented to the reinstatement of desecrated communally sanctioned values. As the locus of magic and ritual, the trial serves the long list of functions beginning with the recognition of crime and criminal and ending by providing the agencies of crime repression with the means of invoking proper authority by which to either absolve the desecrator of his stain or to require that the stain be wiped out by appropriate punishment.

From the point that murder is "recognized" until the case is finally disposed of, the offender is involved in a system of procedures of definition and redefinition of social identities and circumstances. These definitions represent the ways of attending, the "attitude" in Edmund Husserl's sense of this term,[7] with reference to which offender and offense mean whatever they do mean as objects of court treatment. It is with reference to objects which mean as they do in such frames that the significance of the indices of treatment is found.

We have relied upon a personal and summary evaluation

of actual trial situations which were witnessed by the investigator in the area from which the data were taken. To avoid the charge of circular reasoning—that is, the indices of treatment suggest the terms of the social definitions which are then used to explain the indices of treatment—the procedure actually should have been: investigation of the elements of the courts' definitions, to constructed definitions of regard, to explanations of the significances of the distribution of cases as the distributions represent the expressions of repressive concern for violated values. We hope that we are not unduly trying the reader's patience by asking him to allow our types to stand, for the purposes of this discussion. The fact that the types are "intuitively" derived means that the constructions have no better than "if . . . than" status. Their empirical character remains to be worked out by more antiseptic investigative procedures.

The following sequences of key phrases represent elements of the white courts' regard for the four types of cases.

### NEGROES VERSUS WHITES

a. Acceptance of the act as objectively criminal, the objectivity stemming from a deeply sentimental persuasion. It is the specific criminality of the act that comprises the essential meaning of the action for the court. So certainly is the presentation of Negro-white homicide defined as heinously murderous that a definition in any other terms constitutes a distortion of reality.
b. There is a compulsion to allocate responsibility; a compulsion to see that "Justice is done."
c. Trial procedure is marked by its sacred ritual character. There is a sense of administering a sacred trust, this trust being acquired through proper invocation of the ultimate moral authority of "God" and "Society."
d. The court is oriented toward the ultimate non-empirical end of Justice. The means employed are sacredly empirical and non-empirical. The distinction between punishment and dismissal is based on the deep lying sentiment of what Justice requires.
Summary reaction: Get the nigger who is responsible for this.

### WHITES VERSUS WHITES

a. There is a strong persuasion as to the criminality of the act. This persuasion is tempered, however, by the fact that the tying of a suspect to the act, and to some extent the persuasion of criminality of the act itself, rests upon regard for "the evidence."

b. There is a compulsion to allocate responsibility; a compulsion to see that Justice is done.
c. The ritual of the trial is secular as well as sacred. There is a sense of administering a sacred trust, with this trust being acquired through proper invocation of moral and legal authority.
d. There is the orientation toward the ultimate non-empirical end of Justice. The means, however, are secularly empirical and non-empirical in character. The compulsion that Justice be done takes the form that Justice be allocated "in light of the evidence." The distinction between punishment and dismissal is based on the deep-lying sentiment of what Justice requires.

Summary reaction: This man must be tried. If he is guilty he'll get what's coming to him; if he isn't, he'll be set free.

### NEGROES VERSUS NEGROES

a. Though there is a persuasion that the act being considered is a criminal one, there is a lack of persuasion as to its specific criminality. The defendant's "character," for example, is a meaningful component in defining the criminal character of the act.
b. Although there is a marked drive to assign responsibility, it is possible to enter into tactical exchanges regarding the meaning of the sentiment that "Justice must be done."
c. Secular ritual marks the trial. There is little sense of administering a sacred trust. Any authority may be invoked.
d. The court is oriented toward an amorphously formulated meaning of Justice as an ultimate end. Evaluation of crime and criminal is marked by the comparative lack of moral pieties and the presence of utilitarian modes of considering the act. The distinction between punishment and dismissal is based on a utilitarian regard for the consequences of either alternative.

Summary reaction: Murder? Another one? Who is the man? Where is he from? Whom did he kill? Are we going to try him or did he enter a plea?

### WHITES VERSUS NEGROES

a. No particular persuasion of the criminality of the act unless it is an inclination to discount its criminality. Criminality is involved as objectively undeniable where white values are threatened. The fact of the crime taps no deep-lying sentiments of wrong but is seen rather with reference to sentiments of serious misdemeanor. Evaluation may be carried out at the level of utilitarian considerations regarding the consequences for the defendant of a particular evaluation.
b. No compulsion to allocate responsibility; no recognition of the sentiment that "Justice must be done" insofar as this sentiment

bears on the problem of expiation of sin. That Justice must be
done refers instead to the compulsion to establish the reasonable character of the act.

c. Secular empirical ends characterize the orientations of trial
tactics. Authorities for trial action may be sacred or secular.

d. The court is oriented toward the end of Justice which is defined
in secular terms. The presence in the evaluation of choice of interpretation, and the lack of moral compulsions makes possible
pronouncements of degrees of guilt. The distinction between
punishment and dismissal is based on the reasonable justification of either alternative.

Summary reaction: Murder? Why did he kill him?

We shall limit our task of interpretation to the distributions
of indictments, charges, convictions, and sentences as these
are given for the four offender-victim categories in Tables 2,
6, and 7.

In light of the regard types framed above, it is suggested
that the high percentages of indictments for 1° in the cases
of N-W is the result of the fact that indictments for lesser
offenses are not "thinkable." To propose alternative and lesser
definitions of the offense either at the point of indictment or
as future possibilities would simply be a breach of fitness. By
comparison, the high percentage of indictments for N-N occur
precisely because a lesser offense is all too "thinkable." Future
possibilities most definitely provide alternative definitions.
The indictment of 1° for N-W is fixed by criteria of what is
morally required, whereas the indictment of 1° for N-N is
fixed at the point of indictment by amorphous and ill-defined
"experimental" criteria. Not until far along in the trial is the
"real criminality" of the N-N fixed, while the "real criminality"
of the N-W is fixed from the start. An indictment of 1° serves
to get the court machinery underway; among its various meanings this pragmatic one is prominent, as far as N-N are concerned. No such utilitarian consideration is operative for N-W.
Another pragmatic coloring in the elements which lie behind
the high percentage of indictments of 1° for N-N is found in
the fact that such an indictment, in that it denotes high seriousness of offense, is often intended by the white court as a
terrorizing device, and hence is an instrument of white control
over Negro criminality. The same intended effect of terroriza-
tion is found in indictments of 1° for N-W, but we would insist
that it is not calculatedly pursued in the same sense that obtains in cases of N-N.

The different principles of action might be put this way: the indictment of 1° for N-W is reasonable on the grounds that the crime is so heinous that 1° murder best describes it. The indictment of 1° for N-N is reasonable because the "actual criminality" (as the court sees it, remember) is obscure. Where the process by which an offense is finally defined, by the basic rules of trial procedure, is unidirectional such that one can go from a grave offense to a lesser offense, but not the other way around, an indictment of 1° is a way of starting at the beginning thus insuring the catch somewhere up the line. In cases of N-W we would expect to find that trial tactics serve to support or deny the original indictment, while the tactics in cases of N-N would serve to differentiate the indictment into many possible degrees of crime. Such differentiating tactics are employed for cases of W-W, but the "calculus" for W-W differs from that employed for N-N as we shall see in a moment.

Falling between N-W and N-N in relative magnitude, indictments for 1° for W-W are assigned because murder is serious but also because the indictment is a beginning-of-the-line category. In the cases of W-W there is a persuasion to criminality which rests upon the regard for "the evidence." This allows a "calculus" with a difference. Like the N-N, the W-W gets an indictment which is considered "experimental" but it is experimental not on the basis of ambiguous criteria of the definition of the offense, as is the case with N-N, but is experimental on the basis of precisely defined criteria. Murder is real as a solemn crime; what is problematical is the determination of the extent of guilt, and this takes place within a situation where the court is always able to "locate" the defendant and the circumstances of the act with reference to an explicit and intimately known white code. The white man "earns" whatever he gets indicted, charged, or convicted of, and earns it within a game played according to rather rigid rules of procedure; within a game in which there is little place to hide an identity; and within a game to which he contributes as an active and seriously taken contestant. The key to the indictments for W-W is a regard employed by the court which is made up of highly differentiated and precise sentiments. The white defendant may make claims to various strategically significant identities, and in the court's view he may move from an identity of 1° murderer to 2° murderer, but the court always knows specifically what criteria must be fulfilled for the move, and whether or not the defendant has met them.

Indictments for W-N are defined "experimentally" but again with another difference. Indictments are defined "experimentally" in what might be called here "residual terms," and defined on the basis of a lack of persuasion regarding the specific criminality of the offense. Insofar as the offense is defined by indictment as first degree murder, "residual" means that an indictment for first degree murder represents not so much what the offense "is," as the court sees it, but what the offense "is not." Occasionally one finds cases, for example, of a defense attorney allowing an indictment of first degree murder to go without serious challenge and refusing a change of indictment to a lesser offense unless it be to a much less charge, on the grounds that the incongruity between the severity of a charge of first degree murder and the fact that it is a white man who killed a Negro who is being tried for this offense will be such as to increase the possibility of a total rejection of the charge by a jury of sympathetic white men. Insofar as the offense is defined by indictment as less than 1° it is an offense for which a white man who kills a Negro can be reasonably indicted; in effect, the indictment marks off an area of approximate definition. All these definitions, unlike those for N-N, are sharply delineated in the sense that alternative positions for the white defendant are fixed by deep lying sentiments of propriety of court treatment.

We have then a rather paradoxical summary: N-W offenses are heinously criminal, hence the concentratedly high percentage of indictments for 1°. W-W offenses are objectively criminal, hence the high percentage of indictments for 1° and evidence of spread among the other categories of indictments. N-N offenses are ambiguously criminal, hence the concentratedly high percentage of indictments for 1°. W-N offenses are experimentally or residually criminal but exclude ultimate seriousness, hence the high percentage of indictments for 1° and the spread among other indictments.

The problem now faces us of accounting for the fact that each of the four offender-victim categories shows a different percentage distribution of cases remaining at indictment, charge, and conviction, and different patterns of final disposition. The pattern for N-W is marked by the great percentage of cases indicted for 1°, the sustained percentages of severe charges and convictions, and the "all or none" character of the final disposition.

The objective criminality of a N-W murder as far as the white community is concerned makes indictments of less than first degree murder seem morally loose. There is nothing experimental about the indictment nor the concern of the whites for the breach of law. Somebody has to pay; Justice *will* be done. As a member of the outgroup, as a propertyless, non-functioning member in the white community of interest, the Negro's ties to the "rulers" are almost entirely bestowed; his position is weak; the white court *understands* him, *will* understand him, regardless of how he would be understood; he is hardly allowed to redefine his position to the whites; and the character of trial regard is such as to provide him with a situation in which all the strings have been tied. With this combination of factors, the percentage of charges of first degree remains high, much higher than any of the other three categories. The white court's compulsion to see Justice done makes degrees of guilt difficult. The rigidity of conception and procedure is such as to make the trial an all or none proposition. The tendency is therefore to maximized punishment or dismissal. Thus, the percentage of convictions for first and second degree murder is very much in excess of the percentages of any of the remaining offender-victim categories in all of which degrees of guilt are possible. Hence, also, the "U" shaped distribution of dispositions and the startlingly top-heavy distribution of sentences.

A note by way of discounting this hypothesis. One must not overlook the fact that the net thrown out after the murder of a white by a Negro catches many more Negroes than can be directly implicated in the act. Such cases are a source of the high percentage both of acquittals and convictions for lesser crimes. While this fact would serve as a discounting rule, it does not serve to destroy the hypothesis. The fact that many are called but few are chosen still leaves room for an explanation of the grounds of selection, and it is here that the all or none principle we have proposed may be of use.

Cases of W-W and N-N are similar in their patterns as far as charges and convictions are concerned, with the patterns for N-N appearing as somewhat exaggerated images of the W-W patterns. Does this mean that N-N enjoy the same treatment as that afforded W-W only more so? If this is the case, then it is very difficult to make sense of the marked differences in the distribution of sentences for the two types of cases.

The hypothesized regards propose that the two patterns, while they look alike, express quite different states of affairs. The difference is to be made in the fact that for the two types of cases degrees of guilt were possible. How were they possible?

For W-W there was a compulsion to assign responsibility and an orientation to the ultimate end of Justice. In itself this would make for severity of treatment. But withal there was a certain amount of slack which resulted from secular means and consideration for "the evidence" where "the evidence" could be rendered by the contestants in the form of such concepts as "extenuating circumstances," "justifiable homicide," "understandable reaction to prolonged provocation," "moment of insanity." Such concepts, as they were used to depict the circumstances in the lives of white offenders are familiar, legitimately meaningful, acceptable or rejectable according to immediately understandable criteria, criteria which are closely circumscribed by traditional interpretive schemata, familiar in the lives of bonafide in-group members of a white moral community who had been doing business at the stand of trouble for a long time.

Casting this view in other terms, one might say that insofar as cases of W-W were concerned, the court had access to a familiar, unambiguous, and extended vocabulary of persons, motives, and circumstances such that subtle discriminations of identities, motives, and circumstances would command serious consideration to eventuate then in legitimate grounds of argument or agreement. Such subtleties employed in cases of N-W would evoke a feeling of unreality or moral falseness and eventuate in indignation or reprisal; such subtleties proposed for cases of N-N would evoke incongruity and eventuate in laughter.

The result of all this then was a highly discriminative type of treatment. The proprieties in matching offense and punishment were based on the highly articulated character of the meanings of defendant, offense, and circumstance. The result is that all the categories of charge, convictions, and sentences got represented, with the tendencies to severity and dismissal underlined. Herein also lies the significance of the "comb" effect in the distribution of sentences for cases of W-W.

If degrees of guilt were possible for W-W, they were also possible for N-N but with a difference. Unlike the act of W-W, the act of N-N, while it was considered criminal, was seen in a context which did not provide a persuasion regarding specific criminality. Only far along in the trial was judgment passed on the "actual criminality" of the act. The drive to assign responsibility was matched by the absence of an orientation to a sacredly considered end of Justice. It was possible to enter into tactical exchanges regarding the meaning of the sentiment that "Justice must be done." Unlike the cases for W-W, where the allocation of positions and the transformations of position were based on a combination of terms and social logics which were familiar and meaningful to the whites in a context of high seriousness, the allocation of positions and transformations of positions for N-N were based on the familiarities of "contempt," on lack of seriousness, on "strangeness," on the ambiguities peculiar to pictures paintable with a small variety of colors and then in broad heavy strokes, and exemplified in the often encountered complaint, "You never really know why one nigger kills another." For W-W the changes in the definition of offense were made with full cognizance on the part of the law enforcing agencies of the "reason" and "basis" for the change. The case was revalued "as the evidence permits" as this term has meaning in the senses indicated above, whereas in the cases of N-N the change was made according to the paradigmatic formulation of one informant, "No Guilford County jury would give a nigger the chair for killing another nigger. It just doesn't seem worth it."

Such a pragmatic coloring is almost the *sine qua non* of the mode of judgment employed by an in-group member in appraising members of an out-group as persons. It is the coloring of an attitude in which the other person as a social object is a practical rather than an ideal object. The other person is a concrete object, given to the insider as an object in just the way it presents itself. Motives are considered apparent or are not considered at all, but in any case are not problematical. The other person is an object without a personal history, and is an object which has little value apart from and is treated according to its position within a project that is to be realized.

In that the white offender is a problematical figure for the court, in the sense that the court recognizes the legitimacy and necessity for understanding why the white offender "really" killed his victim, the white man is eligible for any conviction. For cases of W-W the conviction of manslaughter, for example, comes after "proper appraisal of the evidence" so that sentences are fixed by very definite sentiments, one element of which is the conception that manslaughter is a minor offense. The white man who kills another white man "earns" his conviction of manslaughter.

On the other hand, this practical object, the Negro offender, is an unproblematical figure as far as the white court is concerned. The white court in professing that "no one really knows why one nigger kills another" is expressing not only the obscurity of circumstances and motivations that the court experiences as a prominent property of the picture of Negro in-group homicides, but is expressing also the question that arises whenever one attempts to add further dimensions of meaning to an object whose practical meanings are apparent and settled: "Very interesting, but so what?" This is translatable into the court's view: The fact remains that he killed him.

If the way of differentiating the meanings of offender and offense are such that the W-W can be convicted of any offense, the regard of the court for cases of N-N is such than manslaughter is peculiarly a Negro's offense. The N-N does not "earn" this conviction as does the white man. Rather, the white court assigns it to him, and assigns it on the grounds that when all interests are considered, manslaughter is the most fitting description of the crime in that it allows that homicide was committed, but that the homicide involved Negroes. Crudely put, it is as if the white court will not allow that the Negro as a person is of sufficient complexity and worth to make a conviction of 1° (and 2° insofar as such a conviction carries the element of severity of offense) reasonably representative of the moral precepts that have been violated. It is in this sense that degrees of guilt are possible.

Not only are degrees of guilt possible for N-N but the lack of compulsion towards an ultimate end serves to obscure the difference between punishment and dismissal. We encounter then the feeling, "Thirty days on general principles" which is meaningful enough to be the premise of treatment. The effects of such an orientation are found in the fact that 74 percent of the cases of N-N drew convictions of 2° murder or less while 54 percent of W-W drew such convictions; only 23 percent of cases of N-N were freed while 38 percent of the cases of W-W were freed; and approximately 57 percent of the cases of N-N charged with 1° drew sentences between 0–19 years which is to be compared with 28 percent for W-W and 7 percent for N-W. Table 8 bears out the fact that if cases of N-W or W-W were called 2° murder, this meant severe punishment. Such was not the case for N-N for whom a conviction of 2° could mean light or heavy punishment.

We shall be unable to fulfill the task of interpreting the cases of W-N. The small number of cases remaining at charges and convictions would reduce our efforts to the kind of sheer speculation that would make the rest of our efforts appear by comparison as rock-founded fact. However, we can sketch the regard and predict on the basis of it what will be found when more cases are available.

The residual meanings of the indictment noted before, the fact that there was nothing deeper than a derivational persuasion of the criminality of the act, the compulsion to establish the reasonable character of the act, the resources of definitive terms accessible to the courts in appraising a white defendant, and the utilitarian regard for the consequences of any judgment would lead us to expect that insofar as the crime was seen as one involving a white versus a Negro the distribution of convictions would tend heavily toward the lesser crimes. Insofar as indictments for 1° murder were returned, there would be marked changes at the point of charge in the direction of charges for the ambiguous "2°-or-manslaughter-as-the-evidence-permits" or charges of manslaughter or less. Indictments for lesser crimes would show relatively little change at charge but marked changes at convictions. Convictions would be for manslaughter or lesser crimes. A much larger relative percentage of acquittals than any of the other four categories would appear, and sentences would be light. Where severe punishments were meted out we would have to predict that the fact that a Negro victim had been involved had little or nothing to do with the punishment. We would expect rather that the court acted in protection of the values of the white community. The fact that a Negro had been killed would have been less important than the fact, perhaps, that the offender had committed "another crime."

# The Victim's Contribution

## *TERENCE MORRIS and*
## *LOUIS BLOM-COOPER*

NOT EVERY crime need have a victim, but in those which do there often exists an especially interesting quality; the nature of the relationship between criminal and victim. More than this; just as the commission of a crime is no isolated, idiosyncratic act, but the culmination of a process in which many factors are at work, so for the most part there are few genuinely random victims of crime. The householder who is the victim of burglary has, as often as not, paid no heed to the state of his locks, left windows unfastened, or has gone away and advertised his absence by omitting to cancel the milk. The motorist who leaves a camera or briefcase on the seat in full view is asking to have them stolen. But victims may go beyond carelessness. The man who had had more liquor than he can take lies in the arms of a prostitute and may lose his wallet if it has not already been emptied by paying exorbitant sums for drinks in the shady "club" where he picked her up. Victims may suffer as a consequence of their own cupidity and foolishly entrust money to "confidence men" who assure them that some financial venture (beyond the reach of the Inland Revenue) is about to produce a fantastic profit. And some women approaching middle age and anxious about their sexual attractiveness are not infrequently the victims of unscrupulous Don Juans who fleece them of their money as well as their modesty. People who are careless about their goods, who are prepared to penetrate the Rialto of the half-world of

REPRINTED with the permission of the authors and the publisher from Terence Morris and Louis Blom-Cooper, "Victimology," *A Calendar of Murder: Criminal Homicide in England Since 1957*, London: Michael Joseph, Ltd., 1964, Chap. VII, pp. 321-326.

prostitutes, "club" owners and criminal lay-abouts, whose greed or whose vanity craves satisfaction, may all fall victim to crimes of one sort or another.

But how much of this applies to murder? Few people, it might be argued, die simply because they have been careless, promiscuous, avaricious or vain. And while it is relatively easy to say that a man has lost his belongings through his own fault, it is much more difficult to say that a man has lost his life through his own fault. For one of the more permanent qualities attributed to the victims of murder is that of innocence. Even a cursory reading of the thumbnail sketches of homicide printed in this book will show that this is often misplaced generosity, for some of the victims might well have been capable of killing on their own account, while others so goaded their killers either by provocation in words or deeds, or by incessant nagging that they directly precipitated their own deaths.

One factor emerges very clearly from these homicide cases, and that is [that] the area of hetero-sexual relationships is one exceptionally fraught with potential violence whether within the marriage or outside it. Relationships between men and women outside marriage are likely to focus on overtly sexual issues which brings in their train deeply charged emotions concerning exclusive rights of possession, and anxieties about unfaithfulness. Love and hate in psychoanalytic theory, are juxtaposed and often intertwined, so that an individual can both love and kill the object of his desire if the normal expression of his feelings is deflected by jealousy. Desdemona, had she been unloved by Othello, might have lived.

There are several cases, too, where murder occurred immediately after, or even during sexual intercourse, instances where true sadism—the infliction of pain upon the love object—occurred, accompanied by masochism—a desire to be hurt by the love object—on the part of the victim. Such complementary sadism and masochism has been observed among animals and is not uncommon among the human species. Within marriage, the frame of reference for the victim-killer relationship is not exclusively sexual. For although sexual infidelity is frequently an apparently precipitating factor, other tensions between husbands and wives may build up. The pattern of neurotic inter-action in marriage is frequently such that, although the relationship may be characterized by continuous conflict, participation in it satisfies the unconscious psychological needs of the partners, and neither has the wish to alter the situation. But, where the effect of conflict is not integrative but erosive, things are very different. Hostility may take a variety of forms—refusal by the wife to co-operate in giving a divorce, pestering or molesting the wife after or during proceedings, or the physical violence of murder. But because the act of murder in most human beings involves the mobilization of intense feeling it is more *possible* in relationships which by their very intimacy produce an intensity of emotion.

Vulnerability exists, not only in emotional proximity, but in certain practical circumstances. Many of these, unlike the circumstances of love and marriage, in no way involve a common psychological bond between killer and victim but are essentially situational hazards. Thus the prostitute whose client is unknown to her, may be murdered simply because she represents a readily accessible sexual object to her killer, to whom anonymity in his victim may be important. More commonly prostitutes are the only women prepared to co-operate in the sado-masochistic sexual perversions which form, for the killer, an integral part of the homicidal drive. While understandably little sympathy attaches in the public mind to the prostitute victim of homicide, the same is not true of other victims of 'sexual' murders, particularly when they are young. Where certain young children are concerned "innocence" is probably a misplaced term, for while little girls cannot be classed directly with adult prostitutes, by no means all of them are lacking in sexual curiosity. It is invariably a drive they but dimly perceive, but one which may draw them into situations where they may become the victims of crime.

Children who take lifts from strangers generally do so either because their parents have exercised little responsibility in instructing them or in direct defiance of parental injunction; in either case there is a situational factor at work. Similarly women who ask for lifts late at night run a risk of being sexually assaulted, largely because the drivers who give lifts to women in such circumstances know that a woman asking for a ride is likely to be of "easy virtue"; if she is not it is often the worse for her, as the sad stories regularly recounted in one Sunday newspaper bear testimony.

Leaving aside those situations in which the victim is likely

to be drawn into the homicidal situation, partly in consequence of some special feature of personality or adjustment,
there are others in which the instinctive behavior of the
victim triggers off the act of killing. The commonest of these
is undoubtedly in the typical capital murder—murder in the
course of furtherance of theft. The housebreaker is disturbed
by the householder (or nightwatchman), who attempts to arrest him, and in panic the housebreaker hits out, often with
some vase, ornament or movable object, killing the citizen
who is attempting to defend his property. The law, as often
as not, assumes that the killer intended to do grievous bodily
harm, and is therefore guilty of murder. In reality this is seldom the case; the housebreaker is normally in a state of great
tension and some regularly urinate on the premises, which
fact is sometimes recorded on their criminal record cards as
a useful piece of information for future detective work. Some
householders on the other hand, especially women, attempt
to defend their property with quite exceptional vigor, frequently screaming loudly. Such behavior is likely to trigger
off a violent attempt to silence the victim on the part of the
intruder who himself is tense and fearful, and the violence of
such panic reaction may well result in death. The ferocity of
resistance on the part of women householders may be connected with the fact that housebreaking is not unlike forcible
rape in the way the victims speak of it.[1] The use of the word
"outrage" is common, and as a woman whose home had been
burgled said to one of the present writers "what is so awful
is the thought of that man being in my bedroom." Although
the severity of injuries sustained by these victims is often
appalling (e.g. Riley 1961) they are not inconsistent with the
behavior of an offender whose panic has released all control
and reduced him to the level of a cornered animal. The law,
however, while not averse in the quieter atmosphere of the
courtroom to applying such descriptions to the killers, is seldom moved to consider "animal" responses in their situational
context when the question of the formation of criminal intent
is under discussion.

"Pleas of panic" in such circumstances are seldom if ever
accepted by the law as provocation, although initial violence
on the part of the victim can amount to such. Costas Panyani
(1960), a Birmingham cafe proprietor, in protecting his wife
and his premises from a group of young hoodlums, stabbed

two of them with a knife lying on the counter. Although these youths had caused trouble before, and were intending to do damage again, the court took a serious view of the crime and sentenced Panyani to 4 years' imprisonment. Chisam (1962), a middle-aged garage owner, fired a gun into the air to drive away some youths annoying him late at night by playing a transistor radio loudly outside his house. The youths forced their way into the house and assaulted Chisam who picked up a swordstick, injuring two and killing a third. His appeal on the grounds of self-defense against conviction of manslaughter under section 2 of the Homicide Act 1957 was rejected by the Court of Criminal Appeal. He was sentenced to life imprisonment. However in Vanstone's case (1962) the court took a different view. Vanstone, a small man of 53, was attacked by Rice a local farmer who, having drunk 15 whiskies, stopped Vanstone while the latter was taking his dog for a walk. Vanstone drew his pocket knife and severed an artery in his 18 stone attacker whom the trial judge called a "powerful drink-sodden bully." Vanstone was acquitted of both murder and manslaughter, and discharged.

What is perhaps most important in any discussion of "victimology" is to distinguish between the legal and the psycho-social aspects of the relationship between victim and killer. The law, both in respect [to] provocation and self-defense, utilizes definite criteria in assessing responsibility, and in awarding penalties it does not regard even legally defined provocation as cancelling out liability for punishment, although the severity of such punishment varies from case to case and court to court. Nor, contrary to what many people believe, does the law give the citizen *carte blanche* to defend himself or his property with any degree of force he chooses to employ.[2] But in examining the social and psychological aspects of the victim-killer relationship it is abundantly clear that homicide "out of the blue," in which the victim is struck down without reacting in any way, is exceptionally rare. Almost invariably there are words or actions (frequently recognized by the law as legitimate, and wholly approved by the community at large) which provoke the killer into the use of force —or in the instance of attempted rape—into still greater force. If householders kept calm, and women passively accepted unwanted interference—counsels of perfection, it is true—they might avoid more disastrous consequences.

But clearly, to expect this is to ask a great deal of human nature, and householders are no more likely to be able to do this than offenders in respect of their behavior. The fact that these reactions and counter-reactions exist is an inescapable fact, but not one which ought to be ignored when "innocence" and "guilt" are under either judicial scrutiny or public discussion. As George Meredith wrote:

> I see no sin;
>     The wrong is mixed.
> In tragic life, got wot,
>     No villain need be! Passions spin the plot:
> We are betrayed by what is false within.[3]

# Victim-Precipitated Criminal Homicide

## MARVIN E. WOLFGANG

IN MANY crimes, especially in criminal homicide, the victim is often a major contributor to the criminal act. Except in cases in which the victim is an innocent bystander and is killed in lieu of an intended victim, or in cases in which a pure accident is involved, the victim may be one of the major precipitating causes of his own demise.

Various theories of social interaction, particularly in social psychology, have established the framework for the present discussion. In criminological literature, however, probably von Hentig in *The Criminal and His Victim,* has provided the most useful theoretical basis for analysis of the victim-offender relationship. In Chapter XII, entitled "The Contribution of the Victim to the Genesis of Crime," the author discusses this "duet frame of crime" and suggests that homicide is particularly amenable to analysis.[1] In *Penal Philosophy,* Tarde[2] frequently attacks the "legislative mistake" of concentrating too much on premeditation and paying too little attention to motives, which indicate an important interrelationship between victim and offender. And in one of his satirical essays, "On Murder Considered as One of the Fine Arts," Thomas DeQuincey[3] shows cognizance of the idea that sometimes the victim is a would-be murderer. Garofalo,[4] too, noted that the victim may

REPRINTED with the permission of the author and the publisher from Marvin E. Wolfgang, "Victim-Precipitated Criminal Homicide," *Journal of Criminal Law, Criminology and Police Science* (June, 1957), 48:1: 1-11.

provoke another individual into attack, and though the provocation be slight, if perceived by an egoistic attacker, it may be sufficient to result in homicide.

Besides these theoretical concepts, the law of homicide has long recognized provocation by the victim as a possible reason for mitigation of the offense from murder to manslaughter, or from criminal to excusable homicide. In order that such reduction occur, there are four prerequisites.[5]

(1) There must have been adequate provocation.

(2) The killing must have been in the heat of passion.

(3) The killing must have followed the provocation before there had been a reasonable opportunity for the passion to cool. Such, for example, are: adultery, seduction of the offender's juvenile daughter, rape of the offender's wife or close relative, etc.

Finally (4), a causal connection must exist between provocation, the heat of passion, and the homicidal act. Perkins claims that "the adequate provocation must have engendered the heat of passion, and the heat of passion must have been the cause of the act which resulted in death."[6]

## DEFINITION AND ILLUSTRATION

The term *victim-precipitated* is applied to those criminal homicides in which the victim is a direct, positive precipitator in the crime. The role of the victim is characterized by his having been the first in the homicide drama to use physical force directed against his subsequent slayer. The victim-precipitated cases are those in which the victim was the first to show and use a deadly weapon, to strike a blow in an altercation—in short, the first to commence the interplay or resort to physical violence.

In seeking to identify the victim-precipitated cases recorded in police files it has not been possible always to determine whether the homicides strictly parallel legal interpretations. In general, there appears to be much similarity. In a few cases included under the present definition, the nature of the provocation is such that it would not legally serve to mitigate the offender's responsibility. In these cases the victim was threatened in a robbery, and either attempted to prevent the robbery, failed to take the robber seriously, or in some other fashion irritated, frightened, or alarmed the felon by physical force so that the robber, either by accident or compulsion, killed the victim. Infidelity of a mate or lover, failure to pay a debt, use of vile names by the victim, obviously mean that he played an important role in inciting the offender to overt action in order to seek revenge, to win an argument, or to defend himself. However, mutual quarrels and wordy altercations do not constitute sufficient provocation under law, and they are not included in the meaning of victim-precipitated homicide.

Below are sketched several typical cases to illustrate the pattern of these homicides. Primary demonstration of physical force by the victim, supplemented by scurrilous language, characterizes the most common victim-precipitated homicides. All of these slayings were listed by the Philadelphia Police as criminal homicides, none of the offenders was exonerated by a coroner's inquest, and all the offenders were tried in criminal court.

A husband accused his wife of giving money to another man, and while she was making breakfast, he attacked her with a milk bottle, then a brick, and finally a piece of concrete block. Having had a butcher knife in hand, she stabbed him during the fight.

A husband threatened to kill his wife on several occasions. In this instance, he attacked her with a pair of scissors, dropped them, and grabbed a butcher knife from the kitchen. In the ensuing struggle that ended on their bed, he fell on the knife.

In an argument over a business transaction, the victim first fired several shots at his adversary, who in turn fatally returned the fire.

The victim was the aggressor in a fight, having struck his enemy several times. Friends tried to interfere, but the victim persisted. Finally, the offender retaliated with blows, causing the victim to fall and hit his head on the sidewalk, as a result of which he died.

A husband had beaten his wife on several previous occasions. In the present instance, she insisted that he take her to the hospital. He refused, and a violent quarrel followed, during which he slapped her several times, and she concluded by stabbing him.

During a lover's quarrel, the male (victim) hit his mistress and threw a can of kerosene at her. She retaliated by throwing the liquid on him, and then tossed a lighted match in his direction. He died from the burns.

A drunken husband, beating his wife in their kitchen, gave her a butcher knife and dared her to use it on him. She claimed that if he should strike her once more, she would use the knife, whereupon he slapped her in the face and she fatally stabbed him.

A victim became incensed when his eventual slayer asked for money which the victim owed him. The victim grabbed a hatchet and started in the direction of his creditor, who pulled out a knife and stabbed him.

A victim attempted to commit sodomy with his girlfriend, who refused his overtures. He struck her several times on the side of her head with his fists before she grabbed a butcher knife and cut him fatally.

A drunken victim with knife in hand approached his slayer during a quarrel. The slayer showed a gun, and the victim dared him to shoot. He did.

During an argument in which a male called a female many vile names, she tried to telephone the police. But he grabbed the phone from her hands, knocked her down, kicked her, and hit her with a tire gauge. She ran to the kitchen, grabbed a butcher knife, and stabbed him in the stomach.

## THE PHILADELPHIA STUDY

Empirical data for analysis of victim-precipitated homicides were collected from the files of the Homicide Squad of the Philadelphia Police Department, and include 588 consecutive cases of criminal homicide which occurred between January 1, 1948 and December 31, 1952. Because more than one person was sometimes involved in the slaying of a single victim, there was a total of 621 offenders responsible for the killing of 588 victims. The present study is part of a much larger work that analyzes criminal homicide in greater detail. Such material that is relevant to victim-precipitation is included in the present analysis. The 588 criminal homicides provide sufficient background information to establish much about the nature of the victim-offender relationship. Of these cases, 150, or 26 percent, have been designated, on the basis of the previously stated definition, as VP cases.[7] The remaining 438, therefore, have been designated as non-VP cases.

Thorough study of police files, theoretical discussions of the victim's contribution, and previous analysis of criminal homicide suggest that there may be important differences between VP and non-VP cases. The chi-square test has been used to test the significance in proportions between VP and non-VP homicides and a series of variables. Hence, any spurious association which is just due to chance has been reduced to a minimum by application of this test, and significant differences of distributions are revealed. Where any expected class frequency of less than five existed, the test was not applied; and in each tested association, a correction for continuity was used, although the difference resulting without it was only slight. In this study a value of P less than .05, or the 5 percent level of significance, is used as the minimal level of significant association. Throughout the subsequent discussion, the term *significant* in italics is used to indicate that a chi-square test of significance of association has been made and that the value of P less than .05 has been found. The discussion that follows (with respect to race, sex, age, etc.) reveals some interesting differences and similarities between the two. (Table 1.)

### Race

Because Negroes and males have been shown by their high rates of homicide, assaults against the person, etc., to be more criminally aggressive than whites and females, it may be inferred that there are more Negroes and males among VP victims than among non-VP victims. The data confirm this inference. Nearly 80 percent of VP cases compared to 70 percent of non-VP cases involve Negroes, a proportional difference that results in a *significant* association between race and VP homicide.

### Sex

As victims, males comprise 94 percent of VP homicides, but only 72 percent of non-VP homicides, showing a *significant* association between sex of the victim and VP homicide.

Since females have been shown by their low rates of homicide, assaults against the person, etc., to be less criminally aggressive than males, and since females are less likely to precipitate their own victimization than males, we should expect more female *offenders* among VP homicides than among non-VP homicides. Such is the case, for the comparative data reveal that females are twice as frequently offenders in VP slayings (29 percent) as they are in non-VP slayings (14 percent)—a proportional difference which is also highly *significant*.

The number of white female offenders (16) in this study is too small to permit statistical analysis, but the tendency among both Negro and white females as separate groups is toward a much higher proportion among VP than among non-VP offenders. As noted above, analysis of Negro and white females as a combined group does result in the finding of a *significant* association between female offenders and VP homicide.

### Age

The age distributions of victims and offenders in VP and non-VP homicides are strikingly similar; study of the data suggests that age has no apparent effect on VP homicide. The median age of VP victims is 33.3 years, while that of non-VP victims is 31.2 years.

### Methods

In general, there is a *significant* association between method used to inflict death and VP homicide. Because Negroes and females comprise a larger proportion of offenders in VP cases, and because previous analysis has shown that stabbings occurred more often than any of the other methods of inflicting death,[8] it is implied that the frequency of homicides by stabbing is greater among VP than among non-VP cases. The data support such an implication and reveal that homicides by stabbing account for 54 percent of the VP cases but only 34 percent of non-VP cases, a difference which is *significant*. The distribution of shootings, beatings, and "other" methods of inflicting death among the VP and non-VP cases shows no significant differences. The high frequency of stabbings among VP homicides appears to result from an almost equal reduction in each of the remaining methods; yet the lower proportions in each of these three other categories among VP cases are not separately very different from the proportions among non-VP cases.

TABLE 1. *Victim-Precipitated and Non-Victim-Precipitated Criminal Homicide by Selected Variables (Philadelphia, 1948–1952)*

| | TOTAL VICTIMS | | VICTIM-PRECIPITATED | | NON-VICTIM-PRECIPITATED | |
|---|---|---|---|---|---|---|
| | Number | Percent of Total | Number | Percent of Total | Number | Percent of Total |
| *Race and Sex of Victim* | | | | | | |
| Both Races | 588 | 100.0 | 150 | 100.0 | 438 | 100.0 |
| Male | 499 | 76.4 | 141 | 94.0 | 308 | 70.3 |
| Female | 139 | 23.6 | 9 | 6.0 | 130 | 29.7 |
| Negro | 427 | 72.6 | 119 | 79.3 | 308 | 70.3 |
| Male | 331 | 56.3 | 111 | 74.0 | 220 | 50.2 |
| Female | 96 | 16.3 | 8 | 5.3 | 88 | 20.1 |
| White | 161 | 27.4 | 31 | 20.7 | 130 | 29.7 |
| Male | 118 | 20.1 | 30 | 20.0 | 88 | 20.1 |
| Female | 43 | 7.3 | 1 | 0.7 | 42 | 9.6 |
| *Age of Victim* | | | | | | |
| Under 15 | 28 | 4.8 | 0 | — | 28 | 6.4 |
| 15–19 | 25 | 4.3 | 7 | 4.7 | 18 | 4.1 |
| 20–24 | 59 | 10.0 | 18 | 12.0 | 41 | 9.4 |
| 25–29 | 93 | 15.8 | 17 | 11.3 | 76 | 17.3 |
| 30–34 | 88 | 15.0 | 20 | 13.3 | 68 | 15.5 |
| 35–39 | 75 | 12.8 | 25 | 16.7 | 50 | 11.4 |
| 40–44 | 57 | 9.7 | 23 | 15.3 | 34 | 7.8 |
| 45–49 | 43 | 7.3 | 13 | 8.7 | 30 | 6.8 |
| 50–54 | 48 | 8.2 | 11 | 7.3 | 37 | 8.5 |
| 55–59 | 26 | 4.4 | 6 | 4.0 | 20 | 4.6 |
| 60–64 | 18 | 3.1 | 7 | 4.7 | 11 | 2.5 |
| 65 and over | 28 | 4.7 | 3 | 2.0 | 25 | 5.7 |
| Total | 588 | 100.0 | 150 | 100.0 | 438 | 100.0 |

|  | TOTAL VICTIMS | | VICTIM-PRECIPITATED | | NON-VICTIM-PRECIPITATED | |
|---|---|---|---|---|---|---|
|  | Number | Percent of Total | Number | Percent of Total | Number | Percent of Total |
| *Method* | | | | | | |
| Stabbing | 228 | 38.8 | 81 | 54.0 | 147 | 33.6 |
| Shooting | 194 | 33.0 | 39 | 26.0 | 155 | 35.4 |
| Beating | 128 | 21.8 | 26 | 17.3 | 102 | 23.3 |
| Other | 38 | 6.4 | 4 | 2.7 | 34 | 7.7 |
| Total | 588 | 100.0 | 150 | 100.0 | 438 | 100.0 |
| *Place* | | | | | | |
| Home | 301 | 51.2 | 80 | 53.3 | 221 | 50.5 |
| Not Home | 287 | 48.8 | 70 | 46.7 | 217 | 49.5 |
| Total | 588 | 100.0 | 150 | 100.0 | 438 | 100.0 |
| *Interpersonal Relationship* | | | | | | |
| Relatively close friend | 155 | 28.2 | 46 | 30.7 | 109 | 27.3 |
| Family relationship | 136 | 24.7 | 38 | 25.3 | 98 | 24.5 |
| (Spouse) | 100 | 73.5 | 33 | 86.8 | 67 | 68.4 |
| (Other) | 36 | 26.5 | 5 | 13.2 | 31 | 31.6 |
| Acquaintance | 74 | 13.5 | 20 | 13.3 | 54 | 13.5 |
| Stranger | 67 | 12.2 | 16 | 10.7 | 51 | 12.8 |
| Paramour, Mistress, Prostitute | 54 | 9.8 | 15 | 10.0 | 39 | 9.8 |
| Sex rival | 22 | 4.0 | 6 | 4.0 | 16 | 4.0 |
| Enemy | 16 | 2.9 | 6 | 4.0 | 10 | 2.5 |
| Paramour of Offender's mate | 11 | 2.0 | 1 | .7 | 10 | 2.5 |
| Felon or police officer | 6 | 1.1 | 1 | .7 | 5 | 1.3 |
| Innocent bystander | 6 | 1.1 | — | — | 6 | 1.5 |
| Homosexual partner | 3 | .6 | 1 | .7 | 2 | .5 |
| Total | 550 | 100.0 | 150 | 100.0 | 400 | 100.0 |

TABLE 1 (Continued)

| | TOTAL VICTIMS | | VICTIM-PRECIPITATED | | NON-VICTIM-PRECIPITATED | |
|---|---|---|---|---|---|---|
| | Number | Percent of Total | Number | Percent of Total | Number | Percent of Total |
| *Presence of Alcohol During Offense* | | | | | | |
| Present | 374 | 63.6 | 111 | 74.0 | 263 | 60.0 |
| Not Present | 214 | 36.4 | 39 | 26.0 | 175 | 40.0 |
| Total | 588 | 100.0 | 150 | 100.0 | 438 | 100.0 |
| *Presence of Alcohol in the Victim* | | | | | | |
| Present | 310 | 52.7 | 104 | 69.3 | 206 | 47.0 |
| Not Present | 278 | 47.3 | 46 | 30.7 | 232 | 53.0 |
| Total | 588 | 100.0 | 150 | 100.0 | 438 | 100.0 |
| *Previous Arrest Record of Victim* | | | | | | |
| Previous arrest record | 277 | 47.3 | 93 | 62.0 | 184 | 42.0 |
| Offenses against the person | 150 | 25.5 (54.2) | 56 | 37.3 (60.2) | 94 | 21.4 (50.1) |
| Other offenses only | 127 | 21.6 (45.8) | 37 | 24.7 (39.8) | 90 | 20.5 (49.9) |
| No previous arrest record | 311 | 52.7 | 57 | 38.0 | 254 | 58.0 |
| Total | 588 | 100.0 | 150 | 100.0 | 438 | 100.0 |
| *Previous Arrest Record of Offender* | | | | | | |
| Previous arrest record | 400 | 64.4 | 81 | 54.0 | 319 | 67.7 |
| Offenses against the person | 264 | 42.5 (66.0) | 49 | 32.7 (60.5) | 215 | 45.6 (67.4) |
| Other offenses only | 136 | 21.8 (34.0) | 32 | 21.3 (39.5) | 104 | 22.1 (32.6) |
| No previous arrest record | 221 | 35.6 | 69 | (46.0) | 152 | 32.3 |
| Total | 621 | 100.0 | 150 | 100.0 | 471 | 100.0 |

### Place and Motive

There is no important difference between VP and non-VP homicides with respect to a home/not-home dichotomy, nor with respect to motives listed by the police. Slightly over half of both VP and non-VP slayings occurred in the home. General altercations (34 percent) and domestic quarrels (20 percent) rank highest among VP cases, as they do among non-VP cases (32 and 12 percent), although with lower frequency. Combined, these two motives account for a slightly larger share of the VP cases (3 out of 5) than of the non-VP cases (2 out of 5).

### Victim-Offender Relationships[9]

Intra-racial slayings predominate in both groups, but inter-racial homicides comprise a larger share of VP cases (8 percent) than they do of non-VP cases (5 percent). Although VP cases make up one-fourth of all criminal homicides, they account for over one-third (35 percent) of all inter-racial slayings. Thus it appears that a homicide which crosses race lines is often likely to be one in which the slayer was provoked to assault by the victim. The association between inter-racial slayings and VP homicides, however, is not statistically significant.

Homicides involving victims and offenders of opposite sex (regardless of which sex is the victim or which is the offender) occur with about the same frequency among VP cases (34 percent) as among non-VP cases (37 percent). But a *significant* difference between VP and non-VP cases does emerge when determination of the sex of the victim, relative to the sex of his specific slayer, is taken into account. Of all criminal homicides for which the sex of both victim and offender is known, 88 involve a male victim and a female offender; and of these 88 cases, 43 are VP homicides. Thus, it may be said that 43, or 29 percent, of the 150 VP homicides, compared to 45, or only 11 percent, of the 400 non-VP homicides, are males slain by females.

It seems highly desirable, in view of these findings, that the police thoroughly investigate every possibility of strong provocation by the male victim when he is slain by a female—and particularly, as noted below, if the female is his wife, which is also a strong possibility. It is, of course, the further responsibility of defense counsel, prosecuting attorney, and subsequently the court, to determine whether such provocation was sufficient either to reduce or to eliminate culpability altogether.

The proportion that Negro male/Negro male[10] and white male/white male homicides constitute among VP cases (45 and 13 percent) is similar to the proportion these same relationships constitute among non-VP cases (41 and 14 percent). The important contribution of the Negro male as a victim-precipitator is indicated by the fact that Negro male/Negro female homicides are, proportionately, nearly three times as frequent among VP cases (25 percent) as they are among non-VP cases (9 percent). It is apparent, therefore, that Negroes and males not only are the groups most likely to make positive and direct contributions to the genesis of their own victimization, but that, in particular, Negro males more frequently provoke females of their own race to slay them than they do members of their own sex and race.

For both VP and non-VP groups, close friends, relatives, and acquaintances are the major types of specific relationships between victims and offenders. Combined, these three relationships constitute 69 percent of the VP homicides and 65 percent of the non-VP cases. Victims are relatives of their slayers in one-fourth of both types of homicide. But of 38 family slayings among VP cases, 33 are husband-wife killings; while of 98 family slayings among non-VP cases, only 67 are husband-wife killings. This proportional difference results in a *significant* association between mate slayings and VP homicide.

Finally, of VP mate slayings, 28 victims are husbands and only 5 wives; but of non-VP mate slayings, only 19 victims are husbands while 48 are wives. Thus there is a *significant* association between husbands who are victims in mate slayings and VP homicide. This fact, namely, that *significantly* more husbands than wives are victims in VP mate slayings— means that (1) husbands actually may provoke their wives more often than wives provoke their husbands to assault their respective mates; or, (2) assuming that provocation by wives is as intense and equally as frequent, or even more frequent, than provocation by husbands, then husbands may not receive and define provocation stimuli with as great or as violent a reaction as do wives; or (3) husbands may have a greater felt sense of guilt in a marital conflict for one reason or another, and receive verbal insults and overt physical assaults without retaliation as a form of compensatory punishment; or, (4) husbands may withdraw more often than wives from the scene of marital conflict, and thus eliminate, for the time being, a violent overt reaction to their wives' provocation. Clearly, this is only a suggestive, not an exhaustive, list of probable explanations. In any case, we are left with the undeniable fact that husbands more often than wives are major, precipitating factors in their own homicidal deaths.

### Alcohol

In the larger work of which this study is a part, the previous discovery of an association between the presence of alcohol in the homicide situation and Negro male offenders, combined with knowledge of the important contribution Negro males make to their own victimization, suggests an association (by transitivity) between VP homicide and the presence of alcohol. Moreover, whether alcohol is present in the victim or offender, lowered inhibitions due to ingestion of alcohol may cause an individual to give vent more freely to pent up frustrations, tensions, and emotional conflicts that have either built up over a prolonged period of time or that arise within an immediate emotional crisis. The data do in fact confirm the suggested hypothesis above and reveal a *significant* association between VP homicide and alcohol in the homicide situation. Comparison of VP to non-VP cases with respect to the presence of alcohol in the homicide situation (alcohol present in either the victim, offender, or both), reveals that alcohol was present in 74 percent of the VP cases and in 60 percent of the non-VP cases. The proportional difference results in a *significant* association between alcohol and VP homicide. It should be noted that the association is not necessarily a causal one, or that a causal relationship is not proved by the association.

Because the present analysis is concerned primarily with the contribution of the victim to the homicide, it is necessary to determine whether an association exists between VP homicide and presence of alcohol in the victim. No association was found to exist between VP homicide and alcohol in the offender. But victims had been drinking immediately prior to their death in more VP cases (69 percent) than in non-VP cases (47 percent). A positive and *significant* relationship is, therefore, clearly established between victims who had been drinking and who precipitated their own death. In many of these cases the victim was intoxicated, or nearly so, and lost control of his own defensive powers. He frequently was a victim with no intent to harm anyone maliciously, but who, nonetheless, struck his friend, acquaintance, or wife, who later became his assailant. Impulsive, aggressive, and often dangerously violent, the victim was the first to slap, punch, stab, or in some other manner commit an assault. Perhaps the presence of alcohol in this kind of homicide victim played no small part in his taking this first and major physical step toward victimization. Perhaps if he had not been drinking he would have been less violent, less ready to plunge into an assaultive stage of interaction. Or, if the presence of alcohol had no causal relation to his being the first to assault, perhaps it reduced his facility to combat successfully, to defend himself from retaliatory assault and, hence, contributed in this way to his death.

### Previous Arrest Record

The victim-precipitator is the first actor in the homicide drama to display and to use a deadly weapon; and the description of him thus far infers that he is in some respects an offender in reverse. Because he is the first to assume an aggressive role, he probably has engaged previously in similar but less serious physical assaults. On the basis of these assumptions several meaningful hypotheses were established and tested. Each hypothesis is supported by empirical data, which in some cases reach the level of statistical significance accepted by this study; and in other cases indicate strong associations in directions suggested by the hypotheses. A summary of each hypothesis with its collated data follows:

( 1 ) In VP cases, the victim is more likely than the offender to have a previous arrest, or police record. The data show that 62 percent of the victims and 54 percent of the offenders in VP cases have a previous record.

( 2 ) A higher proportion of VP victims than non-VP victims have a previous police record. Comparison reveals that 62 percent of VP victims but only 42 percent of non-VP victims have a previous record. The association between VP victims and previous arrest record is a *significant* one.

( 3 ) With respect to the percentage having a previous arrest record, VP victims are more similar to non-VP offenders than to non-VP victims. Examination of the data reveals no significant difference between VP victims and non-VP offenders with a previous record. This lack of a significant difference is very meaningful and confirms the validity of the proposition above. While 62 percent of VP victims have a police record, 68 percent of non-VP offenders have such a record, and we have already noted in (2) above that only 42 percent of non-VP victims have a record. Thus, the existence of a statistically *significant* difference between VP victims and non-VP victims and the *lack* of a statistically significant difference between VP victims and non-VP offenders indicate that the victim of VP homicide is quite similar to the offender in non-VP homicide—and that the VP victim more closely resembles the non-VP offender than the non-VP victim.

(4) A higher proportion of VP victims than of non-VP victims have a record of offenses against the person. The data show a *significant* association between VP victims and a previous record of offenses against the person, for 37 percent of VP victims and only 21 percent of non-VP victims have a record of such offenses.

(5) Also with respect to the percentage having a previous arrest record of offenses against the person, VP victims are more similar to non-VP offenders than non-VP victims. Analysis of the data indicates support for this assumption, for we have observed that the difference between VP victims (37 percent) and non-VP victims (21 percent) is *significant;* this difference is almost twice as great as the difference between VP victims (27 percent) and non-VP offenders (46 percent), and this latter difference is not significant. The general tendency again is for victims in VP homicides to resemble offenders in non-VP homicides.

(6) A lower proportion of VP offenders have a previous arrest record than do non-VP offenders. The data also tend to support this hypothesis, for 54 percent of offenders in VP cases, compared to 68 percent of offenders in non-VP cases have a previous police record.

In general, the rank order of recidivism—defined in terms of having a previous arrest record and of having a previous record of assaults—for victims and offenders involved in the two types of homicide is as follows.

| | PERCENT WITH PREVIOUS ARREST RECORD | PERCENT WITH PREVIOUS RECORD OF ASSAULT |
|---|---|---|
| (1) Offenders in non-VP Homicide | 68 | 46 |
| (2) Victims in VP Homicide | 62 | 37 |
| (3) Offenders in VP Homicide | 54 | 33 |
| (4) Victims in non-VP Homicide | 42 | 21 |

Because he is the initial aggressor and has provoked his subsequent slayer into killing him, this particular type of victim (VP) is likely to have engaged previously in physical assaults which were either less provoking than the present situation, or which afforded him greater opportunity to defer attacks made upon him. It is known officially that over one-third of them assaulted others previously. It is not known how many formerly provoked others to assault them. In any case, the circumstances leading up to the present crime in which he plays the role of victim are probably not foreign to him since he has, in many cases, participated in similar encounters before this, his last episode.

## SUMMARY

Criminal homicide usually involves intense personal inter-action in which the victim's behavior is often an important factor. As Porterfield has recently pointed out, "the intensity of interaction between the murderer and his victim may vary from complete non-participation on the part of the victim to almost perfect cooperation with the killer in the process of getting killed. . . . It is amazing to note the large number of would-be murderers who become the victim."[11] By defining a VP homicide in terms of the victim's direct, immediate, and positive contribution to his own death, manifested by his being the first to make a physical assault, it has been possible to identify 150 VP cases.

Comparison of this VP group with non-VP cases reveals *significantly* higher proportions of the following character-istics among VP homicide.

( 1 )  Negro victims;
( 2 )  Negro offenders;
( 3 )  male victims;
( 4 )  female offenders;
( 5 )  stabbings;
( 6 )  victim-offender relationship involving male victims of female offenders;
( 7 )  mate slayings;
( 8 )  husbands who are victims in mate slayings;
( 9 )  alcohol in the homicide situation;
( 10 )  alcohol in the victim;
( 11 )  victims with a previous arrest record;
( 12 )  victims with a previous arrest record of assault.

In addition, VP homicides have slightly higher proportions than non-VP homicides of altercations and domestic quarrels; inter-racial slayings, victims who are close friends, relatives, or acquaintances of their slayers.

Empirical evidence analyzed in the present study lends support to, and measurement of, von Hentig's theoretical contention that "there are cases in which they (victim and offender) are reversed and in the long chain of causative forces the victim assumes the role of a determinant."[12]

In many cases the victim has most of the major characteristics of an offender; in some cases two potential offenders come together in a homicide situation and it is probably often only chance which results in one becoming a victim and the other an offender. At any rate, connotations of a victim as a weak and passive individual, seeking to withdraw from an assaultive situation, and of an offender as a brutal, strong, and overly aggressive person seeking out his victim, are not always correct. Societal attitudes are generally positive toward the victim and negative toward the offender, who is often feared as a violent and dangerous threat to others when not exonerated. However, data in the present study—especially that of previous arrest record—mitigate, destroy, or reverse these connotations of victim-offender roles in one out of every four criminal homicides.

# Justifiable Homicide by
# Police Officers

## GERALD D. ROBIN

PROBABLY no other type of aggressive behavior has been the subject of as much popular and professional concern and investigation as homicide. Such interest has been restricted almost entirely to criminal homicide, i.e., homicide which is unlawful and therefore subject to legally imposed sanctions. It is frequently not realized that all homicides are not necessarily criminal. Although homicide is the killing of one human being by another, it is the conditions under which the event occurs that determine its criminal or non-criminal nature. At common law non-criminal or innocent homicide was divided into two types: (1) Justifiable homicide, an intentional killing either commanded or authorized by the law. Examples include the killing of an enemy during war, the execution of a legal sentence of death, unavoidable killings in arresting a felon or preventing his escape, and those necessitated in lawful self-defense which places the slayer in imminent peril of death or great bodily harm. (2) Excusable homicide, an unintentional killing done without intent to harm and without criminal negligence, as well as homicide committed in self-defense upon a sudden affray—as when a person kills another after becoming engaged in a sudden affray, in order to save himself

REPRINTED with the permission of the author from Gerald D. Robin, "Justifiable Homicide by Police Officers," *Journal of Criminal Law, Criminology and Police Science* (June, 1963), 54:2:225-231.

The writer would like to express his gratitude to the following individuals for their assistance in the study: Dr. Joseph W. Spelman, Medical Examiner for the County of Philadelphia; Charles E. Hughes, Jr., City Archivist; David S. Brown, Captain of the Homicide Unit of the Philadelphia Police Department; and Dr. Marvin E. Wolfgang, Professor of Sociology, University of Pennsylvania.

from reasonably apparent danger or great bodily harm. The difference between justifiable and excusable homicide committed in self-defense is that in the latter the slayer is regarded as in fault to some extent for becoming engaged in the affray. The main distinction between the two forms of innocent homicide is that in the one the killing is committed under circumstances that constitute merely an excuse, whereas in the other the homicide is fully justified.[1]

The difference between the two types of non-criminal homicide has been emphasized because the present study is concerned with one class of justifiable homicides: the killing of criminals by police officers. Numerically, such killings constitute from 2% to 5% of all intentional violent deaths.[2] On the other hand all forms of innocent and excusable homicide combined account for a sizeable proportion of all killings.[3] It is perhaps because of the infrequency of fatal police assaults on criminals that the literature in this area is almost non-existent. Nevertheless, the subject has a priori interest for all those concerned with law enforcement and the problems of crime. The phenomenon of justifiable police homicide (J.P.H.) is a response to criminal conduct on the part of the decedent. Oddly, the decedent assumes the dual role of victim and offender: he is an offender because he violated the law and a victim because he was killed as a consequence. There can be little doubt that for the V-O's (victim-offenders) of police homicide "Crime Doesn't Pay." Among other things, then, a study of justifiable homicides by police officers is an investigation of the victim's contribution to his own victimization.

## THE APPROACH

The sample studied consisted of all police killings of criminals in Philadelphia from 1950 to 1960, inclusive. The books of the Homicide Unit of the Philadelphia Police Department revealed that there were 32 cases during this eleven year period.[4] Extensive records were maintained for each case, detailing the circumstances under which the killings occurred, various characteristics of the victim-offender, his previous criminal record if any, and interviews with witnesses to the homicide as well as with friends and relatives of the decedent. Thirty of the 32 cases were disposed of by the medical examiner, who at the inquest exonerated the officers involved in the killings on the grounds that death was due to justifiable homicide. In the two remaining cases the officers were held for the grand jury, indicted, tried by a jury, and found not guilty. In all the cases testimony presented at the inquest formed an important basis upon which the medical examiner reached his decision concerning the manner of death. All of these statements were examined by the writer, with particular attention directed to the examiner's summary opinion. From the testimony given at the inquest, combined with police interviews and reports, there emerged a complete and accurate description of the events leading to and the circumstances immediately surrounding the police killings.

## THE FINDINGS

There were 42 police officers who, in the performance of their duty, shot and killed 32 male criminals, or 1.3 officers for each V-O. This does not include officers who fired at the V-O but missed. In 23 cases not more than one officer was responsible for the slaying. All of the deaths resulted from gunshot wounds. Eleven officers sustained injury—from being bitten to multiple stab wounds—in attempting to apprehend the felons.

### Race

Twenty-eight, or 87.5%, of the 32 decedents were Negroes. In contrast, only 22% of the city's population were Negro from 1950 to 1960, while this minority group accounted for just 30.6% of arrests for all offenses reported to the F.B.I. during the same period.[5] In other words, the Negroes' contribution as victims of justifiable police homicide was 2.9 and 4.0 times as great as their contribution to the number of persons arrested and their prevalence in the population of Philadelphia, respectively. The average annual rate of Negro victims of police killings was 5.47 per 1,000,000 Negro inhabitants, compared to a white rate of .25—a ratio of 22 to 1. Regardless of the index used, then, the Negro's tendency to be a subject of police slayings is excessive. This situation, however, is not restricted to Philadelphia. As will be shown in greater detail later, the ratio of Negro to white rates varied from 5.8 to 29.5 among seven selected cities surveyed. For the nation as a whole the ratio of Negro to white rates of the V-O's was 7 to 1, respectively.

The large number of Negro justifiable homicides in Philadelphia subjects, both absolutely and relatively, might be interpreted as an indication of racial discrimination by the police. Such an inference, however, would be unwarranted. To attempt to answer this charge it would be necessary to know the race of the officers responsible for the homicides, the distribution of officers by police districts, the racial composition of the criminals in the city, etc. Moreover, a close examination of the 32 cases indicates that, with few exceptions, the officers who took the criminals' lives acted as any "reasonable man" in their position would have. In many cases the officers exercised considerable restraint in delaying the use of fatal force as long as they did. In each case the officer's reliance on the extreme sanction of effecting arrest was rationally utilized as a last resort. This is supported, in part, by the fact that in 28 of the 32 cases the offenders were warned verbally, by the firing of a shot in the air, or both, that unless they halted they would be shot at. In the 4 cases in which no warning was given, the conditions were such as to preclude it. There is also little doubt that a warning would have had no deterrent effect on these men—it obviously had none on the 28 decedents who were warned. Accordingly, the victims of justifiable homicide were adequately informed of the risks of refusing to submit peaceably.

### Age, Marital Status, Occupation

As a group the V-O's were young: the average age was 27.6 years, the range extending from 15 years to 60 years. Half of the group were under 24 years of age. Only 3 decedents were over 40 years of age, and 2 were juveniles, i.e., below 18 years of age. Of the 27 cases in which marital status was known, 15 of the men were single, 5 were married, 5 separated, 1 divorced, and 1 was a widower. Occupationally the group consisted primarily of unskilled workers. Of the 30 cases in which "usual occupation" was known, there were 3 clerks, 1 machinist, and 1 shoe repair man; the occupations of the remaining men required no special skills or training.

### Time and Place of Shootings

Distribution of the fatal shootings by hours of the day was tabulated for quarter periods, i.e., for six-hour divisions. Any such delineation is of course arbitrary but nonetheless useful in determining whether any relationship exists between time of day and occurrence of fatal attacks. There was a tendency to use fatal force in the late evening and early morning hours (14 cases between 9:00 P.M. and 2:59 A.M.) and somewhat less so toward the late morning hours (8 cases between 3:00 A.M. and 8:59 A.M.). Almost 72% of the shootings occurred between 9:00 P.M. and 9:00 A.M. These figures do not refer to the time at which the V-O's died but rather to the time at which they were shot by the police. This, in turn, depended upon the time the offenders committed their crimes.[6] The concentration of shootings between 9:00 P.M. and 2:59 A.M. is similar to the pattern revealed in studies of criminal homicide.[7] The fatal wounding of the offender typically occurred on the highway, 24 of the men having been shot in the street. Three were shot in retail establishments, 3 in houses, and 2 in transportation vehicles. The interval between the shooting and death of the offender was uniformly short, 29 of the 32 criminals having died by the time they reached the hospital. Of the remaining 3 persons, 2 died one day later and 1 lived for three days.

## Instant Offense, Resistance, Criminal Record

The instant offense refers to the original crime for which the offender was being arrested. This is to distinguish it from additional offenses the criminal may have committed while resisting arrest—itself a violation of the law. These two elements are highly significant because a police officer's right to employ fatal force in making an arrest depends upon them. In attempting to arrest a felon an officer may use all the force necessary, even to the extent of killing him.[8] An officer is not required to engage a felon on equal terms but may use superior force in effecting an arrest.[9] However, the right to kill a fleeing offender is limited to cases in which the officer has reasonable grounds to believe that the person whom he is attempting to arrest is a felon. Mere suspicion that a felony has been committed will not justify the killing to prevent the escape of the suspect.[10] Concerning the apprehension of misdemeanants, although some courts have sanctioned the use of fatal force to accomplish an arrest or prevent escape from the officer's custody, the better opinion is to the contrary.[11] Therefore, if a lawful attempt to arrest a misdemeanant is resisted, to effect the arrest the officer may employ any necessary force short of taking life. If, however, in the course of the conflict the officer is threatened with death or great bodily harm by the offender, he may kill him in self-defense.

Twenty-four of the 32 instant crimes were Part I offenses. These 24 crimes consisted of 5 burglaries, 9 robberies, 7 larcenies, 2 assaults with intent to kill, and 1 aggravated assault and battery. In every one of these cases the officers responsible for the slayings acted in accordance with the law. In the single misdemeanor among these crimes, aggravated assault and battery,[12] the officer killed the offender in self-defense. Of the remaining 8 misdemeanant instant offenses, 3 were disorderly conducts, 4 were weapon violations, and 1 was a case of investigation. In attempting to arrest 7 of these 8 subjects, the officers again acted within the prescriptions of the law: in every instance, although only a misdemeanor had been committed, the killing was necessitated because the officer's life was jeopardized. In the remaining case, that of a man threatening several patrons with a knife, there was some question as to the legality of the officer's action; the defendant was later exonerated in court.

When the officers attempted to arrest the 32 men—28 of whom were solitary offenders—25 exhibited various degrees of resistance, and 7 fled from them. Six of the 25 resisted (pulling away, pushing, jerking away from officer), 2 assaulted the officer, and 17 committed aggravated assault and battery on the lawmen. Without exception, then, the officers' utilization of fatal force was authorized by law, was in the interests of justice, and represented a last resort.

Approximately three-quarters of the V-O's had previous contacts with law. The average number of charges against them was 4.9, with an average of 2.1 Part I charges. In addition, two-thirds of the men had received institutional sentences. A similar proportion of the V-O's had been arrested for offenses against the person.

## COMPARATIVE DATA

In an effort to learn something of justifiable police homicide elsewhere, letters were sent to the police departments of 17 selected cities, nine of which responded with varying amounts of the information requested.[13] In addition, the National Office of Vital Statistics has published annual figures since 1949 on the number of criminals killed by law enforcement officers for the country as a whole. Table 1 presents these data from 1950 to 1960, the approximate period covered in the Philadelphia sample and requested from the cities contacted. The average number of criminals killed per year was 240, with little variation. Only in one year, 1950, was the number of police killings as much as 17.5% greater than the mean. In none of the remaining nine years did the number deviate more than 6.7%

TABLE 1.   *Annual Number of J.P.H. for Country*

| YEAR | NUMBER[a] |
|------|-----------|
| 1950 | 282 |
| 1951 | 227 |
| 1952 | 256 |
| 1953 | 255 |
| 1954 | 244 |
| 1955 | 227 |
| 1956 | 226 |
| 1957 | 228 |
| 1958 | 229 |
| 1959 | 227 |

[a] The 1960 figure is not yet available.

in either direction from the average. Police slayings of criminals were remarkably constant from 1955 through 1959, with an average of 227.4 deaths for these five years and less than 1% deviation from this value in any year. In four years— 1950, 1955, 1956, and 1957—the NOVS also published the rate of police killings by race and sex. The rate of Negro victims was seven times that of the white victims, amounting to 14 Negro decedents and 2 white decedents per 1,000,000 respective population groups. Female victims of justifiable homicide are practically non-existent: 99.6% of the 963 decedents for the four years cited were male; 49.1% of this number were Negro. These figures for Negro and white victims contrast sharply with the Philadelphia findings. However, although the rate of Negro V-O's in Philadelphia is several times that of white V-O's, the City of Brotherly Love is not alone in this respect, as Table 2 indicates. In every city the Negro's tendency toward victimization is disproportionate. Excluding Philadelphia, the general rate for the seven cities

TABLE 2. *Rates of Negro and White Decedents, by City*

| CITY | NEGRO | WHITE | N:W RATIO |
|------|-------|-------|-----------|
| | Rates per 1,000,000 pop. | | |
| Akron | 16.1 | 2.7 | 5.8 to 1 |
| Chicago | 16.1 | 2.1 | 7.4 to 1 |
| Kansas City, Mo. | 17.0 | 2.2 | 7.5 to 1 |
| Miami | 24.4 | 2.7 | 8.8 to 1 |
| Buffalo | 7.1 | .5 | 12.2 to 1 |
| Philadelphia | 5.4 | .2 | 21.9 to 1 |
| Boston | 3.2 | .1 | 25.2 to 1 |
| Milwaukee | 13.5 | .4 | 29.5 to 1 |

is 8.8 times greater for Negro than white decedents; when Philadelphia is included in the calculation the ratio is 9.1 Negroes to each white V-O.

### Age, Race, Previous Record

There was a total of 318 J.P.H.'s from 1950 through 1960 in the nine cities which responded to the researcher's letters. The age of the decedents was known in 159 of these cases, presenting a profile very similar to the Philadelphia data. Half of the group were under 28 years of age; 32% of the men were 20 to 25 years of age. Only 5 of the 159 victims were juveniles, while 8.8% were above 45 years of age. The age of the V-O's ranged from 14 years to 80 years. The race of the decedents was indicated in 269 cases and of this number 61.7% were Negroes. Table 3 reveals some interesting variations in the distribution of J.P.H.'s by city. Chicago accounted for 54.6% of the 350 police slayings (including Philadelphia) from 1950 through 1960 and had the second highest annual rate of justifiable homicides. Miami led the ten cities with a yearly rate of 7.06 decedents per 1,000,000 inhabitants. Boston had the lowest occurrence of slayings, with considerably less than one victim per 1,000,000 population. For the ten cities combined the rate was 3.2 per 1,000,000 population. This rate is appreciably larger than the national rate of 1.45. This may be partially explained by the fact that the cities constituting the total sample are among the largest and most urban in the country. Other things being equal, a larger population base

TABLE 3.  *Rates of Justifiable Police Homicide, by City*

| CITY | 1955 POP. | J.P.H. 1950-60 | X̄ ANNUAL RATE PER 1,000,000 POP. |
|---|---|---|---|
| Boston | 749,320 | 3 | .40 |
| Buffalo | 556,445 | 7 | 1.07 |
| Milwaukee | 689,358 | 10 | 1.32 |
| Philadelphia | 2,037,058 | 32 | 1.42 |
| Washington, D. C. | 783,067 | 26 | 3.06 |
| Cincinnati | 503,274 | 23 | 4.17 |
| Kansas City, Mo. | 466,080 | 23 | 4.50 |
| Akron | 282,478 | 14 | 4.60 |
| Chicago | 3,585,683 | 191 | 4.85 |
| Miami | 270,482 | 21 | 7.06 |

means more potential and actual criminals and consequently the more frequent involvement in those situations in which fatal police force is used. That this is not necessarily the case, however, is evidenced by inspection of Table 3 and by a rank correlation coefficient of .48 between city size and the number of criminals killed by police. Nevertheless, population size certainly is not to be minimized as a determinant of criminal deaths. Another factor influencing the prevalence of J.P.H. is the size of the police force. Effectively, the task of arresting criminals falls entirely to the police, and therefore the number of criminals killed would be expected to vary with police force strength. A rank coefficient of correlation of .37 between these two variables lends some support to this hypothesis. At the same time, Table 4 throws into relief the exceptions to this relationship. The annual rate of J.P.H. per 10,000 officers ranged from 1.05 in Boston to 48.5 in Akron. For all ten cities the rate was 14.0.

## TO KILL AND BE KILLED

An interesting and important practical consideration for those concerned with law enforcement is the likelihood of a police officer's killing a criminal and, conversely, an officer's chances of being killed by a criminal. An officer's chances of causing the death of a criminal while making an arrest is

TABLE 4. *Rates of Justifiable Police Homicide per 10,000 Officers*

| CITY | POLICE FORCE[a] (1955) | ANNUAL RATE PER 10,000 OFFICERS |
|---|---|---|
| Boston | 2835 | 1.05 |
| Buffalo | 1260 | 4.76 |
| Milwaukee | 1635 | 5.50 |
| Philadelphia | 4763 | 6.08 |
| Washington, D. C. | 2253 | 10.65 |
| Chicago | 7720 | 22.53 |
| Cincinnati | 846 | 24.82 |
| Kansas City, Mo. | 593 | 35.41 |
| Miami | 498 | 38.15 |
| Akron | 268 | 48.50 |

[a] SOURCE: *Uniform Crime Reports.*

presented in Table 5 by city.[14] In Akron, the average annual number of officers who fatally wounded criminals from 1950 through 1960 was 63.4 per 10,000 officers; while in Boston the rate was as low as 1.4. Other things being equal, then, the probability of Akron policemen killing a criminal in any given year is 45 times as great as that of Boston policemen. For the ten cities combined the mean rate of J.P.H. was 18.4 per 10,000 officers.

Nationally, there was an average annual rate of 194.2

TABLE 5. *Average Annual Rate of Officers Responsible for Deaths of Criminals per 10,000 Officers, by City*

| CITY | RATE |
|---|---|
| Boston | 1.41 |
| Buffalo | 6.34 |
| Milwaukee | 7.33 |
| Philadelphia | 7.76 |
| Washington, D. C. | 13.75 |
| Chicago | 29.66 |
| Cincinnati | 33.09 |
| Kansas City, Mo. | 47.21 |
| Miami | 50.20 |
| Akron | 63.43 |

officers involved in criminal deaths between 1950 and 1960
per 100,000 police department personnel, or a rate of 5.7 per
3,000,000 population.[15] The average annual number of police
killed in the line of duty from 1950 through 1960 was 52.6,
yielding a rate of 31.7 officers killed per 100,000 police department personnel,[16] or less than one officer killed per 3,000,000
population. In other words, in any given year policemen are
approximately six times more likely to kill than to be killed in
the course of their duty; at the same time the probability of
either event occurring is very small. In this connection, there
is reason to maintain that the popular conception of the
dangerous nature of police work has been exaggerated. Each
occupation has its own hazards. The main difference between
police work and other occupations is that in the former there
is a calculated risk, as indicated above, while other occupational hazards are accidental and injuries usually self-inflicted. That the occupational risks in law enforcement are
less dangerous than those in many larger industry groups is
apparent upon inspection of Table 6. Half of the major occupations had higher fatality rates than that of police officers.
This is not to suggest that courage is not an important pre-

TABLE 6.   *Occupational Fatalities per 100,000 Employees, 1955*

| OCCUPATION | NO. OF EMPL. | NO. OF FATALITIES | FATALITY RATE PER 100,000 EMPL.[a] |
|---|---|---|---|
| Mining | 748,000 | 700 | 93.58 |
| Agriculture | 6,730,000 | 3700 | 54.97 |
| Contract Construction | 2,506,000 | 1900 | 75.81 |
| Manufacturing | 16,552,000 | 2000 | 12.08 |
| Transportation | 2,722,000 | 1200 | 44.08 |
| Public Utilities | 1,335,000 | 200 | 14.98 |
| Trade | 10,728,000 | 1100 | 10.25 |
| Finance, Service, Gov., Mis. | 14,808,000 | 2100 | 14.18 |
| Law Enforcement | 167,862 | 55 | 32.76[b] |

[a] All fatality rates, except those in Agriculture and Law Enforcement, were
calculated from: *Monthly Labor Review*, LXXIX (January–June, 1956),
439, 474–77. The source for the number of employees in agriculture was:
*U. S. Bureau of the Census, Historical Statistics of the United States,
Colonial Times to 1957* (Washington, D. C., 1960), 70.
[b] Calculated from *Uniform Crime Reports*.

requisite in a police officer. Undoubtedly this very quality is largely responsible for keeping police fatality rates as low as they are. Rather, it is to suggest that the general belief that law-enforcement activity is one of extreme peril is not confirmed by an analysis of the facts.[17]

## SUMMARY AND CONCLUSIONS

In the eleven year period from 1950 through 1960 there were 32 cases of police slayings of criminals in Philadelphia. In addition, information concerning this phenomenon was obtained from the police departments of nine selected cities, all having populations of more than 250,000. For all ten cities (including Philadelphia) there were 350 criminals killed during the period in question. Intensive analysis of the Philadelphia data and of the more limited comparative data reveals that definite observable patterns are associated with the justifiable homicide situation and are characteristic of the victim-offenders involved. The Negro's contribution as a V-O is markedly disproportionate, ranging from approximately 6 to 29 times the rate of whites among the ten cities, with a national annual ratio of 7 to 1. The female's participation in justifiable homicide is negligible—there were none among the 350 city decedents, while female victims constituted an insignificant .4% of national police killings of criminals during 1950, 1955, 1956, and 1957. Generally, the victims of such slayings are relatively young: half of the 191 cases in which age was known were below 28 years of age, with only 10.4% above 45 years of age. The ages ranged from 14 years to 80 years; 3.7% of the cases were juveniles. Occupationally the majority of the Philadelphia decedents are unskilled workers. Approximately 72% of the V-O's sustained their fatal injury between 9:00 P.M. and 9:00 A.M., typically on the highway, and were dead by the time they reached the hospital. Three-quarters of the original crimes for which the Philadelphia decedents were being sought were Part I offenses, criminal homicide the only Part I offense not represented. Most of the 32 V-O's forcibly resisted arrest, such resistance ranging from pulling away from the officer's custody to assault with intent to kill the policeman. Almost without exception the victim-offenders were given adequate warning of the possible fatal consequences of refusal to surrender. In every instance the officer acted within the law and exercised mature judgment in the interest of society and in a situation which demanded spontaneous action. About two-thirds of the 32 decedents had previous criminal records, were sentenced to a penal institution at least once, and had demonstrated more than casual violence on prior occasions. There were strong indications of psychotic disturbance in 6 of the 32 men.

The context within which the killings occurred, the serious crimes for which the V-O's were being arrested, their realization of the possible consequences of resistance and flight, and the officer's reliance upon fatal force as a last resort—all these things make it clear that criminals killed by police officers generally are responsible for their own death.

# PART III

# Psychological and
# Psychiatric Aspects

# The Threat to Kill

## *JOHN M. MACDONALD*

CRIMINAL homicide arouses great public concern, yet its frequent prelude, the threat to kill, has received scant attention from psychiatrists and psychologists. The threat is more often made than fulfilled. Yet this is also true of the threat of suicide which has been the subject of countless research projects and reports. The curiously meager scientific literature cannot be attributed to lack of opportunity for study, as many persons who make homicidal threats either seek treatment or are committed to a hospital for psychiatric examination. Thus within 15 months, 100 patients (one in every 16 admissions) were admitted to the 78-bed Colorado Psychopathic Hospital specifically because they had made homicidal threats.

Consideration of the threat to kill will not be restricted to these 100 patients. Statistics on these 55 men and 45 women will be reported as they may throw some light on this neglected problem despite the lack of research controls. Fifty-four patients were admitted on civil court order and 46 were admitted voluntarily. Although no patient was committed by a criminal court, several sought admission as an alternative to the filing of criminal charges. Their ages ranged from 11 to 83 years; 52 were between the ages of 20 and 40, and the mean age was 43½ years.

## THE THREAT

The threat may be uttered succinctly or bombastically, seriously or in jest, in the heat of anger or in deceptive calm.

REPRINTED with the permission of the author and the publisher from John M. Macdonald, "The Threat to Kill," *The American Journal of Psychiatry* (August, 1963), 120:2:125-130.

Read at the 119th annual meeting of The American Psychiatric Association, St. Louis, Mo., May 6-10, 1963.

A young soldier calmly informed a fellow soldier that he was going to kill an N.C.O. That day he shot the N.C.O. and then returned to his barracks where he announced his actions, opening with the remark, "Mission accomplished, mind at ease." He told one soldier to notify his commanding officer and asked another to play the tune, "In the jailhouse now." Another soldier, when informed that he was to be transferred to a mountain camp announced that he would kill himself or someone else first. Arrangements were being made to discharge him from the Army when he shot and killed a man while stealing a car in which he planned to go [be] absent without leave.

In both these cases, the calm statement of intended murder was deceptive. In contrast the threat of murder in the heat of anger arouses a greater sense of urgency, although the danger may be slight. Such threats should not, however, be dismissed lightly. The threat which is expressed in gesture, the hand drawn across the throat or clasped to some weapon has a melodramatic quality which again may be misleading. A change in facial expression, "if looks could kill," sometimes conveys greater menace than the spoken word.

The threat may be made in writing, stated clearly in an extortion note or perhaps disguised in the phantasy of a classroom essay. When a teacher asked the class to write a theme on a book, a 15-year-old student wrote,

This book does not have a title, but it is the story of a boy who was fed up of living. His name, that doesn't matter. It's what he will do will shock you. One night when his parents went to bed, he got up from his bed, took his shotgun, loaded it and went quietly into their bedroom.

His mother and father were sleeping, he took aim shot his father first, his mother screamed he shot her. His smaller brother came running out of his room to see what was the matter, he fired again. What was the reason for this gruesome murder? What made him do it? He hated them. His life ambition was to get a car. They promised him one, but always fell down on their promises. This story is not fiction, although it sounds fantastic, it happened in my family.

That night the student went to his parents' room and wounded both with two shots.

The threat may be made directly to the intended victim or it may be made outside his hearing or presence. It may be made once only or repeatedly over many years so that its ominous significance fades. A person may be falsely accused of having made a threat to kill in order to secure his commitment to a mental hospital, as in the case of a mother who falsely claimed that her son threatened to kill her with a baseball bat. A home visit revealed that the baseball bat was a small light plastic child's bat which could serve no lethal purpose.

In the present study, 81 patients made a verbal threat to kill and in some cases combined words with physical assault. The remaining 19 patients made an undoubted non-verbal threat to kill in the form of physical assault or discharge of firearms. Three of these patients, who were psychotic, denied homicidal intent, but the homicidal nature of their actions was not in question. A chronic paranoid schizophrenic who threatened that she would cut out the tongues of her neighbors with an axe was not included, although such action might well be deadly.

## THOSE WHO THREATENED TO KILL

Forty-eight of the 100 patients who threatened to kill were psychotic and all but 10 had schizophrenia or organic brain disease. The majority of patients with chronic organic brain syndrome had cerebrovascular disease or senility. One young woman was found to have an inoperable cerebral tumor. Paranoid delusions, an important factor in the threat to kill, were present in 35 patients. As will be seen from Table 1 only 3 patients showed mania or psychotic depression.

TABLE 1.  *Diagnostic Classification*

| PSYCHOTIC GROUP | | NON-PSYCHOTIC GROUP | |
|---|---|---|---|
| Schizophrenia | 19 | Passive aggressive | |
| Paranoid state and paranoia | 7 | personality | 23 |
| Chronic brain syndrome | 16 | Sociopathic personality | 13 |
| Acute brain syndrome | 3 | Hysterical personality | 10 |
| Mania | 2 | Paranoid personality | 2 |
| Psychotic depression | 1 | Neurotic behavior disorder | 2 |
| | | Mental retardation | 2 |
| | 48 | | 52 |

In the non-psychotic group of 52 patients, the primary diagnosis was character disorder, except in two patients with mental retardation and two patients with neurotic behavior disorder. Frequently features of more than one form of character disorder were present and some patients also had acute neurosis or alcoholism. Among the 100 patients, alcohol or drugs facilitated expression of the threat to kill in 26 cases. A record of criminal behavior was not common. One psychotic patient had previously been convicted of criminal homicide and had accidentally killed a child in an automobile accident.

Problems in expression of hostility were prominent in both psychotic and non-psychotic patients. Some patients showed sadistic behavior throughout their lives and the threat to kill seemed to be an inevitable part of the total clinical picture. They boasted of their sadistic exploits and took pleasure in describing their hunting triumphs and their skill in karate or judo. One man derived satisfaction from telling his wife again and again of an incident in which he assisted in the birth of a calf by hitching the cow to a post and tying a rope from the presenting legs of the calf to his tractor. He gunned the motor and eviscerated the cow.

Several patients had remarkable private armories including revolvers, as many as 8 automatic pistols, shotguns and rifles of varying caliber. One patient had five large German police dogs and another patient, not in the present study, encouraged his several Boxer dogs to tear other dogs to pieces. He once tossed his child's pet kitten among his dogs while they were fighting with fatal outcome. In the very sadistic patients, the triad of childhood cruelty to animals, firesetting and enuresis was often encountered.

Other patients showed free expression of hostile impulses yet their behavior could not be described as sadistic. Sensitive to criticism and quick to anger they would not hesitate to respond verbally or physically when provoked. At the opposite end of the aggressive spectrum were passive-aggressive and passive-dependent personalities who had difficulty in directly expressing their hostility. In these patients, threats to kill and physical violence stood in contrast to their usual behavior. Sadistic impulses found infrequent expression and the defenses against these impulses were conspicuous.

Thus persons capable of sadistic acts would speak of their

abhorrence of blood and war, their distress over war time atrocities and their aversion to TV programs of murderous violence. In this group were 2 nurses, a former missionary, a minister of religion, and a member of a humane society. Some gave up hunting because of their distress over the kill. The juxtaposition of great solicitude for the welfare of others and threats of homicide was not confined to any single diagnostic category but the contrast in those patients with hysterical character traits was heightened by the dramatic expression of feeling in either direction. Such threats were sometimes acknowledged to be appeals for help.

Pathological jealousy, ranging from baseless mistrust to frank paranoid delusions, contributed significantly to threats to kill. Suspicion of marital infidelity, present throughout the marriage, might reach delusional proportion following business reverse, loss of job, the onset of physical illness, impotence or organic brain disease. Some patients with latent homosexual tendencies, directly or indirectly, encouraged their wives to have an affair and then reacted with great anger. Sadistic attacks also followed requests for the wife to recount in detail marital or premarital sex experiences with other men. Although only one patient gave a history of vasectomy, in another group of consecutive admissions within one year, because of the impulse to kill, 3 of 11 men reported that they had undergone this operation.

Four of the 25 married women under the age of 40 were pregnant when they threatened to kill and a fifth had recently delivered a child. The pregnant mothers all threatened to kill their husbands and three of them also threatened to kill their children. Strong negative feelings over the pregnancy were either freely admitted or suggested by depression in previous pregnancies or attempted abortion. Two mothers who were not pregnant threatened to kill persons who had made disparaging remarks about one of their children and a third threatened to kill her husband because he showed little concern over the illness of his stepson. In each case the mother herself, despite protestations to the contrary, showed evidence of great hostility toward her child.

Twenty patients reported childhood experience of parental brutality which ranged from repeated whippings to loss of teeth, dislocation of a shoulder and other injuries. Several patients overheard a parent threatening to kill and two had themselves been threatened with death. Fourteen patients had experienced direct or indirect attempts at seduction by their parents. Three patients had mothers who were prostitutes, others had blatantly promiscuous mothers and several males had slept with or had been bathed by their mothers beyond the age of ten. Not a few patients had received witting or unwitting parental encouragement of hostile behavior.

Prior to the threat to kill, many patients repressed or projected their homicidal impulses. Thus there would be horrifying dreams or nightmares in which a beloved relative would be killed or injured. Other persons might be accused of planning to murder or harm the very person who would later be threatened with death by the patient. Factors not already noted which precipitated the threat to kill ranged from mild criticism to extremely provocative remarks or behavior. Disparaging remarks especially in the presence of a third person and threats of divorce or separation figured prominently. Apparently trivial precipitating factors assumed much greater significance in the context of the patient's personality development and psychological conflicts.


## THOSE WHO WERE THREATENED

The victim of criminal homicide is more often than not a relative or close friend of the offender. Svalastoga, in a study of 172 Danish murderers, found that of every 10 murderers, 6 selected victims among members of their own family, 3 selected victims among acquaintances and one selected as victim a stranger.[1] In the present study, 8 of every 10 patients threatened to kill members of their own family, one threatened an acquaintance and one threatened a stranger. Some of those patients who threatened members of their own family also threatened sexual rivals or police who were called to the scene.

Wives (27) and husbands (24) were the family members most frequently threatened followed by sons (21), daughters (15), mothers (14), fathers (6), sisters (4), brothers (2), one mother-in-law and one father-in-law. Others threatened included police (9), physicians (4), heterosexual rivals (3), judges (2) and one homosexual rival. The figures in parentheses refer to the number of patients who made the specific threats. Thus 9 patients threatened policemen but more than 9 policemen were threatened. Thirty-seven patients either threatened or contemplated suicide at the time of the threat to kill.

The provocative role of some who were threatened deserves mention. Indeed the recipient of the threat to kill was sometimes the first to criticize or behave in a threatening manner. Harsh, unmerciful comments would be continued long after they had aroused very great distress or anger. Who should be labeled as the aggressor in these circumstances? Wives of very jealous husbands would dress in a very revealing manner and flirt openly with casual acquaintances.

The response to threats of homicide varied from studied indifference and frank disbelief—"Well go ahead and shoot" —to terror stricken panic. Sadistic alcoholic husbands were complemented by long suffering masochistic wives who patiently endured not only threats of death but also repeated physical assault.

Children of these marriages are often exposed to repeated brutality if not the threat of death. Rather than risk separation through divorce or commitment of their husbands to jail or mental hospitals, these women sacrifice their children to preserve the marriage. As the children tend to grow up in the image of their parents, the pattern of family violence passes from one generation to the next. After a particularly severe beating the masochistic wife may take legal action against her husband, but within a short time assault charges are withdrawn or request is made for the husband's discharge from the hospital.

It is particularly important for the physician to see that steps are taken to protect the children. These families may move from one county to another when welfare agencies or courts show concern, and too often the cases are lost in the files of bureaucracy. Alternatively judges and lawyers, with an overscrupulous regard for due process, or an inability to believe that a man who presents a good appearance in court can yet savagely mistreat his children, contribute to society's failure to protect these child victims. The children are either too young to voice complaint or are terrorized into withholding information from court and welfare officials.

A 35-year-old alcoholic often threatened to kill his wife and frequently beat her and the children. After one such threat and a severe beating he put her in his car and drove around with the stated intention of looking for a mine shaft in which to bury her. Once while he was beating one of his children, his wife went to load a shotgun, but he took the gun away from her and clubbed her with the butt. She would turn white according to a neighbor, when she heard her husband's car in the driveway and the children would fearfully scurry around the house picking up their toys and putting things straight in the living room. One child had mild deafness from blows on the head. The wife made no effort to seek help and when her mother notified the court, she opposed the efforts of the court to protect the children from further mistreatment.

The reluctance of some relatives to seek advice or protection was remarkable. A man with many bizarre paranoid delusions repeatedly threatened to kill his wife and over a 2-week period spent much time sharpening 3 knives. His wife revealed this information only after her husband threatened to kill his surgeon. Another wife, who always slept with "one eye open" because of her husband's homicidal threats, agreed to obtain a court order for psychiatric examination only because the police threatened to jail her husband if she did not do so. The police were concerned over the welfare of two young daughters who had been sleeping at night in the family station wagon because of fear of their father.

An elderly man with chronic brain syndrome and paranoid delusions that his life was in danger had for two years been sleeping at night in his barn with a dog and two loaded weapons at his side. He threatened to kill a neighbor and during the two years made many threats to kill his family. One night he hit his wife in the face and pulled her around the barnyard by her hair. No effort was made to admit him to the hospital until he attacked his wife with a fence post. The family were reluctant to agree to continued hospital care and following his discharge from another hospital, they wrote requesting that he should be allowed to have his guns back.

A young paranoid schizophrenic, who had previously been treated with electroshock therapy, beat his father unconscious following an argument. After the assault his behavior was bizarre and he told his mother he had a castration complex. Several months later when his mother asked him to mow the lawn he said, "Do you want to die, because you are going to die?" He then choked his mother till she fell to the floor. She did not reveal this attack to her husband as she wanted to "preserve the peace." A month later he again attacked his mother and was choking her when someone intervened. Following this incident he was admitted to the hospital.

Delay in seeking help was not confined to relatives. A demented old man who lived in a shack with 26 dogs and 58 cats threatened health officials with a loaded shot gun several times during a 3-month period. Another senile, not in this series, called at a police station with a loaded shot gun and stated that he intended to shoot his imagined persecutors. The police removed the shot gun shells, returned his shot gun to him and sent him on his way. He was arrested shortly afterwards following a threat to kill.

Relatives who recognized their danger were often at a loss to explain their failure to seek help. One wife calmly remarked, "Some day he'll kill me." Several wives were reluctant to seek divorce because of their fear of homicide. They lacked confidence in the protection provided by society. Court orders restraining a husband from visiting his wife can be violated and police are seldom able to provide adequate protection. Newspapers contain frequent accounts of murder by husbands under restraining orders. Commitment to jail or mental hospital may provide only temporary security because of the risk of early release. Paranoid patients are often skilled at concealing their symptoms and they may avoid commitment by impressing a lay jury or they may obtain premature release from a hospital.

The reluctance of persons to take action through fear of retaliation is not surprising. However, many recipients of threats to kill do not appreciate their danger. The reaction of denial extends to physicians and others who are consulted. Review of the case records in the present study revealed that some threats to kill were not mentioned in the summary of the medical record. In not a few cases the only reference to the threat was contained in the notes recorded by the physician on admission duty. In other cases the threat was mentioned but discounted, and in one case little credence was given to the statement of reliable informants.

## THOSE WHO LATER KILLED

Six months after the end of the 15-month period during which these 100 patients were admitted to the hospital specifically because they had made homicidal threats, it was known that one patient had killed deliberately and one had killed accidentally. In contrast none of the 1528 other patients admitted during the same period was known to have killed either deliberately or accidentally. Thus patients admitted specifically because of the threat to kill are more likely to kill than patients admitted for some other reason. The statistical relationship between threatening and killing is low but statistically stable ($r_p = .137$. $p < .001$).

A paranoid schizophrenic woman, who had threatened to kill her husband and relatives whom she accused of wanting to take her children from her, gave her 2 children sleeping pills causing the death of one child. In 2 previous schizophrenic episodes she had delusions that her husband wanted to kill her, and in the second she feared that someone wanted to kidnap her children. A 30-year-old man with paranoid personality and pathological jealousy, who had threatened to kill his wife, accidentally shot and killed his brother. He blamed himself, wondered whether the shooting was really accidental and stated that perhaps he really did want to kill his brother.

A third patient, a schizophrenic youth who had threatened to kill a relative, committed suicide within the 6-month period. Careful review of these tragedies showed that signs of danger in one case were not recognized by the family. The other two patients appeared to have responded satisfactorily to treatment of several months' duration. Despite thorough study it was not possible to discover clues which might have indicated the need for readmission to the hospital.

## COMMENT

This study did not provide criteria for the prediction of homicide. The writer, from clinical experience in examining over 100 persons who committed homicide, has the clinical impression that a history of great parental brutality, extreme maternal seduction, or the triad of childhood firesetting, cruelty to animals and enuresis are unfavorable prognostic factors in those who threaten homicide.[2] Paranoid delusions with very great anger denote danger, yet many patients with paranoid delusions do not kill. Features of an hysterical charcater disorder do not preclude danger.

It may be necessary to treat both those who threaten to kill and those who are threatened; the former because their behavior is an indication of poor control over homicidal impulses or a reasonable appeal for help, the latter because of witting or unwitting incitement of murderous hostility. Yet adequate examination and treatment is often dependent upon awareness of the threat to kill and appreciation of its significance.

Unfortunately both those who threaten and those who are threatened are frequently reluctant to seek help. When they do so they may speak vaguely of impulses or threats to harm, or they may minimize the seriousness of the threat or they may even deny that a threat was ever made. Denial starts in the patient's family, continues through community resources and is not confined to lay persons. Even judges, social workers and physicians are not immune.

# The Normal and the
# Sociopathic Murderer

*MANFRED GUTTMACHER*

## MURDER

A CHARACTER in the Elizabethan drama, *The Duchess of Malfi*, declared, "Other sinnes onley speake; Murther shreikes out." There can be no question that in the minds of most individuals murder stands apart from all other crimes. Reiwald, the Swiss criminologist, attests to its universal fascination. He reports that more than ninety-five per cent of all crime novels are about murder.[1]

Despite the importance and the fascination of the crime of murder, the psychiatric literature which bears on it is not extensive. During my years of work in criminal psychiatry, I have had the opportunity of examining more than two hundred individuals who have committed homicide. I shall draw heavily upon this material, and since our clinical studies become part of the public court record, I shall quote freely from them. Most of the cases were referred to our clinic after verdict, to assist the court in disposition. However, many of the defendants were examined prior to trial, at the request of the defense counsel or the prosecutor. It must be understood that the cases, which I have chosen for consideration in this lecture, are not a random sample of murderers in general, and hence some caution must be used in making deductions from our clinical material about the crime of murder.

Of the 175 cases reviewed for this study, 105 were found to have been clearly non-psychotic at the time of the murder,

REPRINTED from *The Mind of the Murderer* by Manfred Guttmacher, by permission of Farrar, Straus & Giroux, Inc. Copyright © 1960 by Manfred Guttmacher.

53 to have been psychotic, and 17 were seriously abnormal individuals but a psychosis at the time of crime could not be definitely established by our examinations. No effort will be made to divide the cases into the responsible and irresponsible, according to the standards set by the Rules in M'Naghten's case, which forms the basis of the Maryland law on the subject. But, I should like to emphasize the fact that in ten per cent of our cases, we experienced real difficulty in reaching a definitive decision as to the seriousness and the significance of the defendant's mental disorder at the time of the homicide. Such cases are particularly difficult to present adequately to a jury under the very restrictive Rules of M'Naghten. In my opinion the true psychiatric picture, particularly in difficult cases of this type, can be much more satisfactorily and justly portrayed in a trial conducted under the Rule of Durham.[2]

Dr. Isaac Ray, in his great *Treatise on the Medical Jurisprudence of Insanity*, published in 1838, gave considerable attention to the crime of murder. He makes a very interesting comparison between the behavior of the criminal murderer and the insane killer, whom he denominates, "the homicidal monomaniac."

He observes that nearly every homicide committed by an insane individual had been preceded by some of signs of insanity. Victims of the insane killer were found generally to be intimate associates, not infrequently his own offspring. Most of the insane murderers exhibited no remorse and freely confessed the deed. The expressed motive for the killing generally seems wholly inadequate to the sane individual. The crimes of the insane murderer are generally extremely gory, while the sane murderer sheds no more blood than necessary. The insane killer rarely plans his crime astutely. He often carries it out with whatever lethal object is at hand and in full view of onlookers. He carries out his crime without accomplices. Experience, during the century and more that has elapsed since Dr. Ray made these generalizations, has validated most of them remarkably.[3]

I should like to add, from an analysis of our material, certain clinical data, which Dr. Ray did not consider in comparing the sane murderer with the psychotic murderer.

A third of our psychotic group had previous psychiatric institutionalization. This was true of only three per cent of the non-psychotic group. Only one-fifth of the psychotic group had prior conviction for assault or for some serious criminal offense, while two-fifths of the non-psychotic group had such convictions. More than a third of the psychotic group were partially or completely amnesic for the crime. This was rarely present in the other group unless the perpetrator was quite drunk at the time of the homicide.

Judges, being continually involved in testing the veracity of witnesses, are often inclined to rely very greatly on their own intuitive judgment in regard to amnesic states. Amnesia is technically a very complex condition; psychological and psychiatric guidance should be sought whenever it becomes an issue. I recall a case referred to our office some years ago by a veteran conscientious jurist who, in determining the severity of sentence, relied greatly on whether the defendant impressed him as truthful or untruthful. A man was charged with the theft of a taxicab. When he was on the witness stand he did not deny that he could have stolen a cab, but insisted that he had no memory of doing so. The evidence was clearly against him; it showed that he had been drinking, left the tavern, climbed into a cab, and almost immediately drove it into a telegraph pole, ending up in a hospital with cerebral concussion. He said he recalled being in the tavern and re-gaining consciousness in the hospital, but he claimed that he was utterly amnesic in regard to taking a cab. The judge grew very impatient with the defendant and tried to badger him into an admission that he had done so, but he was adamant. Finally, more or less it disgust, the judge referred him for psychiatric examination. We were able to point out the great probability of a traumatic retrograde amnesia of sufficient duration to cover completely the period of the theft of the cab, particularly since the offense was preceded by drinking, which is known to facilitate the development of amnesia.

Recently a man was tried for manslaughter in the Baltimore criminal court. According to the police, a car driving on the wrong side of the street at an excessive rate of speed, crashed into a transit bus throwing all four occupants of the car into the  street. The defendant's wife and a male friend of his were dead when the ambulance arrived. The other woman passenger escaped with very minor injuries. The defendant was picked up unconscious and was taken to a hospital where he remained unconscious for at least six hours. A diagnosis of cerebral concussion was made. A blood alcohol determination showed it to be slightly over one hundred milligrams per cent—a finding in that twilight zone in which some individuals are drunk and others essentially sober. The patient insisted that the last thing that he recalled was the four of them leaving a tavern about two miles from the scene of the accident. He had no knowledge of the accident nor of who was driving the car when it struck the bus. When interviewed under light narcosis with sodium amytal he made the same statements. The surviving woman occupant said that she remembered that one of the men took the wheel when they left the tavern, but she was unable to recall which one. It was our belief that the patient was suffering from a genuine retrograde amnesia. The court decided that the case should be stetted since the defendant was unable properly to assist his counsel in preparing his defense.

Most laymen are suspicious of the truth of the defendant when he admits fragments of memory during an amnesic period. They feel that he is admitting memory only of the things that he finds convenient to recall. Actually the reverse is likely to be true. Periods of amnesia can be total and complete, but they are not the rule. There may even be fragments of memory of events occurring during an epileptic attack.

Then there are defendants who profess some memory of events which they actually do not recall. They incorporate, as their own, facts which have been recounted to them regarding the crime. The human mind abhors a vacuum. None of us likes to feel that he has carried out complex acts for which he has no recollection whatever. Some individuals try to piece together the events retrospectively and accept what they have been told, or they invent their own rationalizations, their own specious explanations, rather than admit to themselves that they were completely out of contact and without conscious control and memory.

Nearly half of the "normal murderers" referred for examination had been drinking heavily before the crime. This degree of alcoholism at the time of the commission of the offense was found in only ten per cent of the psychotic murderers.

A suicidal attempt following the crime was rare in the normal group but occurred in a fifth of the psychotic cases. Less than a third of the victims of the "normal murderer" were family members, while nearly two-thirds of the victims of psychotic murderers were close relatives, including mates in a common law relationship.

There are many interesting statistical facts about murder. Since these data are not primarily of psychiatric importance they will merely be detailed and not discussed. In the United States there are about 16,000 suicides and 8,500 criminal homicides[4] a year. In all of England and Wales there are only about 125 murders annually and about 35 per cent of those perpetrating them commit suicide. The total number of suicides in England annually is 5,000.[5] Another striking difference between the homicide figures of England and of this country is that 40 per cent of those tried for murder at assizes in England were declared insane, while in this country the reported figures are from 2 to 4 per cent.[6]

Baltimore, with a population of a million, had 102 homicides in 1958. Only about 6 per cent of Baltimore murderers subsequently commit suicide.[7] In Philadelphia, where there are about 125 criminal homicides annually, less than 4 per cent of the offenders commit suicide.[8] Suicide following homicide is much more likely to happen among whites than among Negroes.

The homicide rate among the colored in the United States is more than seven times that of the white population, while the general arrest rate is only three to one.[9] Professor Wolfgang, of the Sociology Department of the University of Pennsylvania, in his recent research study, *Patterns in Criminal Homicide*, found that in Philadelphia, during a recent five-year period, the Negro homicide offender rate was fourteen times the white rate. After a crude control of the occupational variable, in an effort to compensate for socio-economic differences, the rate for Negroes was at least eight times that of whites. This author quotes studies from Alabama, Massachusetts, Missouri, and Ohio with strikingly similar results.[10] It is interesting that the homicide rate for whites living in the south is five times that of whites living in New England.[11] Suicide in general, in the United States, is three times as common among whites as among Negroes.[12] During 1957 there were in Maryland 278 suicides among the whites and only 26 among the Negroes.[13] Considering their incidence in the population, this is a white to Negro ratio of nearly four to one.

The inordinately high homicide rate of Negroes certainly does not support the view that mental disease is a factor of primary importance in homicide. No authority has asserted that in Maryland mental disease is more prevalant among Negroes than among whites. Accurate comparative data on the incidence of mental disease in racial groups is difficult to find. Probably the most reliable study thus far made in this country is that of Benjamin Malzberg. He finds that incidence of mental disease in Negroes in New York City is increasing very rapidly until their first admission rate to mental hospitals has outstripped the white rate and is now two and a half times the white rate. However, this preponderance may in large part be due to special sociological factors existing in that unique city,[14] and is surely not general throughout the country. Doubtless, complex cultural and sociological factors are controlling elements in the disparate rates for homicide and suicide in various racial groups. Among the psychotic in our series, there were only half as many Negroes as whites, while among the so-called normal murderers there were twice as many Negroes as whites. Therefore, the deduction can be made that white individuals who commit homicides are far more likely to be psychotic than their Negro counterparts.

The sociologists, Andrew Henry and James Short, recently published a monograph on suicide and homicide. Their basic findings confirm the earlier work of European investigators that homicide and suicide rates are constantly inversely proportional to one another, whether the factors under consideration are race, age grouping, or economic conditions. It is as though there is a certain quantum of violent hostility within man and a portion of this must either be directed outwardly against others or inwardly against oneself.

Much has been learned through psychoanalysis in regard to aggressive and hostile impulses. Analysis of the fantasies and dreams of normal individuals has revealed the ubiquity of such impulses. Certain wise men have long known this Goethe said, "There is no crime of which I do not deem myself capable."[15] To be sure, there are certain persons in whom these fantasies appear to be of more malignant character than in others and there are some individuals in whom they occur with such frequency that they dominate their mental life. But psychiatrists must agree with the observation made by Zilboorg that "psychoanalysis has no answer as to what it is that makes man succumb or give in to his fantasies so that they become criminal acts."[16] Clinical psychologists assert that projective tests give an indication of the strength of the controlling mechanism, but we must admit that present devices for measuring social control are quite faulty.

### THE NORMAL MURDERER

Society's greatest concern must be with the non-psychotic murderer; with the individual who exhibits no marked psychopathology, since by far the greatest numbers of homicides are committed by them. It is not enough to say that these are the dissocial individuals who have not incorporated and made a part of themselves constructive parental figures to insure their developing an effective superego.

The late Paul Schilder, a man with a brilliant and a restlessly inquiring mind, published a series of studies on persons' attitudes toward death. In regard to the rather typical young slayer, the holdup man, the killer after an insignificant quarrel, Schilder made this observation: "It is rather that life and death do not seem to play an imporant part in the manifest content of psychic life. Persons of this kind seemingly kill as easily as children in their play, and they are not more concerned about their own death than children are. It almost seems that these 'normal murderers,' who are not otherwise so badly adapted to their reality, show particular infantile trends in their reaction to life and death. One may say they kill because they do not appreciate the deprivation they inflict upon others."[17] In another study the author observes that "the child's idea of death is essentially deprivation. It is ready to believe that this deprivation, like any other, is reversible."

Criminological studies reveal that the great majority of the offenders of this type come from the economically and socially underprivileged strata of our society. Almost without exception one finds in their early backgrounds not only economic want, but cruelities and miseries of every kind. Such early conditioning predisposes to a marked undervaluation of life. To these individuals people are objects to be manipulated for predatory purposes. The Gluecks, in their important studies on juvenile delinquency, have found that the seriously delinquent child was involved in accidents far more frequently than the non-delinquent child. Disregard for their own safety came early and paralleled their disregard for the welfare of others.[18] One can safely hypothesize that the amount of satisfying nurture that the child receives in its earliest years must be a fundamental element in the formation of its attitudes on the value of human life.

The denial of satisfying early nurture must in many instances have a positive aspect, that of frustration. Frustration is known to play an extremely important role in the creation of aggressive and destructive drives, elements in the personality structure of the greatest importance in homicide.

There are many murderers we have examined who could serve as prototypes for the young criminal with a reckless disregard for human life. Take for example Robert T., a twenty-one year old Negro who shot and killed, in a fight, a male Negro twice his age. His father had died when he was five. His mother was an ineffectual woman who died at thirty-seven of heart disease. There were two illegitimate half-brothers who were given out for adoption. In his early life there was a great deal of poverty. He had lived much of the time with a woman he called his aunt, but he does not know whether she was actually related to him. He got to the fourth grade and was then transferred to a special class. He was a very active truant. Robert was twice knocked unconscious, once while a boy, by a toy pistol, and at twenty, by a "boyfriend who hit me in the head with a blackjack when we had a fight." He had had gonorrheal infections which he treated himself with pills from a drugstore.

He had a spotty work record, losing jobs because of absenteeism. The Navy kept him only eight weeks before discharging him. He gambled heavily and used both alcohol and marijuana. His temper was easily aroused, all arguments automatically ended in fights.

When he was eighteen he was fined twenty-five dollars for fighting. A youth had cleaned him out in a crap game. When he refused to return any of the money, a fight started. At nineteen he was sentenced to thirty days in jail because of a street fight in which many youths armed with knives participated. Two months later he robbed a white boy on the street of a small sum of money and was given a penal sentence of two years.

Two weeks before the murder he and the victim had jointly purchased a bottle of liquor. The other man asserted that he was drinking more than his share and jerked the bottle from his mouth; a fight ensued. According to the defendant, this man, at the conclusion of the fight, threatened to kill him.

Robert learned of a youth in his neighborhood who had paid a group of little children fifty cents for a pistol which they had found. He went to this youth and lied, insisting that the pistol was his, but magnanimously gave him fifty cents to reimburse him for what he had paid the children.

For two weeks he carried the loaded pistol in his belt. Then one night he saw the other man on the street, walking with a man and a woman. He shifted the pistol from his belt to his pocket as they approached. He claims that the victim made a menacing gesture. He instantly fired one fatal shot and fled to his girl friend's house, where he had been living.

Robert was given a life sentence in the penitentiary. A recent inquiry reveals that in the nine years that he has been there he has had eighteen disciplinary infractions, including an attempt to choke another inmate, striking an inmate on the head with a brick, and seven fist fights.

Let us consider another example of the "normal slayer." Alvin B. is a huge seventeen-year-old Negro boy nearly six feet tall and weighing two hundred and fifteen pounds, who murdered a policeman. In appearance, he resembles a fine future linesman for a professional football team. By psychological tests he is shown to have bright average intelligence. Some ten months before the homicide he quit in the second year of high school. He had never failed to pass a grade.

His medical history was marked by frequent trips to the accident rooms of the Baltimore hospitals. When he was fourteen, a gang of school boys robbed him of thirty cents and knocked him out, breaking his nose. At sixteen he contracted gonorrhea.

At fourteen he worked one entire summer at a grocery store. For some years he had helped his brother-in-law, who was engaged in gardening and grass cutting. A short time before his offense he worked for a few weeks as a porter in a drug store at $39 a week.

Alvin came from a broken home. He was told that his father left his mother before he was born. He met his father two or three times a month in bar rooms. "He'll give me money if I ask him, but he won't give me nothing unless I do ask." He knows very little about his father, except that he is a construction laborer. His mother does occasional day work. She is an active Baptist. He says of her, "She's a nice mother. She sacrificed herself for us all the time." Occasionally his mother beat him with a strap when he was a small boy. The stepfather, who had married the mother four years before, was a baker. The patient feels quite hostile toward him. "He just nags at you, that's all. He likes to make people feel stupid because he's got an education. He seems to think he's a perfect man, nothing ever suits him." The patient is the youngest of five. The eldest sister, a heavy drinker, had left her husband for another man. The eldest brother had served a five-year sentence for selling narcotics. Alvin lived much of the time with a sister, seven years older than himself, and her husband. He seemed fond of them. He said they treated him well, even permitting him to take girls up to his room. The brother, Lee, who was two years older was involved with the patient in the offense that led to the homicide. Although only nineteen this brother was married and already had two children.

One gains the impression from this patient, as with others of his type, that there is a complete lack of family cohesiveness. His ignorance in regard to his mother's schooling, the occupations of his grandfathers, the name of the bakery in which his stepfather worked, his father's police record, the grade levels in school to which his sisters and brothers went, their church affiliation, etc., are characteristic.

When questioned about the things that give him most pleasure in life, he immediately responded, "girls." Attempts at heterosexual relations began at seven. He had lived with a twenty-six year old girl for nine months and then tired of her. He is a skillful pool player, often running all fifteen balls. He claims to have lost only one fight in his life and was known for his fighting prowess. His mother forced him to go to church regularly when he lived in her house.

The morning of the day on which the offense occurred the patient spent in the poolroom with his nineteen year old brother, Lee. That afternoon he went to see one of his girls. He was taking her to the movies when a friend, Ray, who does not work and has an extensive criminal record, sent word to him to come to his house. He got his brother to go along. When they arrived there they found Ray having sex relations with his wife. Not wishing to interrupt them, they called to him to meet them at the poolroom. An hour later Ray arrived and asked them if they wanted to get some money. Alvin replied, "I guess so." They then went to get Slim. They found him in his car. The four of them rode around, stopping while Ray bought a pint of whiskey, which they drank. On their tour of the city they surveyed various liquor stores and finally picked out one to hold up. Alvin was carrying a loaded pistol, which he had secured some time before through a burglary, Ray was also armed. Slim stayed in his car, the others went in. Three men and a porter were in the store. Ray ordered some whiskey and when the clerk turned around he was facing Ray's gun. Alvin covered the other men. Lee went behind the partition to see if there was a safe. Because of the recent robberies of liquor stores, a police officer had secreted himself in the rear. He grabbed Lee by the neck. Lee shouted "look out." Then the officer started blasting away at Ray, letting go of Lee, and they all fled. Alvin turned and fired at the officer until his gun was empty. Ray jumped into the car that took off. Alvin ran up an alley and met two policemen coming down toward him. He dropped his gun and threw up his hands. One officer shot him in the leg. He said, "I didn't feel much pain. There were lots of officers around me. They tore off my coat to see if they could find my name. They kept wanting to know who the other boys were. I told them I didn't know. Two cops picked me up and put me in an ambulance. They started to hit on my leg where the bullet was at and kept hitting on my head to tell them my name and the names of the others. Then I cussed them and they cussed me. One pulled out his gun and said, 'I ought to kill you.' I was scared so I hit him. I guess I dazed him and then I jumped the other one and grabbed the gun from his hand. He started toward me. That's when the gun went off. The next thing I knew I was out of the ambulance and running. I jumped into a taxi and told the driver to take off. He rammed into the ambulance. That shook me up and knocked the gun out of my hand. I got behind the wheel and tried to put it into reverse. The pain got real bad in my leg. Officers were coming up all around me. I started to run and got shot in the hip and the leg. Then I got shot in the neck as I stooped over. I jumped over a fence and crashed through the back window of a house. I saw a kitchen knife and grabbed it. I ran out the front of the house. There was a taxi with a woman in it. I got in, the woman eased out. The driver said, 'Boy, you are bleeding. What's the matter, have the police been firing at you?' I said, 'No, I was at a bar and got into a fight.' He didn't want to take me. I told him if he didn't I'd run the knife through him. He must have had his blinker light on. A police car came up. I ducked down. Another one came up. They shot into the cab and I got hit in the arm, in the chest, and in the leg. I guess the one in the chest made me kind of dizzy." The hospital report stated that he had seven separate bullet wounds.

When Alvin was asked how he began his involvement in serious crime, he said, "There was an older fellow, twenty-nine, named Slicklow, and me and him made quite a bit of money through burglary. I was around fifteen then. Every-time when I was coming from school, he was waiting for me. He got me cards for bar rooms and started me drinking. He didn't work. He was pimping off a woman. He always had women for me. I guess he just liked me. He said I didn't carry myself like a boy but like a man. I bought a lot of clothes and stuff. He crossed me up one time. He held out a couple of hundred dollars on me, so I told him I'd be his friend but I wasn't going to work with him like this any more. Then I did some hustling with Ray. We murphied a guy, you know, we told him we could get him a woman but it would take a lot of money. When he took out his roll we took it and ran. I done quite a series of robberies with Ray. I kept telling him we ought not to be doing it but he said he'd been doing it for a long time and got away with it pretty good."

The Clinic psychologist, on the basis of his projective tests, reported, "This patient has a somewhat paranoid view of the world, but possibly it has enough reality basis that one cannot say that it is more than a product of aggression. He sees the world as depriving and divides it clearly into the 'haves' and 'have-nots.' His own value system is based on this distinction. He has no compunction about taking from the 'haves' since he is a 'have-not.' He does not feel that he is wrong because society has made him so. He has been de-

prived so now it is up to society to look after him and if they
do not give it, he will take it. Stealing is therefore natural
to him. Murder is incidental."

Despite the fact that he had murdered a policeman, Alvin's
death sentence has been commuted to a life sentence because
of his age.

Certainly one must admit that such individuals are mal-
adjusted to society. But, in all probability, the genesis of such
defective personality structure has resulted from the defective
ethical standards which flourish in the social milieu in which
they were spawned, rather than from hidden neurotic com-
plexes.

## THE SOCIOPATHIC MURDERER

In contrast to these so-called normal murderers let us
consider the case of a sociopathic youth, whose delinquencies
were not merely the outgrowth of cupidity, nor a response to
defective group standards. His depredations were acts of a
war he was waging against society. He was what Lindner
cleverly termed, "a rebel without cause." The climax of his
war came in the holdup of the driver of a milk delivery
wagon, in broad daylight, on a city street. When his victim
offered resistance he promptly shot and killed him.

Herman D. was twenty-one at the time, but he had been
marked as a serious behavior problem before the age of six,
when he achieved the unenviable distinction of expulsion
from kindergarten.

He came from old, well-established Maryland families that
had attained some prominence in the business and social
life of Baltimore. He was the only son of a handsome father
who had been a well-known athlete and who had developed
into a man as hard as steel. He was an extremely selfish
man and he did not want a child because he felt it would
be a nuisance. When his wife tricked him into pregnancy,
he protested violently, but later said he could accept it, if
it were a girl. A malevolent fate presented him with a boy,
to whom he was inhumanly cruel. When the child was an
infant and cried at night he beat it. When the boy did some
pilfering at three he burned his fingers. When he was old
enough to be taken by streetcar to his grandmother's, he
refused to get on the same car with "that brat," but waited

for the next one. On one occasion, before Herman was old enough to go to school, he got away from his father while he was beating him. After that he was tied up before the lash was administered.

The mother was a beautiful woman, but an hysterical, dramatic type of person. The boy loved her with as much passion as he hated and feared his father. When the father was away from home, he occupied the neighboring bed to his mother. They often fell asleep clasping hands. The fights between the parents were frequent and intense. Herman said of their quarreling, "It was like a hangnail. It was always there, it was painful and I wanted to get rid of it." When the boy was nine the mother threatened suicide if he did not reform. A few years later she locked herself in the bathroom and cut her wrists, as a protest against his behavior. Herman broke the door down and applied tourniquets.

According to the many informants interviewed, Herman was an extremely restless, overactive, and utterly fearless child. At seven, having been locked in a third floor room in his grandmother's house as punishment, he slid down the rain spout and started for New York. At nine he climbed to the top of a telephone pole and refused to come down. He had a terrible temper, going into tantrums when thwarted. In one of these he set fire to his clothes.

An uncle, who was a Commander in the Medical Corps of the Navy, had forbidden him access to his country house when he was a child because of his cruelty to animals. He deliberately ran over kittens with his bicycle, he cut turtles in half with a hatchet, and once put out the eye of his Airedale with a dart. He bullied his companions and from the beginning sought social inferiors as friends.

He was expelled from kindergarten and a succession of day schools and military schools because of his rebelliousness. In between his schooling he had private tutors. On reaching his midteens he became a poolroom habitué.

When he was not an inmate of a correctional or penal institution, he worked periodically at various jobs obtained for him. He had developed into a handsome youth and on superficial contact was considered quite charming, especially by women. Although he showed aptitude in several jobs, he quickly tired of them and on all occasions took orders from superiors badly.

When psychiatrically examined, prior to his trial for murder, he was found to have good intellectual endowments, passing tests of intelligence with a medium score for college men. He did particularly well on the vocabulary subtests.

The father said, in giving the history, that Herman had stolen since he was a small boy. At nine he stole a bicycle which he sold. A year later he stole a hundred dollars from a home in which the family was visiting. When he began playing pool for high stakes he stole jewelry and silver from home, but was never caught and consistently denied his guilt. At seventeen he forged checks, signing his mother's name. With the proceeds he ran away to New York. There he lived by means of a racket. He frequented Times Square, posing as a male prostitute. He was clever enough to permit himself to be picked up only by affluent appearing older men. As soon as they got to their apartments and the men had removed their trousers, he grabbed them and made off with them. By this maneuver he obtained their wallets and materially slowed their pursuit. At eighteen he was caught in New York in a stolen car with two older men. He had a pistol on him at the time and was given nine months in the New York City Reformatory. While he was there his parents moved to New York. Shortly after his release he stole one hundred dollars from his father, and returned to Baltimore, where he had an affair with a cabaret singer. He supported himself by burglarizing apartments. When caught he was committed to the Maryland Training School for Boys, from which he soon escaped with two other boys to New York. They immediately burglarized his parents' apartment, outfitting themselves in the father's clothes. They lived for sometime on the loot which they obtained through a series of New York burglaries. Herman visited his mother occasionally when his father was not at home. The father anticipated one of these visits and over the vehement protests of the mother had three detectives awaiting his son's arrival. He was given a minimum sentence of eighteen months in Elmira Reformatory, but had to serve thirty-one before being released. While there he was found to be actively engaged in homosexuality. The institutional psychiatrist concluded, "He is not insane within the meaning of the statute. He is high-strung, egotistic, neurotic, fond of excitement, somewhat suggestible, has poor

ethical sense, is too unstable to settle down to steady employment, and unable to profit by experience."

He was released from Elmira Reformatory on parole and
the parole supervision transferred to Maryland. The parents
had made plans for their son's treatment in an excellent
psychiatric institution, but this was never carried out. A job
was obtained for him at the Glenn L. Martin Aircraft Company. He quit after a month and a half because a boss "rode"
him.

While on this job he met the eighteen-year-old brother of
a co-worker. This youth had just completed a sentence for
the theft of an automobile. The two immediately struck up a
friendship. Under Herman's leadership they planned the
holdup of a driver of a milk wagon. They stole a car and
when they saw the opportunity drove up alongside of the
wagon, demanding the money that the driver had collected,
which amounted to four hundred dollars. The driver attempted
to hit Herman's accomplice over the head with a milk bottle,
and as he did so, Herman shot him in the abdomen, the
bullet passing through the liver.

They immediately abandoned the stolen car for their own.
Then they went for a ride in the country. On their return to
the city, the newspapers were on the street announcing the
murder. They both felt confident that they would not be
caught. That evening they went joy riding with two other
youths. As they went past a college for Negroes, Herman
fired several shots over the heads of some of the students to
frighten them. That night he slept well. In the morning he
learned that his accomplice had been arrested. He left for
New York, where he remained for six weeks in hiding. He
then got a job as assistant purser on a boat going to the West
Coast. He lived in Los Angeles for a year on money sent him
surreptitiously by his father.

Herman was by no means an alcoholic; most of his crimes
were committed when he was entirely sober. But, after having
been in Los Angeles many months he "put one on," stole a car,
and drove it recklessly at high speed. He smashed into another car, turning it over. The police who had been giving
chase shot him as he tried to escape from the car he was driving. After being shot, he ran to the police car twenty yards
away and started off in it, but was apprehended.   He was hos-

pitalized and identified through his finger prints as a fugitive wanted in Baltimore for murder. He was bitter toward the Los Angeles police. When I examined him some months later, he said, "The lousy guy had nothing on me but drunken driving." He was tried before the late Judge Joseph N. Ulman, who sentenced him to be executed. This was commuted to a life sentence by the Governor of Maryland.

The lengthy apologia which Judge Ulman read in court at the time of the sentence is noteworthy. It gave full recognition to the mental abnormality of the youthful murderer, but instead of considering this a mitigating factor, the Judge felt that it called for his extinction. This was predicated upon the belief that the defendant's personality was so warped that it could not be modified by incarceration and that he might well prove to be a danger to the guards of the penal institution to which he would be committed. It was in no small part due to the impact of this statement of Judge Ulman that nearly a quarter of a century later a special institution for the treatment and incarceration of psychopaths, the Patuxent Institution, was established in Maryland. The law provides that defective delinquents, individuals who are not insane but have shown a propensity to become involved in dangerous criminal behavior because of "emotional unbalance," shall be given indeterminate sentences to this institution, which is directed by a psychiatrist and is essentially a hybrid between a psychiatric hospital and a penal institution.

The years that have passed since the trial have proven Judge Ulman's prognostication in regard to his adjustment, or maladjustment, to incarceration only partially true. He has at no time endangered anyone's life during his nearly thirty years in prison. The author holds himself somewhat responsible for the position that Judge Ulman took on this point. I had several conferences with the Judge while he was pondering over the sentence and I expressed the opinion that the prisoner might some day recklessly attempt to fight his way out of prison. I had at that time had less than a year's experience in criminal psychiatry. I do not believe that I would adopt such a view today, based on two facts: Herman's superior intelligence and the evidence that we then had, that he could readily adopt a homosexual adjustment. These data speak against the likelihood of his attempting to force his way out of prison.

The prediction that years of incarceration would not materially modify his antisocial attitudes has been amply born out. More than twenty years after Herman entered the penitentiary the author was requested by the Parole Commissioner to re-examine him. His social alienation and his warped standards were still evident. In speaking of the theft of the automobile in Los Angeles that had been responsible for his capture, he insisted that he had had no criminal intent. He had been out visiting and when he looked for a taxicab in the early hours of the morning, he could not find one so he began to walk. Unfortunately he had on a pair of new shoes that began to become quite painful so there was really nothing that he could do but steal an automobile. One of the sponsors of his parole at that time was a former Catholic chaplain of the penitentiary, although Herman was not a Catholic. The priest had worked out an elaborate plan of employment. The parolee was, during his first six months, to work as janitor in a couple of the small churches in the priest's parish and then he was assured a job in an industrial plant run by one of his parishioners. When questioned about this, Herman replied in his characteristically egocentric fashion, "Oh, I do not mind doing menial work. I'll be happy to help the good Father out." Not long ago this prisoner attained some newspaper notoriety when in support of another parole application, he submitted some forged letters, among them some purported to be from a woman who was planning to marry him.

This man is an excellent example of the sociopath. His delinquencies did not result merely from his having adopted the coloration of his environment; they have much deeper and more twisted origins. If one were permitted to set up an experimental situation to produce just such a character deformity, one would have placed him in the very home from which he came. For such purposes a cruel, rejecting father is almost a necessity. Cruelty breeds cruelty and rejection penetrates to much deeper levels of the personality than does simple neglect. Add to this an hysterical and seductive mother, with the emotionally broken home that is a necessary resultant with two such parents, and you have your chief ingredients. At my last interview with him, Herman said to me in discussing the roots of his antisocial behavior, "As a child I was pretty much bewildered. You know that my father was very stern and my mother very lenient. As far as I can remember, there

was always that difference between them and it created a
sense of bewilderment and insecurity." I recall Harry Stack
Sullivan, a very wise psychiatrist, saying that he felt that a
child developed a healthier personality with two inferior parents who were in essential agreement than with parents of
better caliber who were in constant disagreement. A child
must have a chart to steer by to get its bearings.

The poet Wordsworth said, "The child is father of the man."
In no area of behavior is this more true than in that of crime.
There were ominous portents of Herman's antisocial career
at an early age. His constant pilfering, his expulsion from
kindergarten, his reckless courage and his persistent sadistic
treatment of animals were indicators of the future. Had he
then got into treatment with a competent child psychiatrist
the outcome may have been very different. In all probability
by the time he reached his teens the process had become irre-
versible.

Herman's early stealing was largely from his parents. No
doubt it had its unconscious origins in a feeling that he had
been deprived of the love that was rightfully his and that
this was in a measure compensation. It is significant that
stealing from the parents recurred during later years. His
reckless courage, which persisted in later years, was probably
dependent upon the undervaluation which he placed on life
because he had been deprived of essential early affectional
nurture. The complete lack of feeling which he had about the
murder was surely related to this also. It is normal for very
young children to hurt animals. They are not fully aware of
the effects of what they do. Much of it is motivated by a desire
for experimentation. But the persistence of cruelty toward
animals at a later age is a very malignant sign. It is clear evidence of the child's great unhappiness. The cruelty is essentially retaliatory. The child has been hurt and he derives
satisfaction from inflicting pain. Herman's sexual adjustment
was distorted through his relationships during his early years
with a punitive threatening father and an hysterical, seductive
mother. Despite his outward charm, Herman had made no
lasting friendships throughout his life. He is devoid of loyalty
to anyone. This is a nuclear defect in most sociopaths. This
must be due to an instinctive emotional recoil of the child
raised by rejecting, affectionally inconstant parents. If you
don't invest your love in them you can't be brutally hurt when

they reject you and withdraw their affection. This becomes a strongly conditioned method of response. This is one of the major handicaps in the treatment of such patients. Trust and emotional responsiveness are essential in psychotherapy.

Herman's private war against society was patterned after his early conflict with his father. Modern psychology has postulated the theory, and I believe proven the fact, that a chief determinant in the adult's basic attitude toward law, and authority in general, is his relationship to the first important disciplinary agent in his childhood. This thesis has been skillfully propounded by Judge Jerome Frank in his *Law and the Modern Mind.*

Another dynamic factor that frequently comes into play is that of identification. A boy absorbs his father's attitudes and may even strongly identify with a hostile father, thereby hoping to gain some of his father's strength. However, this is more likely to play an important role in the genesis of the antisocial attitudes of normal criminals.

# Psychological Frustration—
# A Comparison of
# Murderers and Their Brothers

## STUART PALMER

THE FIFTY-ONE men convicted of murder [in a study sample] apparently experienced psychological frustrations which were significantly greater in number and intensity than those experienced by their control brothers. These psychological frustrations arose largely from the following: physical defects which were, in effect, social stigmas; overly rigid, inconsistent, and emotional behavior by the parents, especially the mothers; severely frightening experiences of a definitely traumatic nature; and lack of acceptance, approval, and prestige in school and community. Battered by physical frustrations, the murderers were further beset by psychological frustrations which swelled their reservoirs of aggression to a point where that aggression eventually would, and finally did, burst its confines violently.

Ten of the murderers and two of the brothers were reported by the mothers to have been born with some extreme, severe, visible physical defect. None was born with more than one such defect. These defects were of the type that would be likely to cause others to react negatively, that might well cause the individual social embarrassment in childhood, adolescence, and adulthood.

The preponderance of such defects in the murderer group

as compared to the brothers is statistically significant at the five percent level (using a two-by-two table, $X^2=6.046$). One murderer was born with an abnormally large head; a second with a club foot; several with eyes which were, and appeared to other individuals to be, abnormal. Still another was born with a badly twisted neck, and so on.

The mother of a boy who at nineteen had killed a near stranger after an argument said to me, "I don't know that it had anything to do with the trouble he got in, but he was always so sensitive like about that neck. He thought people was looking at him. I used to tell him, 'Now, nobody's thinking anything about it,' but he had it in his head that they was always looking at him."

Visible physical defects of an extreme nature which occurred *after* birth were over three times as prevalent among the murderers as among the control brothers. Specifically, these defects were present in the cases of sixteen murderers and of five brothers. ($X^2=7.256$; $P<0.01$; two-by-two table used.) No individual had more than one such defect.

These, too, were the kinds of defects which are likely to cause embarrassment in social situations: facial scars, crippled legs and arms, and the like. And that embarrassment can be considered a frustration factor.

Many murderers do not, of course, have any such defects. Still, it is important to note that among the fifty-one murderers there was a total of twenty-six instances of extreme visible physical defects (those which were present at birth combined with those which developed later); among the fifty-one control brothers there was a total of only seven defects. Thus, there were almost four times as many visible defects among the murderers as among the brothers, according to the mothers' statements. It may be that in the cases of the defects which occurred after birth the murderers tended, more often than the brothers, to become involved in situations, such as fights and accidents, where they were likely to be disfigured. Nevertheless, the defects, once existent, can reasonably be assumed to have led to psychological frustration.

Consider now the parents' actions toward the murderers and control brothers. To what extent did the parents cause psychological frustration in their sons? On the basis that a mother's behavior toward a newborn child is likely to be influenced by whether she wished to give birth, the mothers were asked, "How happy or unhappy were you when you found out that you were going to have the child?" The mothers' answers distributed themselves in the way shown in Table 1.

Of course, the mothers' answers may have been distorted. They may not have wanted to admit they had been unhappy about giving birth. Also, knowing now that one son was a murderer, they may have remembered their feelings prior to his birth as more negative than they were at the time. Nonetheless, fourteen of the mothers said they had been somewhat or very unhappy about the prospect of the murderers' births while only four said they had felt that way about the coming of the control brothers' births.

TABLE 1.　*Mothers' Attitudes Toward Prospective Births of Murderers and Control Brothers*

|  | NUMBER OF MURDERERS | NUMBER OF BROTHERS |
|---|---|---|
| Very Happy | 19 | 23 |
| Somewhat Happy | 7 | 11 |
| Neutral | 9 | 12 |
| Somewhat Unhappy | 9 | 2 |
| Very Unhappy | 5 | 2 |
| Don't Know | 2 | 1 |
| Total | 51 | 51 |

In interviewing the mothers, I had the distinct feeling that in actuality they had resented the births of the murderers more frequently than those of the brothers. In some cases, the mother was not married when she became pregnant; in others, she had too many children to handle as it was; in still other cases, she was not well and pregnancy was an added burden. Here are statements by two mothers which bear on this point:

"Well, the truth is, me and my husband wasn't married then—when I found out I was going to have him. He did the right thing, I'll say that. We was married right away. But I was afraid somebody's find out. It was a terrible time."

A trim little woman who had had ten children, one of whom had strangled to death a young girl, said: "I tell you, I had eight of them running around. I was run ragged and I come to find out I was going to have another. This is too much, I said to myself, but what could I do? He came, all right. And what happened? The worst thing that could. He went out and—and—" The mother could not bring herself to say that her son had committed murder.

The mothers were also asked whether they were "getting along" with their husbands "very well," "moderately well," or "poorly" when their sons were born. The responses indicated no real differences in cases of the murderers as compared with the control brothers. Fifteen of the mothers said they were "getting along poorly" when the murderer sons were born, and fifteen said they were "getting along poorly" when the brothers were born.

As I have mentioned previously, the parents seldom separated or divorced. But in a fair number of cases they were clearly very unhappy living together. However, even where there was a wide difference in the ages of the murderers and control brothers, the parents were on the whole probably as unhappy during the infancies and childhoods of the brothers as of the murderers. The main point here is that in about a third of the families, very likely more, the murderers developed in an atmosphere of severe parental discord which was largely kept hidden from public view.

I would characterize the mothers' approach to the murderers, during infancy and childhood, as one of doing generally what appeared to be the accepted thing and of mixing with this a great deal of disguised aggression. According to this view, the mother's aggression could have caused frustration and hence aggression in the child. There appears to me to have been an interplay of aggression and frustration between mother and son with the father somewhat indirectly involved.

The interplay seems to have proceeded frequently in this fashion: the child had been frustrated physically through illness or other factors. This made the child aggressive, especially difficult. The mother, frustrated because of her low station in life and high expectations, directed her aggression against the difficult child, the murderer-to-be. He became all the more aggressive although not necessarily in obvious, direct ways. The mother, upset and exasperated, occasionally

directed her aggression toward the father as well. He retaliated toward her and sometimes toward the child. To the
father, the child seemed to be the root of the trouble.

According to the mothers, they tended rather equally to be
solicitous of the murderers' and control brothers' needs during
infancy. When asked the question, "What did you usually do
when the child cried during his first year of life?" the mothers
responded in this way:

|  | NUMBER OF MURDERERS | NUMBER OF BROTHERS |
|---|---|---|
| Went to Child Immediately | 27 | 27 |
| Waited 5 or 10 Minutes, Then Went to Child | 15 | 19 |
| Let Child "Cry It Out" | 8 | 5 |
| Other | 1 | 0 |
| Total | 51 | 51 |

There was a definite tendency for the mothers to feel that
they had pampered their children during the first year of life.
But the possibility that they actually did so is not borne out by
answers to other questions. For example, the schedules the
mothers followed when caring for the infants were rather
rigid, just slightly more so for the murderers than for their
brothers.

The mothers were asked, "How rigid were you in trying to
keep to a definite time schedule while caring for the child
during the first two years of his life?" In a majority of cases
of both murderers and control brothers, the mothers said that
they were very rigid or moderately rigid:

|  | NUMBER OF MURDERERS | NUMBER OF BROTHERS |
|---|---|---|
| Very Rigid | 18 | 15 |
| Moderately Rigid | 13 | 12 |
| Moderately Flexible | 13 | 19 |
| Very Flexible | 7 | 5 |
| Total | 51 | 51 |

Again, when asked the more specific question, "During the
first two months of the child's life, did you feed him on a fixed
schedule, on demand, or on a combination of the two?" the
mothers' replies indicated that they were slightly more rigid

with the murderers than the control brothers. Here is the distribution of responses:

|  | NUMBER OF MURDERERS | NUMBER OF BROTHERS |
|---|---|---|
| Fixed Schedule | 28 | 20 |
| Demand Schedule | 11 | 15 |
| Combination | 11 | 14 |
| Don't Know | 1 | 2 |
| Total | 51 | 51 |

Going by the mothers' reports, thirty of the murderers and twenty-five of the control brothers were bottle-fed during the first two months of life. Conversely, seventeen of the murderers and twenty-four of the brothers were breast-fed. The remaining four murderers and two brothers were both breast- and bottle-fed. Bottle-feeding is probably less rewarding than breast-feeding. But, the differences in numbers of murderers and brothers so fed are not large enough to warrant attaching any extreme importance to them. However, I was struck by the fact that many of the mothers appeared to have guilt feelings about not having breast-fed their children—murderers and control brothers alike:

"I tried but I couldn't. I should of, I guess. But it wouldn't work and I had to give it up."

"The milk was—what you call sour. I had to use the bottle. What else could I do?"

I asked this mother, "Do you think feeding a baby from the breast is better than from the bottle?"

"That's what I'm saying. But like I told you. The milk was what you call sour. I *had* to use the bottle."

There were no real differences in the ages of the murderers and the control brothers when the mothers started weaning from the breast or bottle. Early weaning can be considered a frustrating experience, and I had thought the murderers might have been weaned relatively early but this was not the case. Six to eleven months was the most common time for weaning both murderers and brothers from the breast. And twelve to seventeen months was the most common time for weaning murderers and brothers from the bottle.

Abrupt weaning, as distinguished from early weaning, can
also be considered frustrating for the child. Therefore, this
matter was investigated. Here, again, there were no real differences between murderers and control brothers. Of the twenty-
one murderers and twenty-six brothers weaned from the
breast, a decided majority of each were weaned in a month or
less. Of the forty-one murderers and thirty-five brothers
weaned from the bottle, a majority of each were weaned completely in three months or less, usually less.

While no important differences were found between murderers and brothers with respect to weaning, there were significant differences as to ages at which the mothers began
toilet training. On the average, the mothers said they started
to toilet train the murderers at an earlier age than they did the
brothers. In the cases of twenty-nine murderers and eighteen
brothers, toilet training was begun before age one year. On the
other hand, in the cases of twenty-one murderers and thirty-
two brothers, this training was begun after age one. Information was not available for one murderer and one brother.

Why, on the average, did the mothers begin to toilet train
the murderers earlier than the control brothers? I suspect that
the mothers were more aggressive toward the infant murderers-to-be than toward the brothers. And the early toilet
training was one indirect way in which the mothers could unconsciously vent their aggression while rationalizing their
actions in the name of cleanliness. As previously mentioned,
it appears that because of early illnesses the murderers were
greater problems to the mothers than were the control brothers. And if the mothers unconsciously resented the potential
murderers for being problems, the mothers' consequent actions only served to increase the magnitude of the frustration.

The average person finds it next to impossible to accept the
idea that if toilet training is begun early and is forced, it is
severely frustrating for the child. He either passes it off as of
no consequence or half-jokingly says, in effect, "Sometimes
you psychologists and sociologists talk as if you think everything a person does depends on toilet training."

Toilet training is neither of no consequence nor does it
in itself determine completely any later behavioral form. But
if a mother is not basically affectionate toward the child and
if she forces him too fast in this regard, he will be greatly

strained to meet her demands. He is likely in later life to be especially anxious about defecation matters and to have a vague but deep-seated feeling of deprivation.

The time required for the mothers to effect the toilet training of the murderers and brothers was also investigated. The differences between the two groups were not large. Nevertheless, the nature of the small differences found is of some importance. The time required to toilet train the murderers tended to be slightly extreme—shorter or longer than to train the brothers. Of the seventeen children trained in one month or less, ten were murderers. And of the fifteen children where training took longer than one year, ten were murderers. This is a pattern that will be evidenced with respect to certain other spheres of behavior: the training of the murderers and their actual behavior were more extreme, tended toward both ends of a given continuum to a greater degree than was the case with the control brothers.

Turning to the matter of sexual training by the mothers, it is clear that as a group the mothers were strongly repressed about sex. They attempted to strait-jacket their children, both the potential murderers and the control brothers, with respect to sex. They succeeded in making the children unduly curious about sex yet guilty when they attempted to satisfy that curiosity. And guilt feelings are frustrating.

The mothers were questioned concerning the extent to which they explained sexual matters to the murderers and brothers when they were about six years old. Forty-nine of the fifty-one mothers said they had explained nothing about sex to the children. The remaining two mothers had explained about sex to a small extent. While the mothers were usually not explicitly asked whether their husbands had explained sexual matters to the children, I gained the distinct impression that the husbands almost invariably did not do so. Discussion of sex was tabooed in the great majority of these families. Here are conversations with two mothers which bear on this point:

Interviewer: "When the boy was around six years old, did you ever explain to him about sex?"
Mother: "No. Well, maybe I should have. Or my husband, maybe he should have. But we just—we just didn't talk about

things like that. Certainly not to the children. Why, my husband and me, we never talked about things like that between ourselves. We, or (brief laugh)—we had the children, of course. We were man and wife, I mean to say. But we never talked about it."

Another mother said, "No, it's not good to tell children those kinds of things. They find out enough, out on the streets, believe me, without being told at home."

"Do you think that sexual relationships outside of marriage are ever all right, under any circumstances?" I asked her.

"No, I don't. Don't believe in it. I never have."

"I don't mean as a general thing. I mean in rare cases where——"

"No cases. It's a sin before God. A sin before God."

"Do you mind my asking you these questions about sexual matters?"

"Well, no. You're supposed to be one of those psychiatrists or so-chiatrists, aren't you? Ask away. I'll say what I said, it's a sin before God."

"How did you feel about your boy getting in the trouble he did?" Her son, at eighteen, had raped and then beaten to death a middle-aged woman.

"How did I feel? I couldn't believe it. But he must of done it. He said he did."

"Do you have any idea why he did it?"

"Well, she was leading him on, from what I heard. But that wasn't all of it."

"What was the rest of it?"

"Bad blood, that was the rest of it. In spite of all I did to try to make him a good boy. It was his grandfather—his great-grandfather, his father's grandfather. He's got that blood in him. That's where it come from."

The mothers were all asked the question mentioned in the conversation above: "Do you think that sexual relationships outside of marriage are ever all right, under any circumstances?" Forty-eight of the mothers said that such relationships were never all right, were always bad. One said they were all right, not bad, under exceptional circumstances. The remaining two mothers were undecided, said they did not know. Given the fact that the forty-eight mothers who answered negatively might have been attempting to impress the interviewers with their morality, their answers still have considerable importance in that they indicate a part of the face the mothers show the world with regard to sex.

The mothers were asked if they had ever made the murderers and control brothers stop sexual self-play and, if so, how old the sons were when they first stopped them. Twenty-nine of the mothers said they had never stopped the murderer sons, and thirty said they had never stopped the control brothers. Most of these mothers claimed that, to the best of their knowledge, these sons had never as children indulged in sexual self-play. Practically all children do engage in this self-play, but many of the mothers apparently had chosen to ignore the matter.

TABLE 2. *Ages of Murderers and Control Brothers When Mothers First Stopped Sons' Sexual Self-Play*

|  | NUMBER OF MURDERERS | NUMBER OF BROTHERS |
|---|---|---|
| 3 Months or Less | 0 | 1 |
| Over 3 Months to 6 Months | 2 | 0 |
| Over 6 Months to 1 Year | 8 | 4 |
| Over 1 Year to 2 Years | 5 | 8 |
| Over 2 Years to 3 Years | 2 | 5 |
| Over 3 Years to 4 Years | 1 | 1 |
| Over 4 Years | 2 | 1 |
| Age Unknown | 2 | 1 |
| Doesn't Apply[a] | 29 | 30 |
| Total | 51 | 51 |

[a] Mothers did not stop sons' self-play.

It is interesting to note in Table 2 that of the fifteen children whom the mothers said they stopped from engaging in sexual self-play during the first year of life, ten, or two-thirds, were murderers-to-be. On the other hand, of the twenty-five children whom the mothers said they stopped after the first year, fifteen, or three-fifths, were control brothers.

The mothers were also asked to what degree, if any, they were emotionally upset the first time they observed the murderers and control brothers in sexual self-play, regardless of whether they stopped them. Again, there are no important differences when the mothers' reported reactions to the mur-

derers and to the control brothers are compared. However, of
the mothers who admitted that they had observed either the
murderers or the brothers or both in sexual self-play, a great
majority said that they were "very upset" rather than "somewhat upset" or "not at all upset."

With respect to their feelings about their sons' sexual self-
play, here is what two fairly typical mothers had to say:

"I didn't know what to do. A little thing like that—playing
with himself. Well, after all, I was afraid he might keep on
doing it, when he grew up, if you understand me."

"I was so upset I had to lay down. I didn't know anything
about those things, then. I came from people where those
things were never mentioned. Never. I was just nineteen or
twenty at the time. After I'd had the other kids I begin to see
it was what they all do but I didn't know that, not then."

The mothers were questioned concerning the worst type
of behavior manifested by the murderers and control brothers
at age five. The answers distributed themselves as shown in
the following table:

| | NUMBER OF MURDERERS | NUMBER OF BROTHERS |
|---|---|---|
| Sexual Self-play | 15 | 13 |
| "Talking Back" to Mothers | 4 | 4 |
| Fighting | 2 | 4 |
| Stealing | 1 | 0 |
| Lying | 0 | 1 |
| No opinion | 29 | 29 |
| Total | 51 | 51 |

As is evident, in the cases of the mothers who answered
the question, sexual self-play was far and away considered the
worst type of act committed by either the murderers or the
brothers. The mothers' most usual action when confronted by
this sexual self-play was to emotionalize—cry or scream—
and sometimes to hit the child as well.

The mothers were asked whether the murderers and control brothers had been sexually attacked during the first
twelve years of life. The mothers said that to the best of their
knowledge three of the fifty-one murderers and none of the

brothers had been so attacked. The difference in numbers is too small to allow the drawing of any conclusions. But it is noteworthy that with respect to this and other types of situations mentioned in this chapter which might reasonably be presumed to give rise to frustration, the differences while small are almost always in such a direction that they indicate greater frustration for the murderer group than for the control group.

The question of how many murderers and brothers were as children severely frightened by other individuals, but not sexually attacked, was also investigated. The mothers said that during the first twelve years of life seven murderers and two brothers had been severely frightened once or more by some individual.

Further, the matter of whether the murderers and brothers were severely frightened by some natural event during their first twelve years was examined. According to the mothers, six of the fifty-one murderers and four of the fifty-one brothers were frightened in this way. These natural events were fires, lightning, falling rocks, and the like. Here, too, the difference is very small. But again it is in a direction which is indicative of greater frustration for the murderer group than for the control group.

We are not concerned in this chapter with the mothers' and fathers' training per se of the murderers and brothers. But we are concerned with the possible psychological frustration that the training might have caused in the children. Therefore, it will be well to consider the extents to which the mothers became angry at the children, cried, isolated themselves from the children, and were inconsistent in carrying out expected punishments and rewards. Table 3 presents this information as provided by the mothers.

With the exception of the responses for "no promised reward," the "very often" frequency occurs more among the murderers than among the control brothers. If one takes all five types of responses and summates the number of cases of murderers where the response was "very often," a total of thirty-four is obtained. And if one does the same for the control brothers, a total of eighteen is obtained. Thus, these five types of responses were directed "very often" at almost twice as many murderers as control brothers. And these

TABLE 3. *Frequency of Selected Responses by Mothers Toward Murderers and Control Brothers During First 5 Years of Life*[a]

| | ANGER | | CRIED | | ISOLATED SELF | |
|---|---|---|---|---|---|---|
| | M | B | M | B | M | B |
| Very Often | 12 | 9 | 10 | 3 | 5 | 1 |
| Occasionally | 18 | 25 | 8 | 18 | 9 | 7 |
| Seldom | 20 | 17 | 33 | 30 | 37 | 43 |
| Unknown | 1 | 0 | 0 | 0 | 0 | 0 |
| Total | 51 | 51 | 51 | 51 | 51 | 51 |

| | NO THREATENED PUNISHMENT[b] | | NO PROMISED REWARD[b] | |
|---|---|---|---|---|
| | M | B | M | B |
| Very Often | 6 | 4 | 1 | 1 |
| Occasionally | 21 | 21 | 18 | 17 |
| Seldom | 24 | 26 | 31 | 33 |
| Unknown | 0 | 0 | 1 | 0 |
| Total | 51 | 51 | 51 | 51 |

[a] "M" designates number of cases of murderers. "B" designates number of cases of control brothers.
[b] Mothers threatened punishment, or promised reward, and then did not carry out the threat or promise.

types of responses I consider to be ones which will cause anxiety and frustration in a child.

The mothers' responses of "cried" and "isolated self" were "very often" directed at the murderers in an especially larger number of cases than they were at the brothers. Crying and self-isolation when young children do things of which the mothers disapprove are, I am convinced, very frustrating for the children. In almost any family, the mother is the symbol of the sources of life to the child. Even if she has not been a particularly attentive mother, she has nevertheless very likely supplied the children with food, warmth, clean or at least dry clothes, and some affection.

A professional thief, who had killed during a holdup but who was not a professional murderer, told me, "Whenever I did anything wrong as a kid, my mother would get very upset and cry. She'd cry and cry and she'd go to her room and lock the door but I could still hear her crying. It made me feel awful. I knew I'd done something but a lot of the time I didn't know what and she wouldn't tell me. She'd just cry."

He was a very intelligent man with a great deal of personal insight. "When I was fifteen or sixteen, I began running around, getting in a lot of trouble. I'm not blaming mother for anything, but sometimes I honestly think I did some of those things just to hurt her for having hurt me. I knew if she found out what I was doing she'd cry, but I didn't care any more if she did."

Another man serving a life sentence for murder told me, "Anything we kids did wrong, she'd go in her room and stay there for three or four hours. Then when she'd come out she wouldn't talk to us for maybe half a day. And it happened more with me than the other kids. I always seemed to be getting in more trouble—at least doing things my mother didn't like. The thing was, she didn't seem to tell us beforehand what we shouldn't do."

Why did the mothers tend to cry and isolate themselves more with respect to the murderers than the control brothers? First, I interpret crying and isolation of this nature to have been veiled acts of aggression on the mothers' parts. Unconsciously, at least, they knew these actions would hurt the children. Second, and as hypothesized earlier, the mothers were perhaps more prone to hurt the murderers than the brothers because, generally, the murderers had been greater problems to them.

The mothers tended to be quite strict with their sons, although not in a consistent fashion. When asked the question, "Were you very strict, moderately strict, or not at all strict in training the child when he was about five years old?" the mothers replied as follows:

|  | NUMBER OF MURDERERS | NUMBER OF BROTHERS |
|---|---|---|
| Very Strict | 25 | 21 |
| Moderately Strict | 18 | 21 |
| Not at All Strict | 7 | 9 |
| Unknown | 1 | 0 |
| Total | 51 | 51 |

The mothers were also asked, "Do you think mothers of today pamper their children too much?" Thirty-one mothers said, in effect, "Yes, definitely." Seven answered, "No," and the remaining thirteen said they did not know.

At the same time, the mothers had, I felt, guilt feelings about their strictness toward their children, especially toward their murderer sons. Going on the assumption that the mothers' guilt feelings would be partially reflected by their responses, they were asked, "How often were you afraid the child would get hurt when he was about five years old?"

Regardless of how frequently the mothers *actually* were afraid their sons would be hurt when about age five, a distinctly larger number of mothers said they were frequently afraid in the cases of the murderers than in the cases of the control brothers. Twenty-four mothers responded that they were "almost always" or "usually" afraid with respect to the murderers, while only eleven said this with respect to the control brothers.

Learning the use of language is a behavioral area in which the murderers experienced a considerable amount of frustration. The mothers reported that, as a group, the murderers first spoke intelligible words at a later age than the control brothers:

| AGE IN MONTHS | NUMBER OF MURDERERS | NUMBER OF BROTHERS |
|---|---|---|
| Under 18 | 15 | 27 |
| 18–29[a] | 34 | 22 |
| 30 or Over[a] | 1 | 1 |
| Never[a] | 1 | 1 |
| Total | 51 | 51 |

$$X^2 = 5.828 \qquad P < 0.05$$

[a] Combined for $X^2$ calculation.

There is, then, a significant difference, as reported by the mothers, in the ages at which the two groups began to speak. How does one explain this? I think the most likely explanation is that the murderers, having experienced more frustration than the control brothers during the first year of life, were somewhat blocked by anxiety. At the same time, slowness in learning to speak is, I think, frustrating in itself. The child cannot communicate his needs as well without language as with it. Therefore, his needs tend, to some extent, to go unsatisfied. Further, parents are apt to be upset with a child who is slow in learning to speak and this causes him added frustration.

This phenomenon has arisen at least implicitly in preceding pages: frustration tends to beget frustration. An individual who has been severely frustrated is unduly anxious and therefore cannot learn as efficiently as he otherwise would. This makes those around him impatient, exasperated with him. They react negatively toward him, thereby increasing his frustration. He responds by some manner of aggression. In the case of slow speech learning by the murderers, I think there was this added element of aggression. The child senses that the parents want him to speak and he aggresses toward them, frustrates them, by slow learning.

This process of frustration begetting frustration seems to be an especially dominant theme in the development of the murderers. It can even grow to the point where the individual seeks frustration. He has learned to expect it and in a certain sense he feels comfortable with it.

About one-fifth of the murderers and of the control brothers, ten murderers and eleven brothers, learned some other language before they learned English. Eventually they all learned English with the exception of one murderer and one brother who were mutes. Learning one language, then learning another which is to become the major tongue, can be construed as frustrating for young children. This is not to say that learning English first, in our society, then learning at ten or eleven a foreign language, to be used as a secondary tongue, is anxiety provoking. But to learn a foreign language at home, then to enter the first grade and be forced to learn English quickly, is frustrating. And that is what most of the ten murderers and eleven brothers were forced to do. They were expected to speak English at school, the parent tongue at home. Conflict, anxiety, and frustration can be assumed to have been the result. Further, the interviews indicated that they experienced embarrassment in school because of their lack of facility with English. Of course, this embarrassment was as true for the control brothers as a group as for the murderers. Nevertheless, it is one more indication of the climate of frustration in which some of the murderers developed.

Learning to read is another important area of language

behavior. Here is the way the murderers and control brothers were distributed with respect to the general difficulty they had in learning to read, as judged by the mothers:

|  | NUMBER OF MURDERERS | NUMBER OF BROTHERS |
|---|---|---|
| Almost No Difficulty | 24 | 34 |
| Moderate Difficulty | 16 | 14 |
| Great Difficulty[a] | 9 | 2 |
| Never Learned[a] | 2 | 1 |
| Total | 51 | 51 |
| $X^2 = 6.430$ | $P < 0.05$ | |

[a] Combined for $X^2$ calculation.

To a significant degree, the mothers reported that the murderer group had greater difficulty learning to read than did the control group. Here is another foundation stone for the theses that murderers have experienced more frustration than nonmurderers and that frustration begets frustration. The murderers were generally highly frustrated when they first went to school. Their resultant aggression brought more frustration upon them. Probably, their anxiety and repressed aggression tended to retard their reading. And this brought on still further frustration.

By and large, the murderers did poorly in school, did not like it, and left as soon as they could, thus virtually precluding any possibility of entering a prestigeful, satisfying occupation. Quite clearly, judging by the mothers' responses to questioning, a distinctly larger proportion of the murderers than of the control brothers disliked grammar school. Of the murderers, twenty-three were reported to have liked the first four years of grammar school, and twenty-three were said to have disliked school during that period. (Five were considered to have been neutral.) On the other hand, the mothers reported that, of the control brothers, thirty-seven liked school while only five did not. (Nine were neutral.) These differences are statistically significant at the one percent level.

A number of behavioral forms which are driven by anxiety and frustration were investigated as to whether they were manifested by the murderers and control brothers during their preadult years. They would serve, as it were, as partial indices of the degree of frustration experienced by the individuals in the two groups. Examples of the behavioral forms are phobias, compulsions, stuttering, and the like. Naturally, in questioning the mothers, it was made clear in everyday terms what is, for example, the actual nature of a compulsion.

Table 4 indicates that seven of these behavioral forms— phobias, compulsions, obsessions, bedwetting, stuttering, sleep-walking, nightmares—were said by the mothers to have

TABLE 4. *Presence or Absence of Selected Behavioral Forms Indicative of Frustration During the Preadult Years of Murderers and Control Brothers*[a]

|  | PHOBIAS | | COMPULSIONS | | OBSESSIONS | | PERSISTENT BEDWETTING | |
|---|---|---|---|---|---|---|---|---|
|  | P | A | P | A | P | A | P | A |
| Murderers | 17 | 34 | 13 | 38 | 4 | 47 | 18 | 33 |
| Brothers | 2 | 49 | 1 | 50 | 0 | 51 | 3 | 48 |

$$X^2 = 14.552 \quad\quad X^2 = 11.922 \quad\quad\quad\quad X^2 = 13.492$$
$$P < 0.01 \quad\quad\quad P < 0.01 \quad\quad\quad\quad\quad P < 0.01$$

|  | STUTTERING | | PERSISTENT SLEEPWALKING | | PERSISTENT NIGHTMARES | |
|---|---|---|---|---|---|---|
|  | P | A | P | A | P | A |
| Murderers | 10 | 41 | 8 | 43 | 11 | 40 |
| Brothers | 5 | 46 | 2 | 49 | 3 | 48 |

$$X^2 = 1.954 \quad\quad X^2 = 3.992 \quad\quad X^2 = 5.300$$
$$P > 0.05 \quad\quad\quad P < 0.05 \quad\quad P < 0.05$$

[a] "P" indicates presence of behavioral form.
"A" indicates absence of behavioral form.

been manifested by a greater number of murderers than of brothers during the preadult years. With respect to presence and absence of five of these forms of behavior—all except obsessions and stuttering—the differences between the murderer and control brother groups were significant at the one or five percent levels.

Phobias, compulsions, and obsessions have much in common. Not only are they indicative of earlier frustration per se, but also there is generally a guilt component in each of the three behavioral forms. Further, they are ways of trying to handle repressed aggression. It is striking that the mothers reported thirty-four instances of phobias, compulsions, and obsessions for the murderer group and only three instances for the control brother group. It is highly unlikely that this vast difference can be accounted for on the basis that the mothers gave distorted answers to questioning.

A considerably larger number of murderers than brothers were said to have been persistent bedwetters or stutterers. These are two types of behavior that not only imply earlier frustration but that when manifested are fairly likely to beget frustration. Both bedwetting and stuttering are socially embarrassing in our society.

Most of the cases of stuttering occurred around ages six or seven and were severe for a year or two. In most instances the stuttering was almost unnoticeable as the children moved into adolescence. However, the stuttering pattern tended to return during adulthood, the mothers said, when the sons were in stress situations. And this was especially true of the murderers.

During the interviews with the mothers, questions were asked concerning how frequently the murderers and control brothers had become emotionally upset at about age five, excluding anger and temper tantrums. To a highly significant extent, the murderers as a group became upset more frequently than did the brothers. Twenty of the murderers were said to have become emotionally upset once a week or more, but none of the brothers were said to have done so this frequently. Here is another piece of evidence to bolster the view that because of early frustration the murderers were as children less emotionally stable than the control brothers.

A further point: according to the mothers, the murderers were, as a group, more solitary in childhood than were the brothers. When asked whether their sons spent a majority of their playing time alone or with other individuals at about age five, the mothers reported as follows:

|                          | NUMBER OF MURDERERS | NUMBER OF BROTHERS |
|--------------------------|:-------------------:|:------------------:|
| Alone                    | 12                  | 2                  |
| With Other Individuals   | 38                  | 48                 |
| Unknown[a]               | 1                   | 1                  |
| Total                    | 51                  | 51                 |

$$X^2 = 8.304 \qquad P < 0.01$$

[a] Not included in $X^2$ calculation.

The whole lower-class situation in which most of the murderers were immersed by circumstances of birth was a broad frustration factor in itself. True, it was equally so for the control brothers. But they had generally not been subjected to the extreme amounts of other frustrations that the murderers had. It is the totality of frustration we are concerned with here. To use an analogy: when you are carrying a hundred pounds on your back for a long distance, the addition of an extra ten pounds seems like a much much greater extra burden than does the same ten pounds if you have been carrying only twenty.

It is true that some individuals seem content with lower-class status and probably do not experience anxiety because of it. By and large, however, the murderers' and control brothers' parents were, in my judgment, people dissatisfied with their lot in the prestige hierarchy of the society, people with strong drives to rise in the social class system. These drives were usually frustrated but they were there. The murderers, and probably the control brothers, had similarly strong upward mobility strivings which were thwarted. The overwhelming majority of murderers with whom I have talked or whose biographies I have read have seemed to me extremely sensitive about their lack of social class prestige.

Related to this is how the murderers and control brothers felt about their occupations. The mothers were asked to judge how well the murderers liked their work just prior to the murders. In the cases of the brothers, the mothers were asked how well they liked their work when they were at ages equivalent to the murderers' ages just prior to the murders. Here are the mothers' judgments concerning how well their sons liked their work:

| | NUMBER OF MURDERERS | NUMBER OF BROTHERS |
|---|---|---|
| Very Much[a] | 10 | 21 |
| Considerably[a] | 4 | 12 |
| Somewhat[b] | 7 | 6 |
| Not at All[b] | 14 | 1 |
| Unknown[c] | 5 | 2 |
| Doesn't Apply[c] | 11 | 9 |
| Total | 51 | 51 |

$$X^2 = 19.006 \qquad P < 0.01$$

[a] Combined for $X^2$ calculation.
[b] Combined for $X^2$ calculation.
[c] Not included in $X^2$ calculation.

There was, then, a tremendous difference in how well the two groups liked their work, if one accepts the mothers' judgments as being valid. It is reasonable to assume that those who do not like their work are frustrated by it and by their general social situation. Again and again I found murderers who said they had had absolutely no interest in the occupation in which they were engaged just before they committed murder.

An Index of Psychological Frustration was constructed in much the same fashion as was the Index of Physical Frustration. One point was given the individual for the known presence in his preadult experience of each instance of fifteen selected types of psychological frustration. For example, one point was allotted for each trauma due to natural events or other individuals which occurred before the age of twelve years, physical beatings excluded. The minimum possible score on this index was zero while there was no limit as to the maximum.

The scores for the murderer group were significantly greater than for the control brother group. Ten murderers had scores of two or less while twenty-eight brothers had these scores. On the other hand, the scores of nineteen murderers were six or higher, but only three brothers had scores at that level. The mean score for murderers was 4.7; for the brothers the mean score was 2.5.

The scores were also analyzed with respect to the differences within pairs of murderers and control brothers. It was found that in thirty-four of the fifty-one pairs the murderers had higher scores than the brothers. In ten pairs, the scores were equal. And in the remaining seven pairs, the brothers had higher scores than the murderers; the difference here was usually one point.

The Index of Physical Frustration and the Index of Psychological Frustration were combined to provide an Index of General Frustration. The score for a given individual on this Index of General Frustration was found simply by totaling his scores on the physical frustration and on the psychological frustration indices. Here, seventeen murderers had scores of five or less on the Index of General Frustration as compared to thirty-six control brothers. At the other extreme, nineteen murderers had scores of eleven or higher while not one of the brothers had a score above ten. To the extent that the mothers' responses reflected the facts, here is great weight in favor of considering frustration as a possible major influence behind murder.

The mean score for the murderers was 9.24; for the brothers this score was 4.20. Comparing scores within pairs of murderers and control brothers, it was found that in forty-two pairs the murderer had a higher score than his brother. In five pairs the scores were equal. And in four pairs the brother's score was greater than the murderer's. That is to say, 82 per cent of the time, forty-two out of fifty-one, the scores agreed with the basic idea stated in the central hypothesis of the study: that the preadult frustration of murderers is greater than the preadult frustration of nonmurderers.

# The Murderer in the
# Mental Institution

## BERNARD A. CRUVANT and
## FRANCIS N. WALDROP

THE POPULAR conception of the primary role of the psychiatrist in medicolegal questions is his appearance in court as an expert witness when insanity has been raised as a defense against a charge of first degree murder. Actually, this is an infrequent part of the psychiatrist's contribution to legal processes, but such instances predominate in public awareness because of the attendant notoriety and because in occasional cases rather brutal crimes have attracted a great deal of public attention and resentment. Despite our awareness of this popular fallacy, we must have been in part influenced and misled by it, for we were surprised, on surveying the literature, to discover nothing dealing with the specific question, What happens to the murderer who is sent to a mental hospital?

This essay is intended as a statistical and descriptive study of the fate of all of the individuals committed to Saint Elizabeths Hospital[1] while under charges or conviction of homicide in any degree during the period July 1, 1925 to July 1, 1951. As can be seen from Figure 1, less than 3 out of each 1,000 admissions had been accused of some variety of homicide. Chance played some role in these figures; a number of our patients had committed serious assaults, and only the in-

REPRINTED with the permission of the authors and the publisher from Bernard A. Cruvant and Francis N. Waldrop, "The Murderer in the Mental Institution," *The Annals of the American Academy of Political and Social Science* (November, 1952), 284:35-44.

efficiency of the aggressor or the hardihood of the victim prevented a fatal outcome.

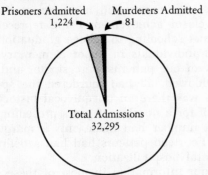

FIGURE 1. *Admissions to Saint Elizabeths Hospital, July 1, 1925–July 1, 1951.*

In order to avoid going beyond the scope of our data, we shall confine ourselves, insofar as possible, to a statement and discussion of our statistical findings, including a few representative cases to illustrate certain points.

The selection of data to be memorialized by tabulation is ever subject to inherent error on the basis of bias, interest, or accessibility of the facts to be tabulated. We attempted to select such material as could be reasonably objective, avoiding clinical interpretations or speculative conjectures whenever possible. We shall present first the statistical data under the headings of the three types of homicide, and, because one can readily overextend the conclusions drawn from statistical particularization, in the commentary that follows we shall present only the most obvious conclusions to be drawn from the material.

## FIRST DEGREE HOMICIDE

In the category of first degree homicide there were 57 patients, of whom 44 were sent to the hospital prior to trial. Fifty-three were males and four were females. Ages at time of the crime ranged from 21 to 50 years, with a modal age of 34. Our patients accused or convicted of first degree murder are about equally divided between white and Negro. It is difficult to draw generalizations from these findings, since, as indicated in footnote 1, during the period surveyed, Saint

Elizabeths Hospital received patients from a variety of sources.

Educational attainment did not seem statistically significant, all levels of achievement being represented, ranging from no formal schooling to college graduation, with a concentration of individuals in upper elementary school level. The majority of our patients were single; and of the seven who were widowed, all had murdered the spouse. In only sixteen cases was there an unequivocal history of excessive use of alcohol for a number of years preceding the crime. A preponderant number had made only a marginal economic adjustment. Fourteen patients had had a definite history of previous mental hospitalization.

Although our information in most of these cases is quite meager, we feel justified in stating that in extremely few cases was there anything that would enable the psychiatrist to predict accurately the subsequent capital offense. It is our opinion that the discipline of psychiatry has not yet developed valid criteria of sufficient degree of predictive reliability to justify hard and fast distinction *before* the act between the individual who is likely to commit a crime of violence, such as rape or homicide, and the one who will not ever translate his emotional conflicts into aggressive, destructive behavior. In this area psychiatric opinion represents only an informed and educated guess, but nevertheless constitutes the most reliable index presently available. It has been our experience that in no other field has the disclaimer of infallibility been met by others wtih so much enthusiastic approval or irritable resentment. Thus, 31 of these patients had no record of antisocial behavior, and in 17 cases there was a record of only minor offenses prior to the homicide. In just nine cases was there a record of a major offense such as a felony involving even a mild to moderate degree of aggression.

Shooting was the most popular method of causing death, possibly for a number of deeply buried psychopathological reasons, but more likely because it is simple, easy, and frequently accomplished by a weapon purchased in advance, often for protection in response to insane delusions. Next most frequent was stabbing, followed closely by bludgeoning. Strangulation and poisoning were rare.

The classification by diagnosis of patients in this group not unexpectedly shows that slightly more than half were afflicted with schizophrenia. The established diagnoses ran the gamut of psychotic and psychoneurotic conditions, but showed predominantly functional as contrasted to organic disorders.

Half of this group were equally Baptist or Catholic, the remainder belonging to various Protestant denominations or claiming no religious affiliation. There were no individuals in the entire group of patients known to be Jewish.

### Disposition

At the time of this writing, 21 of this group remain in Saint Elizabeths Hospital, 7 have died while hospitalized, and 7 were returned to prison to continue serving a sentence. Eleven were returned for trial, of whom 4 were exculpated, 5 received sentences for a lesser included offense, and in 2 cases the final outcome is unknown. Six patients were transferred to other psychiatric institutions, and in 5 instances the patient was discharged from the hospital subsequent to dismissal of the charges and improvement or recovery from his illness.

The decision as to disposition of the accused or convicted murderer who is committed to a mental hospital as insane is obviously complex and difficult. The psychiatrist may be understandably reluctant to return to possible enlargement in the community an individual who has demonstrated his capacity for aggressively destructive behavior by the commission of a crime so serious as first degree murder. Thus it may have been, perhaps, that most of these individuals either remained in our hospital or were returned to prison to continue a sentence, particularly in instances where the sentence was for life or a protracted period of years.

While such conservatism as to disposition might appear justified on a common-sense basis, we have discovered no scientific validation for arbitrary rigidity. Of the limited number who were returned to jail following recovery and were subsequently acquitted or had charges dismissed and who returned to the community, there is no record of their having subsequently committed any serious crime.

Historically, there has been a change in emphasis in hospital policy toward individuals accused or convicted of murder and sent to the hospital for treatment. During the first twenty years of the twenty-six-year period under consideration, the dictates of the ancient talionic law were followed. A person accused of murder was considered to have forfeited his liberty, and, once having been found mentally incompetent and committed to the hospital, he was continued in the hospital virtually without regard to any subsequent changes in his mental condition. With the institution of a program of intensive therapy in the maximum security division of Saint Elizabeths Hospital in 1946, a considerably increased liberality with relaxation of previous rigid standards occurred. Thus, practically all the patients who were listed as returned to prison to continue sentence or returned to jail to await trial represent cases on which such disposition was made in the past six years. In no case was a hospitalized patient accused of murder returned directly to society from the hospital prior to the past five years.

In our review of the records of this group we considered that there was definite or highly suggestive evidence that the patient was of unsound mind at the time of the crime in 42 instances. This is comparable—but not identical—with the finding that 44 of these patients were sent to the hospital prior to trial. Of the 13 who were hospitalized while serving a sentence in prison, 2 became recognizably ill during the first six months of confinement, 5 between one and three years, and 6 after three years of confinement.

## SECOND DEGREE MURDER

In the classification of second degree murderers there were 12 patients (10 males and 2 females), ranging in age at time of the crime from 18 to 45 years, with a modal age of 25.5 years. Eighty per cent were in the third decade of life. All patients had had at least four years of formal education and nearly a half had finished high school or attended college. Four were married, the remainder were single or widowed; again, the three widowed patients had killed the spouse.

Less than half of this group had a definite history of excessive use of alcohol. In none of these cases were we able to establish any connection between a state of intoxication and commission of the crime. This is considered significant in that intoxication is often an element in reducing an accusation of first degree murder to a lesser included offense.

None of the patients in this group had a record of previous mental hospitalization. Six had no known previous antisocial record, two had a record of minor offenses, and four had a record of felonies. Few had an antisocial record which would have occasioned premonition as to the subsequent homicidal behavior.

Two-thirds of the cases were diagnosed as schizophrenic; the others had functional psychoses or were considered sane.

Again, as in the previous group, half of the patients claimed either Catholic or Baptist religious affiliation, and the remainder were listed under various Protestant denominations or professed no religious connections.

In this group shooting and stabbing were equally popular techniques of committing the homicide. There was one instance of bludgeoning and one of murder by strangulation.

Regarding disposition, three patients in this group remain in the hospital, one has died, and three were returned to prison to continue a sentence. Two were returned for trial, one of whom was found guilty and one acquitted. Charges were dismissed on two patients who were subsequently discharged from the hospital into their own custody as recovered from their mental illness. To our knowledge, they are adjusting satisfactorily.

In contrast to the previous group, only half in this category were sent to the hospital prior to trial. In our study of the case records, however, we considered that only a third had shown definite or highly suggestive evidences of mental unsoundness at the time of the crime. Of those who were convicted and sent to prison and then developed mental illness, in only one instance was the illness apparent during the first few years of imprisonment, and five cases in this category had been imprisoned more than three years before the illness developed.

## MANSLAUGHTER

The manslaughter group included 10 patients (8 males and 2 females), ranging in age from 19 to 65 years at the time of the crime, with a modal age of 41. Significantly, the modal age here was seven years higher than for the first degree murder group and sixteen years higher than for the second degree murder group.

Educational attainment in this category was somewhat

lower; three had no schooling, but four had completed elementary school, and one had finished high school. Half were married, and again the widower had killed the spouse.

In only two cases was there a history of excessive use of alcohol, and in no case was inebriation approximate to the crime.

Ninety per cent of the cases had no record of prior mental hospitalization, and half had no known previous record of antisocial behavior. In contrast, however, the five with previous antisocial records had committed offenses of a nature indicating possibly an increased proclivity toward violent behavior.

Diagnostic groupings showed a marked contrast to preceding categories in that the preponderant number were afflicted with organic brain disease, such as syphilis, cerebral arteriosclerosis, and mental deficiency. This accords well with the higher modal age.

In religious affiliation there were four Baptists and one Catholic, the remainder belonging to various Protestant denominations.

Once more, shooting was the most frequent technique of accomplishing the crime, but there was one homicide by poisoning and one by use of an automobile.

Only half of these patients were sent to the hospital before trial, but in our review of the records we believe that 80 per cent had shown almost unequivocal evidences of mental unsoundness at the time of the crime. This is suggestively validated by the fact that of the five convicted and sent to prison, three were committed to the hospital as insane in less than a year after the trial, and only two remained in prison for three years or longer before hospitalization.

Of this group only one remains in the hospital. One has died, three were returned to prison to continue sentence, two were returned for trial, and three were discharged from the hospital into their own custody after dismissal of the charges and improvement in their mental condition. None of those discharged has been readmitted to date.

## DISCUSSION

What we suspect to be the popular conception of the "insane murderer" as a person who suddenly runs amuck and strikes down an unknown and unprovocative bystander is not supported by our study. It is frequently noted in the literature that the murderer's victim is seldom an "innocent participant" in his own demise. This observation seems to us to be as valid for our group, in which the murderer was adjudicated of unsound mind, as it is for the instances where the murderer was not considered insane. Thus, in our 57 cases charged with first degree homicide, the victim was previously known to the patient in 39 cases; in 12 cases accused of second degree murder, the victim was known to the patient in 9 cases; and in 10 cases accused of manslaughter, the victim was previously known in 7 cases. Even in many situations where the victim was previously unknown, his death occurred by ill chance, as, for example, the circumstance of a husband returning home, finding his wife in bed with a stranger, and killing both.

Parenthetically, none of these cases illustrates the conception of the "homicidal sex maniac." We readily concede that there are instances of "beserk insane murderers" and "insane sex killers," but these cases are extremely rare exceptions in our experience.

In connection with another popular conception, there was little evidence in our entire group that alcoholic inebriation directly precipitated the crime of homicide. In fact, the percentage of those even with a history of excessive use of alcohol, though fairly high, is not significantly different from that of the general hospital population.

Preponderantly, the patients under study had made only a marginal or dependent economic adjustment. This is in contrast to some reports about murderers in general.

Among our 81 patients, there were two who did not fit into any category, inasmuch as they had killed a nurse or physician in another mental hospital and were transferred to Saint Elizabeths Hospital without charges.

Approximately 70 per cent of the victims were of the same sex as their murderer. Therefore, males were predominantly the murderers and the victims.

Again in contrast to what we believe to be the popular notion, the "insane murderer" does not execute his crime with a more conspicuous lack of planning, motivation, or rationale than the murderer whose mental faculties are not in question. For example:

## CASE 1

A 38-year-old colored male was described as timid, shy, and seclusive. His behavior was always exemplary and he had never been arrested except for a traffic violation. Drafted into the Army in 1941, he became tense and emotionally upset while in England in 1943 and was discharged for disability. Hospitalized in a Veteran's Administration Hospital, he was signed out by his mother against advice.

For some time prior to admission he was noted to be increasingly sullen and suspicious, seemed unable to hold a job, and complained about the "delicacy" of his health. Following his mother's death he began to brood and expressed feelings of hopelessness. He moved into the home of his sister and brother-in-law, but lived on very poor terms with them. On one occasion the brother-in-law came home drunk and consumed some food the patient had placed in the icebox. An argument ensued, during which the brother-in-law behaved in a threatening fashion. The patient seized a .22 rifle and shot the brother-in-law five times, with fatal consequences. Immediately the patient became tense and agitated, repeating over and over "What have I done?" and proceeded to call the police and an ambulance.

In the hospital he initially made a fairly good adjustment but gradually showed more severe impairment, with the development of marked aggressiveness, alternating with states of seclusiveness and untidiness. After a few years he began to dress consistently in a bizarre fashion and kept his ears constantly stuffed with paper in an effort to prevent auditory hallucinations which had not been obviously manifest on admission.

Even in instances of what were apparently completely "senseless, insane crimes," there was often more than a thread of emotional continuity. For example:

## CASE 2

A 32-year-old white male seemed to become progressively upset in anticipation of his appearance before his draft board. Three months prior to the crime he began to exhibit "antiwar religious fanatacism." On the day before he was scheduled to report before his draft board he was noted by his sister to be praying, reiterating constantly "Thou shalt not kill!"

While his sister was writing a letter she looked up suddenly and noticed that the patient had a knife poised above her head. She screamed and jumped up with such force that she tore the arm from the chair, and the patient was shoved backward. The noise awakened her husband, who grappled with the patient. After inflicting several wounds on the brother-in-law, the patient broke away, chased one of the children, who managed to elude him, and then dashed out into the street and fatally stabbed an innocent passerby. He was chopping senselessly at the top of an auto with his knife when he was finally subdued with great difficulty by an auxiliary policeman.

In the hospital he was resistive, negativistic, inaccessible, incontinent in his habits, and made repeated attempts to choke other patients. There has been a progressive increase in severity of his illness to the point of complete disorganization of behavior and mentation.

There were only five patients who had committed apparently senseless crimes. Much more common was the following:

## CASE 3

A 34-year-old white male college graduate of comfortable economic status was accused of the murder of his four-year-old daughter. For some months prior to the tragedy he had been depressed and contemplating suicide. With increase in severity of his illness, he became hopeless about the future and began to worry that his illness had "contaminated" his wife and daughter.

Despite his complete obsession with this delusional belief, he evidenced careful planning in inviting them for a drive through scenic mountain country with intention of killing them and himself. When he stopped the car to permit his family to enjoy the view, he came up behind his wife and daughter with a hammer, beating them with it until the handle broke, and then struck them repeatedly with a car jack handle. When they were both unconscious, he dragged them back into the car, got in and drove off the cliff. When he regained consciousness in the wreck, he realized he had not been killed, kicked a window out of the car, took a piece of glass and cut his throat and wrist and the throats of his wife and child. When he still survived, he found a broken bottle which he also used to cut himself. When found by policemen from a state patrol car, he was attempting to set fire to the upholstery with a cigarette. Amazingly, he and his wife survived.

In the hospital he was at first quite depressed and retarded, but under treatment improved considerably and remained in good contact at all times.

In second degree murder one would, by definition, commonly expect the exhibition of marked impulsivity with evidence of great emotional turmoil and obvious mental distress as factors mitigating the degree of the crime. Yet only half of the cases in this group were considered a priori as mentally ill and sent to the hospital before trial, as compared to approximately 75 per cent in the group accused of first degree murder, the prototype of a crime involving *mens rea*. Further, although we believe that there was fairly clear clinical evidence of mental unsoundness at the time of the crime in 80 per cent of the patients accused of first degree murder, we found such evidence in only a third of the records of patients sent to the hospital in the category of second degree murder. However, where mental illness was present in this group, the crime tended to be more obviously bizarre or irrational than homicides in the other groups. For example:

## Case 4

A 25-year-old Catholic female with a sixth-grade education was accused of killing her year-old daughter. Following the birth of her second child, she had become nervous and easily upset by the infant's crying. On the day of the homicide, she impulsively seized the infant, took her into the bathroom, and there repeatedly cut her throat with a knife. Upon psychiatric examination she was confused, depressed, and disoriented. The patient had had no record of any previous mental illness or any antisocial behavior.

An even more bizarre crime was the following:

## Case 5

A 25-year-old Negro male was riding in a streetcar when one of the passengers stepped on his foot. An altercation ensued which was terminated when the patient pulled a pistol out of a small bag that he was carrying, and shot and killed the other passenger. He then calmly left the streetcar, and was not arrested until a month later. He was released on bond, and, without knowledge of the authorities, went to a Veterans Hospital in another jurisdiction, where he received electric shock therapy. He was eventually identified and sent to Saint Elizabeths Hospital.

In the group of patients accused of manslaughter, a substantially larger number were obviously of unsound mind at the time of the crime. This is consonant with the statistical finding of higher modal age and the preponderance of organic brain disease. In most instances the homicide was the result of mental confusion or defects in judgment. For example:

## CASE 6

A 42-year-old white male became confused while driving his car, and, in attempting to pass a streetcar on the wrong side, he ran down and killed a prominent banker. Upon examination he was discovered to have syphilis of the nervous system. Previous to the crime there was no record of hospitalization or antisocial behavior. The charges against him were dismissed. After intensive treatment for his syphilitic infection, he improved greatly and was discharged as a social recovery.

## CASE 7

A 65-year-old white male, who had been making a marginal adjustment as a street vendor, was employed by a housewife to install a gas pipe. He was not aware of a defect in the pipe or a regulation requiring such installaiton to be made by the gas company. With the leakage of gas, the woman died of asphyxiation and her husband was rendered unconscious. On examination the patient was found to be suffering from marked confusion and clouding of consciousness, the result of advanced cerebral arteriosclerosis.

It is our clinical impression that mentally ill people who have committed violent and serious offenses against society are not a group apart from other mentally ill persons who have not translated their emotional conflicts into overt assaults upon others. The psychotic patients who have committed a homicide run the gamut of psychiatric disorders, and as a continuum are not clinically distinct from psychiatric patients in general. Some mentally ill patients who exhibit the most acutely disturbed and destructive behavior have never demonstrated sufficiently directed and organized aggression to kill another, while others who are quite meek and inoffensive have on occasion killed suddenly.

Further, it is our experience that the psychotic murderer responds to the same methods of care and treatment as other mental hospital patients. Maximum security and other extraordinary precautions need to be determined for each patient individually, and not on the arbitrary basis that he has been accused of a crime. One of us in a pilot study of several years' duration[2] has demonstrated that many of the security measures previously deemed so necessary for patients of this category have been based largely on preconceptions of physicians and hospital staff rather than on actual experiences with patients.

## CONCLUSIONS

1. In the period July 1, 1925 to July 1, 1951, there were 32,295 persons admitted to Saint Elizabeths Hospital, of whom only 81 had been accused of some variety of homicide. These latter cases were studied on a statistical and descriptive level.

2. Homicide is an infrequent consequence of mental disorder. However, many mentally ill people may commit serious assaults and fail to kill only by chance or through inadequate design, itself also the result of the mental illness.

3. Because of the limited number of cases, few sweeping conclusions can be drawn as to the importance of such factors as educational attainment or economic or marital status. Interestingly, however, all those who were widowed achieved this status by their own hand.

4. Only 15 patients had a history of previous hospitalization for mental illness. Careful study of these case records indicated little that would have been useful, in the present status of our knowledge, for accurate prediction of the subsequent homicide, when they were compared with the unselected records of thousands of other mentally ill patients, except by *post hoc* reasoning. Similarly, the record of antisocial behavior was not considered of substantial value in predicting the specific crime. None of the patients had committed a previous murder, and only a small number had records of major offenses.

5. Alcoholic inebriation was not indicated as an immediate precipitant of the crime in any instance, and the frequency of a history of excessive intake of alcohol was not significantly different in these patients from that found in other mental patients or in the general population.

6. Most of the patients accused of first and second degree homicide were afflicted with one of the functional mental disorders, predominantly schizophrenia. In contrast, most of the patients accused of manslaughter were afflicted with an organic type of psychosis, and were, by and large, much older at the time of the crime than were the other patients.

7. Statistics as to the disposition of the mentally ill patient

accused of homicide can be better understood from a study of the attitudes of the psychiatrist, or the community in which he lives, than from an objective evaluation of the patient distinguished as a distinct clinical psychiatric entity primarily on the basis of his having committed a homicide.

8. If there exists a popular conception of the "insane" murderer as a person who suddenly runs amuck and strikes down a perfect stranger, it is not confirmed by our studies. Such cases do occur, but they are extremely rare, as is also the frequency of the "maniacal sex killer" as conceived in the popular press.

9. Mentally ill people who commit a homicide do not constitute a psychiatric entity as distinct from other mentally disordered patients, and they respond in the same way and in the same degree to the identical methods of care found useful with mentally ill patients in general. Special precautions as to security and management, when indicated, must be individually prescribed for each mentally ill person, and cannot be arbitrarily decided on the basis of the previous occurrence of a homicidal transgression. That special precautions are frequently arbitrarily prescribed is, in our experience, more often than not the result of preconceptions entertained by the psychiatrist, or of social pressures, expressed, implied, or assumed.

# A Psychiatric Study of a
# Mass Murderer

*JAMES A. V. GALVIN and*
*JOHN M. MACDONALD*

ON NOVEMBER 1, 1955, eleven minutes after leaving Denver, a 4-engine airliner exploded and crashed with the loss of 44 lives. Two weeks later a 23-year-old man confessed that he had placed in his mother's luggage, a time bomb consisting of a timer, hot shot battery, blasting caps and 25 sticks of dynamite. Following a plea of insanity, he was committed to hospital for psychiatric examination. Friendly and cooperative, yet somewhat reserved in his manner, he volunteered that he had no intention of faking insanity although he thought it would be easy for him to do this by saying that he heard voices. Indeed he stated that it had been suggested to him that he should say that he had seen visions and that he acted under instructions from God.

He claimed innocence and said that he had never had any wish to kill his mother. He knew it was wrong, both morally and legally, to blow up an aircraft and he would never do such a thing. A variety of reasons was given to explain his confession. He could not stand the questioning; when he told the truth and was not believed, he figured "to heck with it"; he was manhandled and threatened with bodily injury. At his subsequent trial, there was no evidence of threats by

REPRINTED with the permission of the authors and the publisher from James A. V. Galvin and John M. Macdonald, "Psychiatric Study of a Mass Murderer," *The American Journal of Psychiatry* (June, 1959), 115:12:1057-1061.

Read at the 114th annual meeting of The American Psychiatric Association, San Francisco, California, May 12-16, 1958.

F.B.I. agents. Indeed, the F.B.I. selected a man smaller than the patient to act as principal questioner.

Nothing untoward occurred prior to the tragedy. His mother who had been living with him decided to visit a relative in Alaska. He tried to persuade her to remain till Thanksgiving but without success. At the airport, it was found that her luggage was 37 pounds overweight. His mother wished to avoid the surcharge but the patient assured her that she would need all her luggage. On her request he took out 3 insurance policies, each with a different beneficiary. He fumbled this task and had to throw away 2 policies. The policies were to have been for $6,250 but by mistake he deposited extra coins in the machine for his policy thus giving it a value of $37,500.

After the plane left, he had dinner with his wife and child in the airport restaurant. During dinner he became nauseated and vomited in the rest-room. When he learned that the plane had crashed he cried till he did not have any tears left to cry. Although he denied having made any callous remarks about the plane crash, he did in fact, remark to his family one day, with reference to some shot-gun shells in his mother's luggage, "Can't you just see those shot gun shells going off in the plane every which way and the pilots and passengers and grandma jumping around."

On November 10, he told a comparative stranger that the center of the plane on which his mother had died had been blown to only small strips of metal. He went on to say how easy it would be to blow up a plane and estimated that it would require 2 gallons of nitroglycerine and a timing mechanism which could be placed in a suitcase and slipped on the carts which carry baggage to the planes. He mentioned the irony of the crash. If the plane had not taken off 20 minutes late it would have crashed in the mountains and no one would ever have suspected sabotage. (At that time the possibility of sabotage had been raised in the newspapers.)

On November 13, he was questioned by the F.B.I. and was arrested following his confession. During the interrogation, the F.B.I. offered to let him go back home and he had since asked himself a "million times" why he hadn't accepted the offer.

## FAMILY HISTORY

The patient knew little about his father who left his mother when he was 18 months of age. His mother who had a daughter by a previous marriage then went to live with her mother and returned to work.

During the patient's childhood, she was very generous in providing toys and money for her children but spent little time with them. She appeared to have been quick tempered, somewhat domineering and not an affectionate mother. The patient was quick to defend her, but it was evident that he had felt rejected by her from an early age.

"We loved one another but she wasn't a person you could call 'mom.' She wanted you to call her by her Christian name. You couldn't put your arms around her. You couldn't show your affection like that to her. I always depended on her a lot. If she got mad at you she'd stay mad for 15 years."

Her gifts were accompanied by demands and whenever she caused particular feelings of anger, she would effectively prevent their expression and arouse a sense of guilt by some generous monetary gift. At the same time, she would play the role of a martyr. According to a relative, she was once found unconscious after a suicide attempt with drugs. There was no family history of psychosis.

## PERSONAL HISTORY

Little is known of his early development. Childhood neurotic traits included cruelty to animals, bed wetting and fear of being left alone. It was reported that he once set fire to a garage while playing with matches. When his grandmother died he was placed in an institution for fatherless boys where he remained from 6 to 11 years of age. Bed wetting which had occurred almost every night stopped almost immediately after he was sent to the institution. His adjustment there was not good and the school records noted that he felt his mother did not love him because she had put him in an institution. When he was 9 his mother married a wealthy rancher but she refused his repeated requests to be allowed to come home. Several times he ran away from the school to his stepfather's ranch but each time he was returned to the institution. At 11, he was caught stealing and the institution then insisted that his mother should look after him.

At 14 years of age, he left school to work on his stepfather's ranch. At 16 he enlisted in the Coast Guard. His mother aided him in his deception that he was 18 years of age. Within 6 months he went absent without leave and subsequently he was discharged from the service. "It seems that I gave the Commodore the wrong answer, because as soon as he and his hat came back to earth, I was sent back to New York and they asked me to stay in a Marine Hospital."

At the time of the neuropsychiatric examination he stated, "I just took a notion I'd get out of the service by going A.W.O.L. I was fed up with saying Yes sir, No sir, and getting punished for things that didn't seem very important. I had $200 and I went to New York, Chicago, Georgia, Washington, D. C. I was hitch-hiking. I had a lot of fun drinking, dancing, going to parties. I don't feel sorry about it, but I'm not happy about it; its just one of those things, but I don't want a bad conduct discharge. If I stay in the Coast Guard and don't get leave, I'll go over the hill again to see my mother."

He claimed that he was given 5 or 6 electric shock treatments while in hospital and was able to give a convincing description of EST. This claim was not confirmed by the Coast Guard records which stated: "This man is an exceedingly immature individual who has exhibited poor judgment and who tends to act on impulses. He is a dependent person, with strong ties to mother. He tolerates frustrations, even those in the normal course of work, very poorly. Other evidences of his poor judgment and impulsive behavior are to be seen in his sleeping on watch, stealing food while on watch, and returning to work drunk."

During the 2 years following his discharge from the Coast Guard, he held over 25 different jobs, principally in construction work and as a truck driver in various parts of the United States and Alaska. He attributed his frequent job changes to poor business conditions or unfair treatment by his boss. In March, 1951, he forged over 40 checks for a total value of approximately $4,500. He then flew to Seattle, purchased a car and travelled extensively. He was arrested in September, 1951, in Texas, after crashing through a road block at high speed and was sentenced to 60 days imprisonment for bootlegging and carrying a concealed weapon.

His true identity was discovered and he was returned to Denver to face trial for check forgery. Early in 1952, he was released on 5 year's probation upon condition he repay $1,800 during this period. His stepfather repaid the remaining $2,500. In 1953, he married a girl he had met the previous year while taking courses in business administration at Denver University. Although he had been friendly with several girls prior to his marriage, this was the first girl he had "really cared for." "To me it's the only thing that matters, it's hard to describe. Some people take their wives for granted. I couldn't. If I came home and she wasn't there I had to find out right away where she was. I wanted to put her up on a shelf and not let anyone else touch her or see her." There were 2 children of the marriage.

When his stepfather died in October, 1954, his mother inherited over $90,000. She insisted on his returning to the university and reluctantly he agreed. In 1955, she purchased a drive-in for him and went to live with him. Although his mother had told him that he was to be in charge of the business, she interfered considerably in its management and there was increasing friction between them. During this year he became very irritable and short tempered. At the same time, he continued to be very dependent upon his mother. The drive-in was not a financial success and in September, 1955, it was closed for the winter months. The patient then worked as a night mechanic. This was his 45th job since leaving school.

His health record was not [showed nothing] remarkable and he was in good physical health. In 1955, he was sterilized because his wife had almost lost her life during the delivery of her second child.

### Personality Before Arrest

Although he made friends easily, he had only one close friend apart from his wife. In groups he was self assertive and liked to be a leader rather than a follower. Since working in the drive-in, his usual cheerful, if somewhat impatient disposition, had changed and he was subject to moody spells following arguments with his mother and at these times he liked to be by himself. He disliked routine tasks and would often start some project but not finish it. His only hobby was working on his car and he spent his leisure time working about the home, watching sports or reading novels. Although he had no strong religious beliefs, he attended church 2 to

3 times a month after his marriage. He tried to avoid fights and claimed that he did not lose his temper easily. He did not take drugs and his average weekly consumption of alcohol was a pint of vodka and 3 to 4 cans of beer. He denied day-dreaming but said he tended to tell exaggerated stories about himself and his achievements.

### Mental State

A tall well built young man, he was polite, friendly and courteous in his manner. Although ready to talk on imper-sonal topics he became somewhat reserved when questioned about his mother and about his experiences with the F.B.I. Thus certain information which one might have expected from vague general questions would be forthcoming only in response to very specific inquiry.

Although usually cheerful and outgoing, at times he ap-peared preoccupied and depressed. His cheerful mood might have been considered inappropriate in the circumstances, but he was being encouraged almost daily by an attorney to expect a favorable outcome at the trial. Between interviews he carried on lively conversations with others in the ward and he entered with zest into recreational activities.

There was no evidence of phobias, obsessions, thought disorder, hallucinations or delusions. Testing of sensorial function showed no abnormality and he appeared to be of average intelligence. Although there was ample indication of poor judgment in his past life he showed good judgment in his handling of situations in the ward.

### Readmission to Hospital

In our opinion, he was considered to be legally sane and the diagnosis was sociopathic personality. One month after his return to jail, he made a suicidal gesture by tightening his socks around his throat. He did not suffer any ill effects but the following day he was readmitted to hospital because of bizarre behavior. He claimed that people were against him and were trying to poison him. A patchy amnesia, intermit-tent disorientation, absurd as well as correct answers to sim-ple arithmetical problems, together with other symptoms suggested a Ganser state or simulated insanity.

On the 4th day in hospital, he confessed with considerable abreaction, that he had placed a time bomb in his mother's luggage. He revealed that before coming to hospital the second time, he had learned that his attorney had discovered where he had bought the dynamite, timer and battery. This had dashed his hopes for acquittal and depressed him considerably. His original intention had been to blow up the drive-in; however, after his mother refused to stay until Thanksgiving, he decided to blow up the airoplane instead.

"I tried to tell her how I felt about it. She just said she wouldn't stay, she wouldn't give me any reason at all, no reason why she didn't want to stay. I thought it was the last time she was going to run off and leave me. I wanted to have her to myself for once. Since I was just a little kid she'd leave me with these people, those people, I wanted to get close to her, everytime I'd get close to her she'd just brush me off like I was a piece of furniture, as if I didn't mean more to her than nothing. If she gave me money I was supposed to realize that was enough. I just wanted to do things with her, to sit down and talk to her—just like everybody else's mother would do.

"I just had to stop her from going—yet it seemed I had to be free from her, too. She held something over me that I couldn't get from under. When the plane left the ground a load came off my shoulders, I watched her go off for the last time. I felt happier than I ever felt before in my life. I was afraid to do anything without asking her and yet I wanted to go ahead on my own without having to ask her. Down deep I think she resented me, little things she would do to aggravate me. It's such a relief to tell somebody what I did. It was such a terrible thing I couldn't bear to tell anybody. I deserve to be taken out and shot. I can't find an excuse for something like that." He wept as he made these statements and he begged the physician to tell his wife that he was guilty of the crime.

In subsequent interviews, he was alternately callous and remorseful regarding the tragedy. "I just felt if it killed somebody that was tough. It seemed the odds were big enough, there was more fun that way. I just didn't think about the other people on the plane. I don't think it's hit me yet. I guess I thought I could keep it all inside of me and forget about it. I finally decided I couldn't live with it myself."

He revealed previous delinquent acts. He once set fire to a garage causing $100,000 damage because he had been refused discount on car repairs. Four suicide attempts were described. On the projective psychological tests he had deliberately given false answers and he had lied when he said people were trying to poison him. After 11 days in hospital he was again returned to jail. The opinion was that he was legally sane. Later he said he had faked his attempt at suicide in the hope that he would be found insane.

## DYNAMIC FORMULATION

Our dynamic formulation was based partly on conjecture. Little is known of the relationship between this man and his mother in infancy. In later life she constantly followed a pattern of rejection, punctuated by episodes of indulgence. The consequence was that this young man had an extremely intense ambivalent relationship with his mother. He continued to hope for real and lasting affection from her, but his experience made him view her as rejecting, frustrating and a great cause for anger. In his ambivalent relationship he repressed and suppressed very much of his hostile feelings and when he spoke of his mother it was usually in loving terms.

With his warm accepting wife he had not only adult and mature satisfactions, but also important infantile satisfactions which permitted a partial mastery of the conflict with his mother. With both wife and mother he had great separation anxiety. The final determinant of his crime was his anger because his mother would not remain with him over Thanksgiving. His helplessness when threatened by his separation anxiety added to his hostility against his mother. In the year before the tragedy he was miserably unhappy with his mother.

He denied conscious knowledge of his own father. We thought his teachers were for him a shadowy father figure. He viewed them as unjustly demanding, implacable and unreasonably punitive. The authority figures were merged together into "society" so that his poorly directed anger and indignation against them justified, for him, his antisocial behavior.

After his marriage, his sociopathic patterns seemed to become less. There were some social aberrations but he did work steadily, was successful in his university examinations and spent much time with his family. The experience arising out of his marriage of increased drive satisfaction on both adult and pregenital levels had slightly changed his anger and rebellious attitude toward society.

The period of relative social adjustment was ended by his mother's return into his life. The recapitulation of the infantile situation with her engendered so much strong emotion that his substitute gratifications paled into [in] significance. He became more and more hostile, he began to have increasing phantasies of violence and at the end of the year he acted these phantasies out. He at once destroyed his tormentor and in a counterphobic way dealt with his fear of separation from her.

There was remarkable lack of conscious guilt in this man throughout his life. While reassured by people around him, confidence and cheerfulness could be maintained for a time. When he realized that he would be found guilty he faked a suicide attempt and made a belated attempt to simulate insanity. Much affect accompanied his confession in hospital, but there was little conscious guilt: rather he was filled with fear, anxiety and despair.

There was ample evidence of unconscious guilt and an unconscious wish to be punished. When he bought the electric timer he gave his home telephone number. He did not hide or destroy the things he took out of his mother's suitcase to make room for the bomb. His behavior following the tragedy seemed almost designed to draw attention to himself as the guilty person. He did not avail himself of the legal defenses against questioning by the F.B.I. When he had been tried and found guilty he energetically opposed appeals to higher courts.[1]

## SUMMARY

Careful examination including review of the psychological test data failed in our opinion to reveal evidence of psychosis. The diagnosis of sociopathic personality was based upon the history of poor social adjustment, intolerance of frustration and discipline, antisocial behavior, nomadism, poor work record, egocentricity and lack of judgment. . . .

# The Sudden Murderer

*JOSEPH W. LAMBERTI, NATHAN*
*BLACKMAN and JAMES M. A. WEISS*

IN JULY, 1956, a social maladjustment study unit was organized at Malcolm Bliss Psychiatric Hospital to serve as an interdisciplinary research, teaching and consultation center, focusing on problems common to psychiatry and law; and contributing to the study, understanding and eventual social readjustment of individuals involved in aggressive antisocial or delinquent acts.[2, 14] Between July 1, 1956, and December 30, 1957, 153 patients were seen at this unit. Many of these patients presented problems in which diagnostic and psychodynamic formulations were fairly obvious, regardless of the nature of the offense or of the referring agency.[4] However, in one group of patients—those who, without any prior pattern of antisocial behavior that might indicate the individual concerned would commit such a crime, suddenly attempted to kill or did kill another person—the crime as a function of the personality of the individual concerned was much more difficult to understand. This paper is a preliminary report of an investigation of the common factors in the life patterns and offenses of the thirteen persons from our 153 cases who fit this category—thirteen whom we called "sudden murderers."

Such a person was Al, a 22-year-old twice married white male, who was charged with murdering a 30-year-old divorcee (the cousin of his first wife) in a brutal fashion, carrying her remains in a laundry bag in the trunk of his car for several

REPRINTED with the permission of the authors and the publisher from Joseph W. Lamberti, Nathan Blackman, and James M. A. Weiss, "The Sudden Murderer: A Preliminary Report," *The Journal of Social Therapy* (1958), 4:1 & 2:2-14.

weeks, and finally dumping her in a creek near his home in another state. Although he confessed after apprehension, he later claimed that he did so under duress and that he was innocent, although the evidence against him was overwhelming.

Al was a native of a rural southern state. His father was a coal miner, but due to chronic illness was incapacitated most of the patient's life. There were two older brothers and two younger sisters. His mother, according to Al's account, was unusually overprotective and domineering.

Al apparently joined the Army as soon as possible both to escape from his mother and to gain financial security with the least effort. He said he spent some time on the Korean front. He denied any serious trouble in the service and said he was honorably discharged. There is no information to deny or corroborate this statement. His attitude towards the Army was one of being victimized by moneyed interests engaging in a useless war, but he said that he "put up with all this" because he knew that "it could not last long."

His major conflict seems to have been over his extreme dependency on and fear of women. His mother and younger sisters ran the household. He insisted that the Army forced him to marry his first wife after she became pregnant, and that his mother's objections to the marriage were powerless. As he and his first wife were unable to get along, they finally separated, and he said he sued for divorce. The murdered woman, cousin of the first wife, had been active in trying to keep his first marriage intact. Al at first denied that the cousin took sides, but later said that she sided with the first wife.

His second wife he had known from childhood and he married her in February, 1956, seven months before the birth of a son. At first Al denied that the child was conceived before they were married, but later said he didn't know that his wife-to-be was pregnant at the time. He married his second wife before the legal waiting period after the divorce from his first wife was over. Hence, he said, his mother and sisters maintained that he was not legally married.

He felt that his mother, sisters and first wife all joined forces and pestered him continuously in an attempt to break up his second marriage. They also caused him to lose one of his jobs. After he and his second wife began fighting, he decided to leave home so that his family "would leave my [second] wife alone." He came to St. Louis without his wife and child ("because it was too cold for the baby to travel") to find a job and settle down—or to take a vacation, depending on which time he was telling his story.

It just so happened, he said, that by chance he met his first wife's cousin in St. Louis and he spent much time with her —but with other people around. She worked in an aircraft plant and he applied for work there, too, but was unsuccessful in obtaining a job because he never seemed to be able to locate his Army discharge papers.

During this time he became involved sexually with the cousin while she maintained his support. However, after a while she lost interest in him and was becoming involved with other men. Following an argument in regard to this behavior, during which she rejected him in a belittling manner, he suddenly lashed out in homicidal fury, beating her with a milk bottle and then strangling her with his hands and a lamp cord.

In the hospital, Al appeared to be a neatly dressed young man with a bland, flat affect even when talking about disturbing subjects. Only after considerable "pushing" would Al show some agitation. He was extremely vague about the details of his crime, although he read all the lurid accounts in the newspapers and detective magazines. He said that he felt he was an utter failure, that everything he tried to do went wrong and that the important women in his life lost no time in telling him so. He projected almost all the blame for failure onto interference from other people and said his only chance for success was to be left alone and given a chance to start over again. However, he seemed to have no idea as to how he would stop this alleged interference if he were given a chance to start over.

He felt that he had been to a mental hospital "to find out if there is anything wrong" with him. He said he believed there was not; that, after seeing other patients, he was thankful that he was not thus afflicted. He denied, incidentally, any family history of delinquency or mental illness. If freed, he said, he would not "mess up again" but would like to make a career of "working in hospitals helping other people." Although his ward behavior was unusually cooperative and he went out of his way to assist debilitated and withdrawn patients, he verbalized his feeling of edginess and irritation toward other patients and said that even the ordinary ward noise disturbed him. His attitude was that, if he were not freed, "they might as well shoot me."

He appeared to consider himself a well-controlled, mild-mannered person who had no difficulty getting along with other people. However, he suggested that, if he were pushed too far, he might lose control of his temper to the point where he wouldn't know what he had done afterward.

The case record of Al is in many ways typical of the pattern found in the lives and offenses of all thirteen sudden murderers referred to our unit. Ten of these committed actual murder and three were charged with assault with intent to kill, rather than with murder per se, as their victims did not die. None of these offenders was involved in murder for profit or for obvious personal advantage, and none of them had patterns of consistent repeated criminal activities. In age, our thirteen patients ranged from 15 to 56, although only one was under 18 and only one was over 45. The median age was 25 and, in general, these patients could be characterized as belonging to the young adult group. Eleven men and two women were involved; eight were white and five (all male) were Negro. All thirteen were native-born. Five were single, four were married and four were divorced.

In terms of family background, a consistent pattern began to emerge. In every case the patient was reared by at least one natural parent—his mother. Most patients (nine cases) lived with both natural parents while being reared. Two lived with mother alone (one's father having died and one's parents being divorced) and two lived with a natural mother and a stepfather (both mothers having divorced the natural father). No patient was reared by a natural father alone, or by foster parents, or in institutions. Most patients came from large families—although three were only children, seven were reared in families with five or more children and the three others came from families with at least three children. Of those who were not only children, seven were intermediate in age among the siblings, two were the oldest and one was the youngest.

The families of origin lived in rural farming areas for six

cases, in urban areas for five and in peripheral urban or small-town areas for two. Geographically, most families were relatively stable, living in the same area throughout the patients' childhood (seven cases), and in three more cases some degree of geographic stability was noted. Only in two cases were the families relatively mobile geographically. However, the economic condition of the families during the rearing period was marginal for most (nine cases) and could be considered as "comfortable" in only four cases. A history of severe physical or mental disorder in father, mother or siblings was not common, although three patients noted physical disorder in one or more close relatives, one patient's family had a history of chronic alcoholism, one patient's family had a history of serious physical ailments, serious mental disorder and chronic alcoholism, and one patient's family had a history of serious mental disorder and criminality.

The families of origin were, in general, overtly cohesive— the pattern of the "broken home" was not apparent in our data. In only one case was there a family pattern suggesting poor cohesiveness, and some cohesiveness was noted in eight cases, with marked cohesiveness in four. The apparent quality of the relationship between mother and father was not generally good, however: it was rated as poor in nine cases, fair in three cases and good in only one case. It was clear the mother was the dominant parent in ten cases, and father in only three. In no case was there a history of cooperation without domination between the two parents.

A striking finding was the overt attitude of the parents toward the patient during the childhood period. No father had a warm or even overprotective relationship to the child: father's attitude was generally characterized as hostile, rejecting or overstrict (five cases) or indifferent (two cases). Father was absent during the rearing period in three cases, and his attitude toward the patient was unknown in three cases. Even more consistent was mother's overt attitude toward the patient during the childhood period, for it could be characterized as overprotective in eleven cases (being unknown or undetermined in the remaining two). In no case was mother's attitude that of warmth or even indifference or overt hostility. At the same time, the patient considered himself to have been, as a child, attached to the mother in eleven cases and hostile to her in only one (the attitude of child toward mother is unknown in the other case). However, except for three cases in which the overt emotional ties of the patient to his father are not known, the attitude toward father was generally hostile (eight cases) or indifferent (two cases). The closeness of the emotional tie to mother is demonstrated by the fact that only one patient out of thirteen ever made a complete break away from home (with severance of contact with all family members).

The patients were not generally well educated—none had attended college and only one had completed high school. Three attended high school, three completed grammar school (eight grades) and four attended grammar school. In two cases the degree of schooling was unknown, although it was evident in both that they had not gone any further than high school. Five of these patients were unskilled laborers, three were engaged in clerical work, one owned a small business and four were dependent on others. Job stability was not good, however; of the ten patients who had ever been gainfully employed, eight had never held a job for as long as a year, although two patients had been employed at steady work at one job for more than five years.

Economically, the patients' status could be characterized as marginal in eleven cases and "comfortable" in only two cases (of the four dependent on others, in only one case was the provider characterized as affording a "comfortable" economic status). Four men of the eleven had served in the armed forces—two of these received honorable discharges but never advanced in rank and two received other than honorable discharges (although neither received outright dishonorable discharges). In only two cases was there a record of past criminal activity, one man having committed forgery (he was put on probation) and one having committed car theft (he was sent to prison for a short time.) Both female patients, however, had a record of illegitimate pregnancy. Although, as noted above, these patients came from families that were relatively stable geographically, they themselves generally had patterns of relative mobility from place to place (eight cases); only five had patterns of relatively stable geographic location.

Of the twelve patients 18 and older, four had never married (nor had the one 15-year-old boy in our series). None of the eight patients who married appeared to have achieved good relationships with their spouses. Four patients who had married only once showed records of a marital relationship marked with frequent bickering or disagreement or infidelity or other difficulty. In four cases, marriage ended in divorce (for one marriage in two cases, and for two marriages in two cases). In addition, the pattern of overt sexual behavior of these thirteen patients appeared to be that of "normal" heterosexually oriented persons in only two cases, six patients having been involved in consistent promiscuous heterosexual behavior and five patients having a history of markedly inhibited sexual behavior. In no case was there a record of definite overt homosexual behavior. In general, these patients did not have a history of severe physical disease or defect, although one was partly deaf and one had a past history of chronic headaches of indefinite etiology.

In one case was the body configuration of these patients markedly dysplastic in any way. There was a primary tendency toward mesomorphism in seven cases, toward ectomorphism in five cases and toward endomorphism in only one case. Surprisingly, the intellectual capacity of these patients was rather high. Psychiatric histories and interviews and psychological tests (in most cases) indicated that seven patients were of average intelligence, four were considered to be dull normal and two were of borderline intelligence; no patient was considered to be in the mental defective range.

Analysis of the character and personality structures was based on extensive and intensive psychiatric interviews and observations in a mental hospital. All patients were rated on the basis of such interviews and observations by a large group of psychiatrists, clinical psychologists and psychiatric social workers and the traits examined were then categorized under the following headings: self-assertion (the faculty of asserting one's rights, demands, opinions, and so on); social assertion (the quality of asserting will and ambition with regard to the social environment, as well as the surface ability to get along with others); overt defiance or hostility, overt submissiveness and/or dependence, ambivalence to authority, general feelings of insecurity or anxiety, feelings of not being wanted or loved or of not being recognized or appreciated, feelings of helplessness or powerlessness, fears of failure and/or defeat, feelings of resentment, depressive trends, tendency to blame others for one's troubles, feelings of isolation, feelings of sexual inadequacy, and tendencies toward extroversion or introversion.

Striking and consistent patterns were noted in several of these character and personality traits. In general, these patients showed some degree of ambivalence in their attitudes toward authority, and some degree of feeling not wanted or loved or recognized or appreciated. Most of them showed as well some degree of fear of failure and defeat and some feelings of resentment. Most patients showed some surface ability to get along with others, but all tended to blame other people for their troubles and all expressed definite feelings of isolation. In general, they expressed marked feelings of sexual inadequacy. All showed some small degree of chronic depression, although this was not marked in any case. Most of these patients could be characterized as introverts, only one being definitely extroverted and one being an ambivert. All of the findings were substantiated by batteries of psychological tests.

For some traits, however, there were marked differences between the findings on psychiatric examination and interview and those on the psychological tests. Self-assertion and social assertion were present to some degree in several cases in terms of overt behavior, but were definitely lacking in *all* cases on the tests. In the same way, although four patients showed only minimal or absent overt feelings of submissiveness or dependency, all showed marked submissiveness or dependency feelings on the tests. Only about half of the patients overtly expressed marked feelings of helplessness or powerlessness, but all demonstrated these feelings in tests. The minimal depressive trends noted in overt behavior were in most cases *not* evident on the tests.

The history of the crime itself provides certain insights of value. It was noteworthy that in all cases there was a period of overtly adequate adjustment immediately prior to the offense. This period of adjustment was of varying duration: from one to three months in four cases, three months to a year in six cases and one to five years in three cases. During this period of overtly adequate adjustment nine patients were employed at steady work (eight were working with apparent effectiveness and satisfaction, one with increasing resentment and difficulty), two were in a dependent status (one was a juvenile and one a housewife), and two were unemployed. During this period nine patients had apparently stable relationships with a spouse or an illegal heterosexual partner.

In twelve cases there appeared to be some later precipitating factor or "insult" that threatened the patient's stability in his most important relationships. (In the remaining case it was not clear whether there was such a factor.) The incidents that precipitated the offense were: (1) a belittling rejection by the patient's sexually provocative paramour, (2) a sadistic threat by this female patient's male sexual partner to his wife, who represented to the patient an accepting maternal figure, (3) the threat of impending marriage, (4) the refusal of his child to conform to the demands made by the patient, (5) the withholding of the patient's pay check by his employer, (6) the "teasing" of the patient in regard to his girl friend by his supervisor, (7) the refusal of his stepfather to pay the patient for work performed, (8) provocative hostile remarks made by the second husband of the patient regarding his sexual abusiveness toward her children, (9) criticism of the patient's drinking by his domineering wife, (10) an altercation with a friend about the patient's job problems, (11) rejection of the patient by his girl friend and belittling remarks made by the girl friend's new lover, and (12) the ejection of the patient from a public library by a library guard.

The time period elapsing between this precipitating "insult" and the crime varied: three patients reacted within a few minutes, four within a two-day period, two in periods longer than two days but less than two weeks, and two took several months to react. (In two cases the time period is unknown.) The method of killing or attempted killing was violent in all cases: eight persons shot their victims, four beat them with blunt instruments (and two of these also strangled or attempted to strangle their victims), and one knifed his victim. In five cases the victim was the sexual partner of the subject (three of these were legal spouses and two were illicit but continued partners), in two cases the victim was a stranger of the same sex, in two cases the victim was an employer or supervisor of the same sex, and in four cases the victims were in other roles (stepfather, stepson, friend, and one girl friend's new paramour). The conjectured symbolic role of the victim was not consistent, as it was thought to be paternal in five cases, maternal in three cases and self in five cases. In eight of the crimes evident sexual hostility was involved; in five only a more generalized hostility was apparent.

After the crime, five patients either called the police or acted in such a way that someone else was sure to call the police, and then admitted their crimes without hesitation. Six patients did not turn themselves in to the police but made no active efforts to escape apprehension and, when apprehended, also admitted their crime. Two patients made active but poorly planned efforts to escape apprehension and both of these later denied that they were guilty of the alleged crime although the evidence of their guilt was overwhelming in both cases. Seven patients were bland and unconcerned after the crime (although one of these patients was anxious and somewhat depressed about her possible future disposition), five were "righteous" and one patient appeared to be resentful and hostile but not righteous. No patient showed strong feelings of guilt, none showed evidence of marked or even moderate depression and none was overtly anxious about having committed a crime. Eleven patients admitted or expressed a definite sense of relief after committing the crime, in such phrases as "I'm glad I did it" or "I'd do it again."

From the foregoing data, it appears that persons who have committed or attempted to commit sudden "inexplicable" murders have certain consistencies in their life patterns. Although the families of origin are generally large and of marginal economic status, they tend to be relatively stable geographically, living in the same area throughout the patients' childhood, and there is a definite tendency toward cohesiveness and toward an apparent family attempt to conform with social norms. (The immediate family rarely demonstrates a history of criminality or serious mental disorder, or even of serious physical disorder.)

At the same time, there is a strong tendency for mother to dominate in the family pattern, and mother and father do not generally get along well. Father is consistently a negative figure (either absent from the family picture or indifferent or overtly rejecting toward the child). Mother is even more consistently overprotective. With such conflicts around them, these persons as children must develop a strong sense of insecurity and inadequacy. To defend against this and against marked feelings of anger and rage, which they are not able to express openly because of their introjected need to conform, they make strong use of the psychological mechanism of projection.

Such conflicts become more difficult to handle as these individuals grow older. Despite reasonably adequate intellectual capacities and good physical constitutions, they generally do not do well in school, at work or in the armed forces, and tend to drift from place to place, perhaps looking for greater "opportunities," which, of course, they are not able to handle successfully even if such opportunities become available. By the time these persons reach the young adult period they are quite aware of their failure to achieve adult roles and they have feelings of not being wanted or loved, of not being recognized or appreciated and of being isolated from other persons. Although, overtly, they are able to maintain some surface ability to get along with others, some degree of self and social assertion, more covertly they feel markedly deficient in these areas: covertly, they feel helpless, powerless and dependent.

Such conflicts are bound to reach greatest intensity during periods of apparent adjustment—when social and interpersonal expectations of adaptability and conformity to adult standards are increased. Then the discrepancy between such demands and the individuals' inability to meet them adequately becomes more and more painfully obvious, the sense of isolatedness more and more unbearable and the intrapsychic tensions increasingly stronger and more difficult to cope with. At such a time, then, some "insult" (an "insult" that might seem irrelevant or trivial to the casual observer) may trigger a sudden discharge of tension into a wish-fulfilling, furious, violent, hostile lashing out—the sudden murder —which may be directed against a clearly significant person or against a stranger or passer-by.

In terms of diagnosis, these patients present certain problems. Complete physical and laboratory examinations made it clear that none of those in our series were suffering from organic brain disorders or mental deficiency. (In one case electroencephalographic examination indicated certain minor deviations which, however, were not thought by the consultant in neurology to be of any etiological significance in the patient's disorder.) It was also clear that none of these patients were suffering from affective psychotic reactions, psychoneurotic disorders or transient situational personality disorders as primary diagnostic possibilities.

The disorders of most patients appeared to resemble the long-standing personality disorders. Like the classical antisocial psychopaths, our subjects seemed to suffer disturbances in the processes of projection and identification,[10,13] to be concerned with conflicts relating to unrequited love, guilt, and hostility,[9] and to have suffered affect starvation in the formative childhood years.[8] Like the psychopaths described by some authors,[1,3,5,12] the sudden murderers had a shadow family life and developed attitudes resulting in social isolatedness with limited or nonexistent positive relationships. *Unlike* the psychopaths as described by these and other authors,[6,7,11] however, the sudden murderers did *not* have a history of continuous and repetitive trouble with the law, nor did they lack a sense of responsibility. Rather, their difficulties came about because of their needs to conform and because of their inability to act out hostility in ways that they would feel might still be socially acceptable.

In general, the sudden murderers demonstrated certain qualities of the schizoid personality (emotional coldness and isolatedness, difficulty in forming close relationships with other persons and difficulty in directly expressing hostility), and certain qualities of the passive-aggressive personality (feelings of helplessness, inefficiency and persistent reaction to frustration with resentment). Two patients were, however, overtly and blatantly schizophrenic, with fundamental disturbances in reality testing, regressive behavior and strong delusional or paranoid trends evident at the time of the crime and on initial examination following the crime. In two other cases diagnosis was especially difficult on initial examination, but after six months under close observation in a mental hospital regressive behavior with delusional material and paranoid and autistic thinking became apparent, so that a final diagnosis of schizophrenic reaction was made.

The life pattern, personality trends and offenses of those later diagnosed as schizophrenic were generally similar to those of the nine other patients. However, in certain ways the schizophrenics did differ: three of the schizophrenics demonstrated markedly inhibited sexual behavior and the only two patients of the thirteen who had good job stability were both later diagnosed as schizophrenic. In relation to the crime itself, the schizophrenics tended to have the longest time periods of overtly adequate adjustment immediately prior to the offense (one to five years in three cases), and in all four cases where the time lag between the precipitating "insult" and the crime was more than forty eight hours, the offender was later diagnosed as schizophrenic. In addition, following the crime, the four schizophrenics all either called the police or acted in such a way that someone else was sure to call them and their reaction afterward was "righteous" in every case.

Follow-up investigation in January 1958, (ranging from four to eighteen months after final disposition at this unit) indicated that the behavior patterns of all thirteen offenders were essentially unchanged from the time period of our last observations, and that the four patients diagnosed as schizophrenic (all of whom had been committed to a state mental hospital) were still clearly psychotic, while the remaining patients (who had been sentenced to varying terms in the state penitentiary) were still clearly not psychotic.

Although this study indicates that there are certain common consistent factors in the life patterns of persons who commit or attempt to commit a "sudden" murder, it is quite possible that some of these factors are not specific for this group of offenders but apply to all offenders of any kind referred to our unit. For this reason we are currently analyzing data from other "control" groups of offenders for comparison.

In summary, this preliminary study of eleven men and two women who—never having been in serious trouble before —suddenly committed or attempted to commit murder shows that there are consistent patterns in their life histories and offenses. Such persons appear to be quite different from the usual delinquent or criminal. The "sudden murderers" come from cohesive family backgrounds, where conformity to the rules of the social system was emphasized. Failing in the attempt to conform because of underlying conflicts, such persons have tended to blame other people and, as a result, to feel alone and isolated.

It is when such persons seem to be getting along quite well, when others expect them to be even more conforming and mature, that these men and women become most aware of their shortcomings. Then they become more and more tense and more and more angry. At such a time even a slight insult or provocation sets off the violent surge of rage that results in murder.

After the crime, the murderer is almost always bland, relieved or even righteous, for the end-result of his crime is to remove him from further responsibility to act as an adult.

This study has resulted from research being done at the Social Maladjustment Study Unit of the Malcolm Bliss Mental Health Center in St. Louis, whose goal is to contribute to the understanding and prevention of adult antisocial behavior and to the treatment of criminal offenders.

# Suicide in Murderers

## T. L. DORPAT

A STUDY of 114 consecutive suicides showed that five had committed murder just prior to their own suicide. In addition to presenting the five cases, this paper suggests a consistent pattern for the act and presents an hypothesis on the underlying psychodynamics.[1]

Suicide following murder is not rare—more murderers kill themselves than are executed.[2] A number of studies show the incidence of suicide in murderers to be between 4% and 35%.[3-5] In the largest series from the United States, the rate was 9%.[5]

## CASE REPORTS

### CASE 1

A Negro man, aged 39, known as a "woman chaser," was subject to periods of depression. His wife learned about his most recent affairs and filed for a divorce, after which he moved out of their apartment. Two weeks later he shot and killed his wife and then himself.

### CASE 2

A Caucasian man, aged 28, had courted a beautician for several years, and for some time had lived with her. She moved out of his apartment after a quarrel. One morning, as she opened the beauty parlor, he shot and killed her and then killed himself.

REPRINTED with the permission of the author and the publisher from T. L. Dorpat, "Suicide in Murderers," *Psychiatry Digest* (June, 1966), 27:6:51-55.

### CASE 3

A man, aged 59, was an alcoholic who had been married twice. He had been moody and depressed, and said that he had nothing to live for. His paramour, a married woman, had threatened to leave him. One day both were found shot to death. He had the revolver in his hand.

### CASE 4

A man, aged 61, an alcoholic and paranoid schizophrenic, had become increasingly paranoid and withdrawn. A few days before his suicide, his wife had called her daughter saying that she was frightened. She said that he had warned her he would not tolerate a separation. Her body was found near the door to their trailer, as if she were about to leave, and he was found shot to death on the couch.

### CASE 5

A man, aged 41, an alcoholic and single, while drinking began arguing with two men in his hotel room. He shot both men (killing one and wounding the other) before killing himself.

In addition to the five cases from this suicide study, three other cases involved men who killed themselves immediately after killing their wives in a setting of prolonged marital conflict and severe psychologic disturbance. In two cases, there had been a recent threat of separation or divorce, and in the third a separation had occurred just prior to the murder and suicide.

## DISCUSSION

The following constant factors were present in the cases cited. Together they could be considered a murder-suicide syndrome.

1. The suicide followed immediately after the murder.

2. There was an intimate relationship between a man and a woman.

3. The man was disturbed, frequently psychotic.

4. The histories indicated that the relationship was marked by prolonged, bitter conflict, and that the murder and suicide came at a time of violent emotional struggle between the two.

5. Frequently the act followed a real or threatened separation.

A review of the literature was made to see if other studies described the same pattern of dynamics, but no systematic psychiatric investigations could be found. More meaningful data, largely of a statistical and descriptive nature, were discovered in the criminologic and sociologic literature. In a study of 621 murderers, Wolfgang[4] found that 24 (4%) of the murderers later killed themselves; 22 of the 24 were men. In most cases, he found the relationships between the murderer and his victim had been long and intimate. In these cases, the suicide followed almost immediately after the murder.

That the men were seriously disturbed and often psychotic was supported by the study[6] of 27 murderers, in which it was determined that suicide attempts and suicide tendencies were more frequent in the psychotic group than in the non-psychotic group. An investigator[7] reported a psychotic man who killed his wife, and then made a suicide attempt (nearly fatal) when he was threatened by commitment to a mental institution. In a study of 175 murderers,[3] it was found that suicide attempts following the crime were rare in the "normal" group, but occurred in a fifth of the psychotic cases. Less than one-third of the victims of the "normal" murder were family members, while nearly two-thirds of the victims of psychotic murder were close relatives, usually their wives.

Out of a total group of 389 suicides,[8] 18 were preceded by murder or attempted murder. In most of these cases, a man killed a woman and then immediately attempted to kill himself.

The threat of separation is mentioned in a study[9] of wife murderers. The subjects were unable to continue living with their mates, but were equally unable to be separated from them. Following the murder, it was observed that many had an impulse to suicide and some attempted suicide. An investigator[10] has described the role played by separation in precipitating a broad spectrum of psychiatric and psychosomatic illnesses. This factor in the etiology of suicide behavior was also studied by this author.[11]

## REGRESSION OF IMPAIRED EGO

How, then, can the psychodynamics of the murder-suicide syndrome be reconstructed? To the borderline schizophrenic or psychotic male, the threat of separation from the woman he needs brings about massive rage and a further regression in an already impaired ego. The murderer attempts to master the fear of passively experiencing the separation by actively bringing about that which is feared.

There is also regression to the undifferentiated phase of psychic development in which there is fusion of the self and object. Hatred may be turned either against the self or the object, or both. Research[12] showed that at the time of suicidal crises several patients felt diffuse anger toward both their analyst and toward themselves. They could not tell if murder or suicide, or both, was their aim. In the present study of attempted and completed suicide, it was also found that people who showed suicidal behavior were often unsure of the object of their hatred.[1,11] Threats of murder were frequent before the suicide or attempted suicide. One woman who ran excitedly out of her house with a loaded revolver, after a quarrel with her husband, said, "I didn't know who I wanted to kill most, him or me, or both."

Our findings agree with Cavan's observation,[8] that the murder and suicide appear to be part of the same act. If guilt for the murder and the need for punishment were the only motives for the suicide, one would expect to observe two separate but related acts. Because the murder and suicide occur together, would it not be more reasonable to suppose that the murderer wishes to die with his victim, and not because of killing her? Dying together is meant to gratify sexual fantasies and fantasies of reunion. Death has been equated with reunion in folklore and myth. Conscious religious beliefs stress reunion with loved ones in paradise, and it is not uncommon in marriages of long standing to find that the death of a spouse is followed in a short time by the sudden death of the grieving one. Fantasies of reunion after death are also frequently observed in suicidal patients.[11]

The work of Ernest Jones, in his two papers entitled "On Dying Together," supports the plausibility of the hypothesis that the murderers wished to die with their victims.[13,14] Dr. Jones proposed that the idea of a personal death does not exist for the unconscious, but is always replaced by that of sexual communion or birth. The ideas of sex, birth and death are extensively associated with one another, and he claims that the fantasy of dying together gratifies childhood sexual fantasies.

## SUMMARY

A study of eight cases, as well as the literature on murder followed by suicide, revealed a consistent pattern. The murderer was a psychotic, or a severely disturbed man, who killed himself immediately after murdering his mistress or wife. The murder came as a reaction to separation in a relationship marked by prolonged turmoil. It is hypothesized that the threat of separation brought about an ego regression in which rage was directed at both of the subjects, and that the murder-suicide was an acting-out of fantasies of reunion.

# Etiological Factors in
# First-Degree Murder

*GLEN M. DUNCAN, SHERVERT H.*
*FRAZIER, EDWARD M. LITIN,*
*ADELAIDE M. JOHNSON, and*
*ALFRED J. BARRON*

MURDER is a tragic phenomenon. Sociologists, criminologists, jurists, dramatists, and novelists have studied it widely. To the present, little has been known of the causation of lone murder (unrelated to murder committed by gangs). The question arose in our minds as to how this problem could be approached and the causation defined. Since capital punishment is the law in the United States in all but seven states, removal of the person charged with murder presents an obvious difficulty to long-term investigation, but we were fortunate in working in a state in which there is no capital punishment. A pilot study of the problem was set up.

Fifteen years ago the collaborative technique in therapy and research in neurosis, psychosis, perversion, and delinquency first established itself as a tool for investigation. This technique consists of equally intensive studies of the patient as well as the parents and other significant relatives of the patient. Pooling of the information thus gained enables investigators to validate omissions, distortions, and falsehoods and suggests fields or avenues for further inquiry. Such studies may range from exploratory interviews to long-term

REPRINTED from *The Journal of the American Medical Association,*
November, 1958, Vol. 168, pp. 1755-1758. Copyright 1958, by American
Medical Association.

Read before the meeting of the American Orthopsychiatric Association, New York, March 6-8, 1958.

analytic study of the unconscious. It is now established that, in cases of individual delinquency in children from so-called good families of all economic classes, the parents unconsciously foster and promote this behavior as a solution to their own unintegrated pathological needs. Similarly, there are adolescents whom we have studied who commit serious crimes, such as murder or sexual assault, and who also reveal a history of unwitting parental fostering of the offense. Timely intervention by pediatricians and general practitioners aware of such mechanisms has been of great value to the child and family. Wider knowledge of family patterns which predispose to adult murder might well be lifesaving.

## AIM OF PRESENT STUDY

With the collaborative technique as a mode of inquiry, this project was devised as a pilot study to search for possible common factors in the life stories of a number of adult persons convicted of first-degree murder and imprisoned for life at the Minnesota State Prison at Stillwater. There is no capital punishment in this state. The study was made possible by the understanding and cooperation of the warden, Mr. Douglas C. Rigg, and his staff, to whom our grateful thanks are due. Since the terms of our study required that special attention be focused on the attitudes and behavior of the parents of these persons, only those prisoners whose parents were available for interview were included in the study.

Since our aim was to explore solely the possible causes of homicide, we did not concern ourselves with the questions of management, treatment, or punishment of the convicted person. This contentious field of forensic psychiatry was not entered. However, it was hoped that material would emerge in the pilot project which could be further validated by study in other states without capital punishment and which might assist criminologists in prophylaxis against murder and against the continuance of a family pattern which predisposes to such criminal violence.

We emphasize that no study was made of murderers associated with gangs or of those to whom crimes of violence were part of the cultural way of life. We believe that such offenses are sociologically determined and are more or less predictable and that prevention is largely a broad social problem. It was with the individual, isolated murderer, with no record of violent crime, that this study was concerned.

## CRITERIA FOR SELECTION

The investigating procedure was as follows: Prisoners were selected according to certain criteria; namely, they were to be normally intelligent white men convicted of first-degree (premeditated) murder, who did not deny the crime and who were of middle-class background from families of good social standing. There should have been no history of addiction to drugs, alcoholism, organic disease of the brain, or epilepsy. There must have been no known history of psychosis prior to the murder. Both parents were to be available for interviews.

It should be noted that this was a preliminary study not involving extensive investigation of the parents' or prisoners' unconscious. It is to be hoped that this study will be followed by a more intensive collaborative investigation of the conscious and unconscious mental processes of prisoners and their parents.

In each instance it was made quite clear that the psychiatrists were in no way connected with the prison management, the courts, or the legislature. Participation of a prisoner would not influence his treatment or sentence in any way whatever. The prison psychologist, whom they trusted, explained the investigation to the subjects in advance and also introduced the psychiatrist to the subjects in each case. No information which the prisoner or relative wished to have maintained confidential was disclosed to anyone outside the research team. Parents and prisoners were told that their cooperation would help the investigators learn something which might be of service in the prevention of tragedies similar to their own. Of course, interviews were conducted in private.

In view of these provisions, there was minimal temptation to distort material in order to protect the prisoner or to modify his sentence. Only by such procedures could meaningful data be gathered and some measure of truth ascertained. Aside from important biographical facts, special attention was paid to the feelings and attitudes of each person interviewed and to understanding what contribution these might have made to the eventual crime. The psychiatrists were thus alerted to any attitude or manner of the parents which might have allowed their child to sense that a violent solution to disputes with others was an acceptable thing.

When six subjects had been selected, interviews were arranged with them and with their parents. In interviews with prisoners, the first striking impression was the readiness with which they discussed the crime and the events leading up to it. They also invited return interviews, although they knew that no legal advantages would accrue to them as a result of additional consultations. They did not try to escape responsibility for the crime or to lay the blame on others. Almost without exception, when the stories of prisoner and family were at variance the prisoner was found to be telling the truth. We wish to acknowledge our indebtedness to the prisoners and to their families for their ready cooperation and willingness to participate in the interviews.

These studies led to the conclusion that, among these prisoners, remorseless physical brutality at the hands of the parents had been a constant experience. Brutality far beyond the ordinary excuses of discipline had been perpetrated on them; often, it was so extreme as to compel neighbors to intercede for the boy. In no case was any effort made by the prisoner to conceal the crime or to evade capture.

The most striking aspect of the interviews with the parents was the remarkable aptitude of these persons for evasive shifting of blame. Nor was there any suggestion from them of self-criticism or guilt over their sons' upbringing or downfall. They repeatedly and steadfastly lied on many important matters of fact, often differing sharply from their spouses or offspring, and often they remained unshaken by glaring discrepancies.

We shall present reports of two of the six cases.

## REPORT OF CASES

### CASE I

In a jealous rage, a 30-year-old man found an ax and, in the presence of neighbors, killed his former sweetheart. Originally, he had seduced her away from his brother when the latter went to Europe on military duty.

This man, the second of six children, had been the target for the most violent uncontrolled brutality on the part of the father, who, although he had a good job as a shop foreman, was a philandering alcoholic and a physical and mental sadist in his relationships with the prisoner's mother. The father's wild beatings of the boy were so frightening that neighbor men often interceded. The mother said she continued to live with the father only "to be sure he did not kill one of the boys," while at the same time her husband doted on the older daughter, of whom the prisoner was violently jealous. The father often beat and choked the mother in the children's presence. He shouted that she was a whore and that he would kill her some day. From the time the boy was 3 years old, the mother said, he recurrently ran away from home because he was so terrified of the father. From the time the boy was 14 years old, his father accused him of vicious sexual practices with girls, a charge which was not true at the time. The mother said that the father constantly "spoke evilly about other people's sex lives" in the presence of the children. At no time did the father ever accept any responsibility for his brutal acts, and he never expressed any remose. The boy never dared to bring a young friend into the home.

The mother offered no protection to the child against the father's attacks, but she did console him afterward. She never called the police to protect the boy. She and the prisoner leaned on each other emotionally, and apparently he was always tender with her. At no time did the mother express any guilt or responsibility for having kept the boy in such a savage environment, and at the time we saw her the next oldest son was experiencing a similar life with the father. The prisoner said that without her warmth and comfort he would have killed himself long ago. He cried and moaned about his love for her for 15 minutes when she was first mentioned in the interview. He could not recall any conscious hostility toward his mother.

He always felt that his fiancée was better than he and above him socially. He made no protests when she had promiscuous affairs with others and left him. Later, for a time, he tried to win her back, after she had married. However, he began to live with a woman 10 years his senior, an occurrence which prompted his former fiancée to divorce her husband and to attempt to woo him back, promising marriage. As a result of this, he abandoned the woman with whom he had been living, whereupon the former fiancée began to go out with other men. The prisoner found an ax and killed her.

Several facts stand out in this case. First, the patient had strongly identified with his father. He saw how sadistic his father was toward the mother as well as toward himself. Although consciously he loved his mother, he hated her unconsciously for not protecting him from the years of savage attacks. Similarly, she seduced him with consolations after the assaults and sought his sympathy as years went on and her plight continued. The prisoner stole his brother's girl, felt she was above him, and then for a brief time consoled himself with an older companion. Finally, the savagery he had felt and learned at the hands of his father came out toward the alternately unfaithful and seductive fiancée. She was merely repeating the lifelong behavior of his mother, who alternately abandoned him to this father's brutality and then wooed him back with sentimental consolation.

His mother said that the father made no secret of his violent attacks on her sexually, verbally, and physically and that the sons knew all about these attacks. It was only by a stroke of luck that this prisoner actually was not killed by his father. The mother had always feared it and believed the father capable of it. The prisoner had known of his mother's fear for years. This boy, by direct example, learned that frustration and anger were to be handled by violence. He learned that men are brutal to women. The tremendous unconscious hatred for his mother, who submitted to the father and then turned to the prisoner for love, finally overwhelmed him at the expense of his alternately promiscuous and seductive fiancée.

## CASE 2

This prisoner was 27 years old when he strangled his sweetheart. When we saw him he was unable to account for his killing her. "Those 12 months with her—I wouldn't trade them even to being in this prison for life." He murdered her when she refused to marry him.

He said he wondered if he had not "misidentified" his victim with her interfering mother, of whom he said in all seriousness he would "gladly wring her neck." He also remarked, "If it hadn't been Rosie I killed, it would have been someone else—it was inevitable."

He was exceedingly bitter toward his own mother. "Mom hated me since the day I was conceived. I was an unfortunate burden on her. It wasn't my fault I was born. She has punished me ever since, though, for it. I can remember all the unmerciful beatings she gave me. She is happy now that she has completely destroyed my life."

He said she was vicious; she would choke him and beat him so hard with a barrel stave that he became bruised and bleeding. She used to say to him: "What did I ever do that God thinks I deserved to have you wished on me!"

His mother constantly belittled his father, and, whenever the father protested these humiliations, she threatened him with the "disgrace" of separation. "She destroyed any standing he might have had in my eyes," said the prisoner.

The mother told us of how her father "ran out" on the family when she was 5 years old, and she said he never supported them (a pattern her son repeated in the action of causing two unmarried girls to become pregnant and then abandoning them). Throughout her childhood the mother had been accused by other children of being illegitimate. No mention was allowed of the father by the family, and she had never heard other mention of him until she was 10 years old. It is clear how this hostility toward her father had carried over toward the son.

She reported that "the whole idea of John was a big mistake." She added that she had been angry about the pregnancy, blaming her husband's carelessness. She readily confirmed to us her son's account of her cruel and unusual punishment of him. It was remarkable to the interviewer how devoid she was of any sense of guilt about her rejection and cruelty. She explicitly said of his tantrums and ungovernable rages that "he acted how I felt." Local feeling in the community had been against the boy from the age of 5 years because of his violent temper, and from the age of 7 years he had been wrongly but persistently accused, over many years, of pushing a young companion to his death from a roof.

"His whole childhood was filled with anger," said the mother. She said she always thought he would get into trouble. "He grew up thinking the same way. He felt everyone was against him." At the time we saw her, she said she was glad the son was in prison and she hoped the authorities would never release him.

In this instance we have ample evidence for the prisoner's modeling himself after his vindictive and remorseless mother. She made it clear that the behavior of the son was in accord with her feelings. Satisfactory identification by the boy with his acquiescent, unprotecting father was not possible. The only close friend the boy had was an orphan boy older than himself who had lived with the family for a short while. As a boy, the prisoner often would stay away from school to dig worms for, and to go fishing with, a group of older men, who made much of him. His mother was aware of his truancy with these older men.

In the later life of this prisoner it seems that the mother of his sweetheart was the nominal target for his hostility, but when the girl herself spurned him he had no compunction about turning his vengeance on her. His lack of sense of guilt or restraint was modeled after those defects in his mother.

## COMMENT

The most striking common feature in four of the six cases was the continuous, remorseless brutality which the prisoners in question had suffered at the hands of one parent, in the face of the compliant acquiescence of the other.

We discovered evidence in the case of the remaining two that the prisoners were psychotic at the time of the murder, and, of these, one was clinically psychotic during the study. In these two cases there was no history of gross brutality.

An example of the level of the brutality in the four cases was an incident in which the father held up his nude little boy by the heels, belted him, then dropped him on his head to the floor. Recurrently, some prisoners, when children, had been flung bodily across a room. Only by chance were some of them not fatally injured. Although such violence was a common factor in the four cases, it should not be concluded from them that violence is the major factor in the etiology of murder. This, at present, we cannot say. Imitation and identification with violent parents, however, constituted the commonest pattern found.

Another impressive feature was the absence of a sense of guilt on the part of the parents, yet, when the circumstances of their own upbringing became clear, the source of their hostility and of their lack of remorse was obvious. The interviewers were startled by some of the transparent evasions and calculated lying manifested by most of the parents. Yet, in contrast, the prisoners were found, by investigation, to be giving true accounts of events. The probable reason for such a situation was that the prisoners had nothing to lose by telling the truth, wheras the parents were still trying to absolve themselves from any responsibility for the tragedy. This observation confirmed findings long known to prison authorities, namely, that prisoners are most cooperative when given the opportunity to be so.

Still another interesting observation was the fact that these psychiatrically unsophisticated prisoners showed a surprising degree of insight in relating their criminal violence to their family experiences. Furthermore, documented evidence showed that no prisoner had attempted to escape from the scene of the crime and that none had denied committing the offense. All defended their actions, but none disputed the fact of the killing or of the premeditation.

Of interest to psychiatrists was the constant finding of deep, unconscious homosexual tendencies, a finding which is not surprising in view of the brutality disclosed. Often these tendencies were revealed in frankly paranoid behavior. In three of the cases such trends were reinforced by contrasting favorable treatment of a sister.

In contradistinction to previous experience with individual juvenile delinquents and adolescents guilty of serious crime in whom unconscious parental fostering was a powerful factor driving the child toward acting-out, these adult persons, convicted of first-degree murder, revealed a minimum of unconscious parental fostering. Instead, the acts of violence seemed to be much more on a conscious imitative level, reflecting actual childhood experience.

An interesting aspect of the investigation was the consistent pattern of behavior and personality of the victims. Female victims were by turns seductive and rejecting; male victims were threatening figures who carried weapons.

It seems to the investigators that factors of brutality such as have been outlined above must come under the scrutiny of pediatricians and family physicians. Direct inquiry into the mode of punishment and discipline should be made by physicians whose practice includes the care of children. It is felt that intervention by them in known sadistic family patterns may well avert a later violent crime.

Clearly, since the studies here reported are preliminary and not statistically valid, additional extensive and intensive work must be done with similar subjects. To this end, work is already under way by us with teen-age first-degree murderers.

## SUMMARY

Six prisoners convicted of first-degree murder and their parents consented to undergo investigation by the collaborative technique in a pilot study. White male prisoners were selected who were of at least average intelligence, from middle-class families, not members of a gang, not alcoholic or epileptic, and with neither organic disease of the brain nor a history of psychosis.

Remorseless physical brutality inflicted through the childhood and adolescence of the prisoner at the hands of parents was a common factor in four cases. The other two prisoners proved to have been psychotic at the time of the murder, and these two had not been treated with such gross brutality.

Unconscious fostering by parents, such as has been described frequently in individual delinquency, was not observed in these cases. Rather, the prisoners learned to behave like their brutal aggressors and learned by conscious example that violence was a solution to frustration.

The need for family physicians and pediatricians to be aware of, and to intervene in, such brutal family patterns is emphasized with a view to preventing possible tragedy.

# PART IV

# Some
# Cross-Cultural
# Evidence

# Patterns of Homicide
# Among Tribal Societies in
# Africa

## PAUL BOHANNAN

IN A NUMBER of the [African] societies studied, some homicide occurs in dangerous but not illegal institutions in which people participate at their more or less consciously acknowledged risk. Homicide occurs with some regularity in the course of action associated with such institutions, but is "accidental" and not necessarily part of that institution. Members of the society are aware that the institution is dangerous, and that participation in it may lead to such accidents. Our own society institutionalizes automobile racing, which is admittedly dangerous. Even automobile riding demands a certain calculated risk. In all instances save those which involve gross negligence, homicide which occurs in such an institution is classed as non-culpable.

A second type of homicide is also non-culpable, but whereas the first type occurs as a fairly regular but accidental or unfortunate event and is outside the recognized and intended course of events of any institution, this second type is institutionalized. Here homicide which is classed as non-culpable actually occurs as an institutionalized, recognized activity. Omitting genocide (which Africans do not practice) and infanticide (which they no longer practice), there are two areas in which a society may institutionalize non-culpable homicide: the jural area and the ritual area. Institutionalized homicide in jural institutions is found in the Western world as execution of convicted perpetrators of specific crimes. It is carried out by officials of the state. In the societies examined here, "execution" is performed by other agents, but is still considered non-culpable and an institutionalized jural necessity.

Ritual killing, which is also a form of institutionalized homicide, is rare in this sample. It is suggested, and two or three cases of it appeared, among the Tiv, who, under certain conditions, consider it non-culpable. One Alur case is mentioned.[1]

We shall examine our material and these two types of non-culpable homicide before proceeding to those instances which are considered culpable in the societies in which they occurred.

Three of the seven societies represented here recognize institutions which are dangerous in that their activities increase the likelihood of homicide. Among the Tiv, the communal hunt with poisoned arrows is admitted to be extremely dangerous. Over 17 per cent of the Tiv homicides recorded occurred within this institution. The Luo of Kenya practice ritual wife-capture at marriage. They recognize it as a dangerous institution. They take both ritual and practical precautions to see that it does not end in "real" violence and in killing, but when it does so they make (or, in the indigenous system, made) ritual and domestic adjustments, not predominantly jural ones. The percentage of Luo homicides which fall into this dangerous institution pattern is much lower than that for Tiv, but it is nevertheless culturally significant. The Alur also have their "dangerous institution": dances which are attended by rival groups. The danger of these dances was recognized, and several days' ritual precautions were taken to guard against untoward incidents arising from them. Although these "immaterial sanctions," as Southall has called them, were highly effective, some homicides did indeed occur at these dances. Such non-culpable homicides were unsanctioned and were usually unpunished.

In most African societies either today or in the recent past, some forms of homicide are positively sanctioned: this sort can be compared to execution. It is the duty—at least the right—of a person to kill some people in some situations. One such situation is the ritual of sacrifice. In some areas, such as nineteenth century Dahomey and Ashanti, human sacrifice was generally used as a means of executing criminals, although slaves might also be sacrificed. Many African peoples acknowledge—or in the recent past acknowledged —the necessity for human sacrifices in specific religious institutions. Occasionally newly institutionalized homicide, definitely extra-societal, such as Mau Mau killings or the Diretlo murders of Basutoland, springs up in Africa even today. Insofar as these institutions are acknowledged by the peoples of the tribes where they are found, homicides occurring in connections with them must be considered as ritual, non-culpable homicide. They are branded criminal by the British-dominated law in all cases, and by "native law and custom" in many, but not in all.

Tiv, even though they are extremely upset when such killings are believed to have occurred, acknowledge the right of the "league of witches" or *mbatsav* to make certain human sacrifices. It is difficult to draw an objective line between those cases which a people such as the Tiv consider legitimate and those they consider criminal because the view of different individuals may vary depending on relationship to the victim and other factors. Because most of the "victims" are "killed by witchcraft"—death considered by Europeans to be from normal causes—these cases do not enter the criminal records. Ritual homicide is rare in Africa, by European definitions. If we accept African definitions, it is much more frequent.

Much less equivocal is the non-culpable homicide that occurs within jural institutions. In Western society, most cases in which policemen kill in the course of their duties are dismissed as excusable or justifiable homicide. Cases in which the victim of homicide was involved in commission of a felony at the time of his death are often dismissed by coroners' courts or otherwise excused as justifiable. The difference between excusable and justifiable homicide in interpreting African data would be mere pedantry. But examining the sort of victim and the situation found in non-culpable homicide elicts African patterns which are comparable with, though notably different from, those found in other societies.

First of all, thieves either now are or in the past have been the victims of non-culpable homicide in most of the tribes examined here (the point was not mentioned for the Luo or

Nyoro). Among the Soga, thieves were formerly subject to
execution by their victims, though today Soga concur that
such killing is felonious in spite of the fact that 15 per cent
of Soga killings are classified as "self-help justice." There are
examples of thief-killing for the Tiv, Alur, Gisu, and Luyia.
Among Tiv, they accounted for over 6 per cent of the homicides for which records existed, of Alur, 4.2 per cent. Killing
thieves has, of course, been universally proclaimed culpable
homicide by the British governments. However, judges tend
to be lenient to this type of killer.

Witches were or still are "fair game" in many African
societies, and killing a witch was sometimes considered not
only non-culpable but justifiable. The witch-killing pattern
emerges unequivocally for the Luo, the Alur,[2] the Gisu, and
the Nyoro. Luyia, with one example of a woman killing a
female witch, shows the pattern, but in only a very small
number of cases. Usually the witch is killed because he or she
was bewitching the killer's kinsman. Among the Nyoro particularly, the witch is likely to be female. The Tiv situation
of witch killing is more equivocal. Killing a witch may be a
jural act. Much more common, however, is killing a person
thought to be killing one for ritual purposes. Instead of a
jural or ritual act, this is an example of self-defense when
the legal or ritual force of the community is directed against
one. By their act of choosing a victim, the rationale goes, the
community has placed him outside the pale of the law—he
may fight with any weapons available to him. In all such
homicides, which appear as a form of self-defense, the British
judges tend to be lenient.

Killing an adulterer, although it is of course everywhere
considered a felony under British law, was not considered
by Gisu, Alur, or Luyia to be culpable. British judges, unless
premeditation can be proved, usually consider adultery a
mitigating circumstance in homicide cases, sufficient to reduce the charge to manslaughter.

Other non-culpable homicide patterns were mentioned for
the Gisu, the Soga, and the Luyia: the Gisu claim that provocation by certain insults makes resultant homicide non-culpable; Soga (and probably all the others) defend their right
to kill in self-defense; Luyia claim that killing in revenge for
killing is not wrong, though they realize that it is today considered a crime under British law.

Finally, we must note the different attitudes that exist depending on tribal membership of the offender and the victim. Southall notes in some detail the differential attitude Alur have toward killing tribesmen and foreigners: Alur not only kill non-tribesmen more readily, but they claim that killing a non-Alur is less heinous. Although it is not recorded in the Tiv essay, I have on several occasions been told the same thing by Tiv—one man who had just been released after serving three years of a sentence for manslaughter of a non-Tiv thought his sentence grossly unjust because he had killed a mere stranger.

Africans tend to evaluate the culpability of homicide not only in over-all terms of the institutions with which it is associated, but also by the relationship between the offender and the victim. The Fallers noted that Soga sometimes gives the relationship between killer and victim as the reason for homicide. Even we, of course, recognize some degree of differential moral turpitude depending on the relationship. This problem becomes of major concern in analysis of culpable homicide.

By far the most homicides in our samples are culpable: homicide that is branded as wrong in the society in which it occurs and that indicates the anomic state of the institution with which it is connected. The most important single factor to keep in mind in a comparative study of criminal homicide is that it, like any other culture trait, must be studied firmly within its social and cultural setting. To lift a homicide out of its social context for comparison with a homicide in some other society or at some other time is to rob it of its significance and meaning. For homicide in a society does have meaning: after eliminating non-culpable homicide, we have a series of situations with which at least some people in the society could deal only by killing. Repetition of these situations indicates weak points, or points of stress, within the social organization of the group concerned.

Several factors are to be noted in studying the repetitive situations of homicide typical of various societies. First is the relationship between the criminal and his victim. Criminologists have only recently become interested in this relationship and, as we shall see, have not yet faced the task of interpreting the place of this relationship in a more general social and cultural setting. Wolfgang[3] has shown that some concern for the matter goes back as far as Tarde, but the only major source of theory on which he could draw for his Philadelphia material was Hans von Hentig's book, *The Criminal and His Victim*. We shall in turn interpret our data in connection with Wolfgang's Philadelphia study, since it is by far the most advanced and thoughtful analysis of the subject.

Hentig's and Wolfgang's books have shown that kinship and family relationships between homicide offenders and victims in Western society are comparatively simple—compared, that is, to Africa. Obviously this is a function of a simpler kinship system and of the reduced range of family relationships in modern Western life. Here I shall examine the African material on the basis of sex distinctions, comparing it with some material from modern Europe and America. Then I will proceed to a fuller comparison of the relationships themselves, first kinship relationships and then others.

Wolfgang has shown the necessity for keeping the offender and the victim figures separate when discussing homicide. In Philadelphia during 1948–1952, the time covered by his study, Negroes were 73 per cent of the victims and 75 per cent of the offenders; males were 76 per cent of the victims but 82 per cent of the offenders. Table 1 shows the rates per 100,000 in Philadelphia.

TABLE 1.   *Homicide Rates in Philadelphia,*
*per 100,000 Population*

|  | VICTIM | OFFENDER |
|---|---|---|
| Negro |  |  |
| male | 36.9 | 41.7 |
| female | 9.6 | 9.3 |
| White |  |  |
| male | 2.9 | 3.4 |
| female | 1.0 | .4 |
| Both |  |  |
| male | 9.0 | 10.2 |
| female | 2.6 | 2.0 |

We cannot present data strictly comparable with Wolfgang's because the population counts and homicide records with which we worked in Africa are vastly inferior to those with which he worked in Philadelphia. However, two significant factors do emerge. First, it is obvious that homicide rates among American Negroes are several times as high as those among African Negroes. Material from British East Africa (where the records are best and the police systems efficient in most areas) allows the comparisons made in Table 2.

TABLE 2. *Annual Homicide Rate of Offenders per 100,000 Population*

| | |
|---|---|
| Soga | 4.0 |
| Luyia | |
| from | .7 |
| to | 7.9 |
| Uganda Tribes | |
| from Amba | 1.1 |
| to Sebei | 11.6 |
| Philadelphia Negroes, 1948–1952 | 24.6 |

If it needed stressing, here is overwhelming evidence that it is cultural and not biological factors which make for a high homicide rate among American Negroes. More homicides may go unreported in East Africa than in Philadelphia, but the difference would still be significant.

It is, of course, not our purpose to analyze the anomic position of the American Negro. But we note that insofar as homicide is indicative, his position is more grave than is that of socially dislocated African Negroes.

Second, African rates tend not only to be lower than American Negro rates, but lower than American rates for the general population, and strictly comparable with rates from Europe, as well as with other primitive societies where the information is available.

Differences between males and females both as victims and offenders have been of primary concern in most studies of homicide because the difference is so startlingly significant. In his Philadelphia study, Wolfgang found that 76 per cent of the victims and 82 per cent of the offenders were male, while only 48 per cent of the population of Philadelphia were males. Taking both Negro and white races, the male rate per 100,000 was 9.0 for victims and 10.2 for offenders,

TABLE 3.  *Annual Homicide Rate of*
*Offenders per 100,000 Population*

| | |
|---|---|
| 18 American cities, 1948–1952[a] | |
| from Milwaukee | 2.3 |
| to Miami | 15.1 |
| Uganda Tribes | |
| from Amba | 1.1 |
| to Sebei | 11.6 |
| U.S., 1946 | 6.3 |
| Britain[b] | .5 |
| Bison-Horn Maria[c] | 6.9 |
| Ceylon[b] | |
| from Muslims | 2.5 |
| to Sinhalese | 7.4 |

[a] Wolfgang, *op. cit.,* pp. 25.
[b] J. H. and M. A. Straus, "Suicide, Homicide and Social
Structure in Ceylon," *American Journal of Sociol-*
*ogy, LVIII,* pp. 461–469.
[c] Verrier Elwin, *Maria Murder and Suicide,* London,
Oxford University Press, 1943.

whereas for females it was only 2.6 and 2.0. Wolfgang's summary of the literature on this subject[4] showed his figures
approximately representative for America: most of the studies
he cites found that between 70 and 80 per cent of the offenders
were male; a few studies found an even higher proportion
of males. In some European countries, he found, the proportion of females is very much higher: in England between
1900–1948, the proportion of females was 57 per cent of
victims and 32 per cent of offenders, showing a ratio among
offenders of 2 males to 1 female, compared with the Philadelphia rate of 5 males to 1 female. Pollak noted[5] that in
Italy during the late part of the last century, the rate was
63 female offenders per 100 male offenders, that is, almost
40 per cent of offenders were women.

The proportion of female offenders in the African societies
studied here is even smaller than it is in most Western com-
munities. The highest proportion of female offenders, 9 per
cent, was found in three tribes—Gisu, Nyoro, and Luo—
while in all other cases the proportion was well below 9
per cent. The Philadelphia figure for female homicide
offenders is 17.6 per cent. However, this figure is made up
of two subcultures—Negro and white—which show very

different homicide patterns. Of all Negro offenders, women are 20 per cent in the Philadelphia sample; of all white offenders, women are only 10 per cent. The African data, thus, indicate not only that Negro women are offenders in Africa even less often than Negro women in Philadelphia, but even less often than white women are offenders in Philadelphia. It may be argued, but is difficult to prove, that African women use poison and "get away with murder." However, this charge is brought against women everywhere in face of overwhelming lack of evidence.[6]

TABLE. 4.   *Proportion of Female Offenders and Victims of Homicide*

| | TOTAL CASES | FEMALE OF- FENDERS | PER CENT TOTAL OF- FENDERS | FEMALE VICTIMS | PER CENT TOTAL VICTIMS |
|---|---|---|---|---|---|
| Tiv (accidents omitted) | 122 | 5 | 4.0 | 22 | 18.0 |
| Gisu | 99 | 9 | 9.0 | 17 | 17.0 |
| Nyoro (intentional) killings only) | 34 | 3 | 9.0 | 21 | 62.0 |
| Soga | 100 | 2 | 2.0 | 45 | 45.0 |
| Luyia (those found guilty of murder or manslaughter) | 80 | 4 | 5.0 | 19 | 24.0 |
| Luo | 47 | 4 | 9.0 | 12 | 25.0 |
| Alur | 47 | 2 | 4.0 | 8 | 17.0 |
| Philadelphia | | | 18.0 | | 24.0 |
| Britain | | | 32.0 | | 57.0 |

It is among victims that the greatest differences appear in the African societies. The number of female victims of homicide runs from 17 to 25 per cent among five of the tribes studied here (Table 5). This figure compares with 23.6 per cent in the Philadelphia sample (24 per cent for whites, 22 per cent for Negroes). In two of the African tribes, however, the proportion of female victims soars. Among Nyoro they reach 62 per cent of intentional killings, and among Soga 45 per cent of the total homicide victims. This high incidence of female victims occurs among the only two tribes of Interlacustrine Bantu represented here, suggesting that the posi-

TABLE 5.   *Sex of Killers and Their Victims*

|                        | TIV    | LUO  | NYORO | GISU | LUYIA | SOGA | ALUR |
|------------------------|--------|------|-------|------|-------|------|------|
| ♂ kills ♂              | 75.4%  | 71.7 | 35.4  | 69.5 | 70.0  | 55.0 | 47.6 |
| ♂ kills ♀              | 16.4   | 21.7 | 55.8  | 15.1 | 20.0  | 43.0 | 14.3 |
| ♀ kills ♀              | 1.6    | 2.2  | 5.8   | 2.2  | 3.8   | 1.0  | 2.4  |
| ♀ kills ♂              | 1.6    | 2.2  | —     | 7.7  | 1.2   | 1.0  | —    |
| Multiple victims or offenders | 5.0 | 2.2 | 3.0 | 5.5 | 5.0 | — | 35.7 |

tion of women in those tribes is a focal point for difficulty. Both Beattie and the Fallers have in fact indicated in their essays that such is the case. Yet, there are two other tribes in our sample—the Gisu and the Luyia—who have been influenced by the Interlacustrine Bantu, particularly the Baganda. In neither case have the domestic institutions—if that is indeed what the high female homicide victim rate illustrates—been seriously affected by Interlacustrine patterns or attitudes.

When we consider the sex both of victim and of offender, as is set forth in Table 5, we find that for most of the tribes (the exception is Nyoro) the majority of cases are male victims of male killers. This figure runs from 55 per cent of cases among the Soga to over 75 per cent of cases among the Tiv. Only the Nyoro have the maximum in another area— 56 per cent of cases are men killing women, whereas only 35 per cent are men killing men. This fact may be accounted for by the fact that the Nyoro sample takes only cases in which intent was proved; the Alur sample shows 39 per cent of cases with female victims also show intent, whereas 61 per cent do not.

Veli Verkko has, on the basis of Scandinavian and some comparative data,[7] put forward some hypotheses about the proportion of female participation in homicide. Reduced to its simplest terms, he has postulated that the percentage of female participants (both victims and offenders) is high in areas where homicide is of low frequency, and low in those areas of high frequency. In other words, according to his hypothesis, homicide by female offenders is fairly constant, and the variation in rates found in various societies and at different times is accounted for by male offenders.

Among Philadelphia killers, Wolfgang found Verkko's hypothesis verified, but he rejected Verkko's explanation that the fact can be accounted for by biological qualities of the sexes.[8] Murderousness can no more be assigned as an attribute of one sex over the other than it can be assigned to one race over another, unless all other possibilities have been exhausted. Preliminary questions lie in the area of the adjustment of women to the roles that they play in their societies.

The African data do not verify Verkko's hypothesis. In all the societies we have considered, the homicide rate can be considered to be low, by Verkko's definitions. The range of female offenders is also low in all cases, while the proportion of female victims ranges from 17 to 62 per cent.

Although Verkko's hypothesis about female homicide rates is not valid for Africa, it would seem to be possible to formulate an hypothesis under which both Verkko's results and our own may be admissible: it may be that, in the vast majority of societies, men kill in the same situations and similar patterns as do women—and in some others besides. Save in situations of serious and widespread domestic stress, it is the "some besides" which most affects the rates and the changes of rates. This hypothesis makes two assumptions: that woman's primary concern is in the domestic institutions, that men must in addition adjust to other institutions. Although women may be better adjusted to the institutions in which they participate, their range of participation is in most societies narrower. The second assumption is that the homicide rate is composed chiefly of anomic homicide.

There is, however, more to the study of offender-victim relationships than differential sex rates. Criminologists themselves have done some further work in this regard, but for many of them statistics and rates become an end instead of a means.

The first step that faces any student of the relationship between offenders and victims in homicide cases is how to classify them. There is no "natural" classification; rather, the classification must vary with the society of analysis. How, then, do we compare the various societies and their typical classifications? I have worked in an *ad hoc* way, beginning with Wolfgang's categories, which he derived from police files in Philadelphia, and I have added whatever categories I have needed to get three African societies and a Danish sample sensibly onto Table 6. This process has meant sub-

TABLE. 6. *Victim–Offender Relationships*

| | ALUR | TIV | GISU | SOGA | PHILA-DELPHIA NEGROES | 172 DANISH KILLERS |
|---|---|---|---|---|---|---|
| Kinsmen | | | | | | |
| Spouses | 8.9 | 8.8 | 11.0 | 37.0 | 19.5 | 12.2 |
| Other affines | — | 5.5 | 5.0 | 8.0 | | |
| Parents | 2.2 | — | 11.0 | — | | 4.0 |
| Children | 4.4 | | | | | 33.1 |
| Agnates | 6.7 | 24.4 | | 5.0 | | |
| Others | — | 5.5 | 11.0 | 6.0 | 4.4 | 7.5 |
| Sex partner or rival | | | | | | |
| Paramour, mistress, or prostitute | — | 2.2 | — | 2.0 | 10.0 | 8.7 |
| Paramour of mate | — | 7.7 | 3.0 | — | 3.0 | |
| Rival | — | | | 5.0 | 5.0 | |
| Homosexual partner | — | | | | .5 | 1.7 |
| Total | 22.2 | 54.1 | 41.0 | 63.0 | 42.4 | 67.2 |
| | | | | | | |
| Close friend [same village or lineage] | — | | 17.0 | 6.0 | 31.0 | 4.0 |
| Acquaintances | 46.7 | 14.4 | | | 14.0 | 21.0 |
| Stranger | 8.9 | | | 10.0 | 8.0 | 7.6 |
| Enemy | 15.5 | | | | 3.0 | |
| Felon or officer | 4.4 | 8.8 | 17.0 | 1.0 | .5 | |
| Innocent bystander | 2.2 | | | | 1.0 | |
| Total | 75.7 | 25.2 | 34.0 | 11.0 | 57.5 | 32.6 |
| | | | | | | |
| Relationship unknown | — | 23.3 | 24.0 | 20.0 | | |

dividing the categories almost every time a new society is added. If the categories are broad enough to be comparable, they are also more or less meaningless in specific instances. Obviously, "family relationships" will not work as a category in tribal society on the same basis as it will work in modern Western societies. I have changed this category to "kinsmen (including affines)"—whereupon most of the material other than spouses and parents from Western society has to be put in a category called "other," for it is hopelessly miscellaneous. Less obvious—but more difficult—is the notion of "close friends" and "acquaintances" as cross-cultural categories. Friendship lacks the biophysical basis of comparison that is evident in kinship. It also lacks any full-fledged cross-cultural analysis that can be used as a background for classification. There is not, so far as I know, a cross-cultural study of friendship.

However, when the data is forced onto a chart, to give us at least primary comparability, several points do emerge. When Tiv kill kinsmen, they kill agnates; when Soga and Philadelphia Negroes kill kinsmen, they kill spouses; when Danes kill kinsmen they kill their children; when the Gisu kill kinsmen they kill parents and spouses—theirs is, in fact, the only high incidence of killing parents. It also indicates that Philadelphia Negroes have much higher incidences of killing mistresses, sex rivals, or mates' paramours than do Danes or Africans. It shows that killing of felons is very much higher among Tiv and Gisu than among Soga or Philadelphia Negroes. These indications have to be explained.

First, however, we must examine in greater detail the patterns for killing kinsmen. Comparison is difficult because kinship systems and kinship institutions vary so greatly from one culture to another. For example, Svalastoga uses, for Danish material, the categories spouse, children, parents, secondary relatives.[9] As anthropologists are all aware, not a single one of these categories is unequivocal in the African situation—not even the first. "Parents" is likely to include mothers' sisters and fathers' brothers in many African societies. "Children" often includes all one's clansmen younger than oneself. And "secondary relatives" may be a satisfactory catch-all in European studies but, when applied to Africa, hides the most important aspects of the problem. Even when the precise biological relationship can be traced between an offender and a victim, it must still be evaluated in the kinship nomenclature and system of the society in which it occurs, else it will be without meaning. I have therefore tabulated the relationships first in general categories (Table 6) and then in descriptive categories (Table 7). Several interesting correlations emerge from this classification. We

TABLE 7. *Kinsman Victims*

| | GISU | TIV | LUO | LUYIA | NYORO | SOGA | ALUR |
|---|---|---|---|---|---|---|---|
| **Kinsmen** | | | | | | | |
| **Ascending Generation** | | | | | | | |
| Father | 7 | 0 | 0 | 3 | 1 | 1 | 1 |
| Class. father (inc. FaBr) | 4 | 5 | 0 | 4 | 0 | 0 | 0 |
| Mother | 4 | 2 | 0 | 0 | 1 | 0 | 0 |
| Class. mother | 1 | 0 | 0 | 0 | 1 | 0 | 0 |
| Mother's brother | 1 | 1 | 0 | 0 | 0 | 0 | 0 |
| Other | 0 | 2 | 0 | 0 | 0 | 0 | 0 |
| **Ego's Generation** | | | | | | | |
| Brother | 5 | 7 | 1 | 4 | 1 | 1 | 2 |
| FaBrSon | 0 | 1 | 0 | 2 | 0 | 0 | 0 |
| Sister | 0 | 0 | 1 | 0 | 0 | 0 | 0 |
| Other | 0 | 1 | 0 | 2 | 0 | 2 | 0 |
| **Descending Generation** | | | | | | | |
| Brother's Son | 0 | 4 | 0 | 0 | 0 | 1 | 0 |
| Child | 0 | 1 | 0 | 0 | 1 | 0 | 0 |
| Son | 0 | 0 | 0 | 1 | 0 | 0 | 0 |
| Daughter | 0 | 1 | 0 | 1 | 0 | 0 | 2 |
| FaBrSoSo | 0 | 1 | 0 | 0 | 0 | 0 | 0 |
| FaBrDaSo | 0 | 1 | 0 | 0 | 0 | 0 | 0 |
| **Affines** | | | | | | | |
| **Ascending Generation** | | | | | | | |
| Father-in-law | 2 | 0 | 0 | 2 | 1 | 0 | 0 |
| Mother-in-law | 1 | 0 | 0 | 0 | 2 | 0 | 0 |
| Father's Wife | 0 | 1 | 0 | 2 | 1 | 0 | 0 |
| BrWiFa | 0 | 0 | 0 | 1 | 0 | 0 | 0 |
| Other | 0 | 1 | 0 | 0 | 0 | 1 | 0 |
| **Ego's Generation** | | | | | | | |
| Wife | 7 | 8 | 6 | 5 | 8 | 39 | 2 |
| Husband | 4 | 1 | 0 | 0 | 0 | 0 | 0 |
| Brother-in-law | 2 | 1 | 0 | 1 | 0 | 0 | 0 |
| Brother's Wife | 0 | 1 | 1 | 1 | 1 | 0 | 0 |
| Co-wife | 0 | 0 | 1 | 1 | 1 | 0 | 0 |
| Son's Wife's Fa | 0 | 0 | 0 | 1 | 0 | 0 | 0 |
| HuBrWi | 0 | 0 | 0 | 0 | 1 | 0 | 0 |
| BrWidow's Hu | 0 | 0 | 0 | 1 | 0 | 0 | 0 |
| Other | 0 | 0 | 0 | 0 | 0 | 6 | 0 |
| **Descending Generation** | | | | | | | |
| Mistress' Da | 0 | 1 | 0 | 0 | 0 | 0 | 0 |
| Co-wife's Da | 0 | 0 | 1 | 0 | 0 | 0 | 0 |
| HuBrDa | 0 | 0 | 0 | 1 | 0 | 0 | 0 |
| Son's wife | 0 | 0 | 0 | 0 | 1 | 0 | 0 |
| Other | 0 | 0 | 0 | 0 | 0 | 1 | 1 |

shall first list them before going more deeply into the institutional patterns of the societies in which they occur.

Only two kinship relationships between killer and victim were found in all tribes of our sample: in all tribes, wives were killed and brothers were killed. No other relationship between killer and victim is found in them all. Killing the father, fairly common among the Gisu and present among the other Bantu tribes, was absent among Tiv and Luo. However, killiing fathers' brothers was of extremely high frequency among the Tiv, present among the Gisu, but not noteworthy elsewhere. Tiv and Luo are also the only tribes that show no examples of killing parents-in-law.

Although all tribes showed uxoricide—some of them very high rates of uxoricide—only two (Gisu and Tiv) showed any examples of killing a husband. In the one Tiv case, there was no intent—which leaves the Gisu as the only tribe in which husband-killing is present to any appreciable degree (4 per cent of the total cases, 4 of the 9 cases of female offenders). Killing of the wife's brother occurs in three of six societies (twice in one; once in each of two others); and killing the brother's wife occurs once in each of four societies. Two Nyoro killed mothers-in-law because they claimed that these old women encouraged their wives to break up their marriages. The only other mother-in-law victim was among the Gisu.

When generation is considered, still other patterns emerge. Gisu is the only tribe in which there are more victims in the ascending generation than in the killer's generation—La-Fontaine's explanation of tense intergenerational conflict is borne out: in tribes such as Luo and Soga, the intergenerational conflict is at a minimum; conflict centers in ego's

TABLE 8. *Summary of Kinsman Victims, by Generation*

| | ASCENDING GENERATION | | | KILLER'S GENERATION | | | DESCENDING GENERATION | | |
|---|---|---|---|---|---|---|---|---|---|
| | *Kin* | *Aff.* | *Total* | *Kin* | *Aff.* | *Total* | *Kin* | *Aff.* | *Total* |
| Gisu | 17 | 3 | 20 | 5 | 13 | 18 | — | — | — |
| Tiv | 10 | 2 | 12 | 9 | 11 | 20 | 8 | 1 | 9 |
| Luo | — | — | — | 2 | 8 | 10 | — | 1 | 1 |
| Luyia | 7 | 5 | 12 | 8 | 10 | 18 | 2 | 1 | 3 |
| Nyoro | 3 | 4 | 7 | 1 | 11 | 12 | 1 | 1 | 2 |
| Soga | 1 | 2 | 3 | 3 | 45 | 48 | 1 | 1 | 2 |

generation—in both cases, in the marriage relationship. The Nyoro are interesting for the fact that the marriage relationship is the pivot of conflict, but it extends into both the ascending and descending generations.

With one exception, the tribes represented here do not kill kinsmen of the descending generation. There are no cases at all among the Gisu, and only negligible numbers of cases among the other tribes—save the Tiv, in which almost a quarter of the victims are in the descending generation from the killer.

Another factor which lends itself to ready comparison— and the meaning of which must also be explained—is differential use of weapons for homicide in various societies. It has been repeatedly stressed by criminologists that killers commit homicide with whatever weapon may be handy. The implication is that the weapons used are no more than a reflection of patterns of cultural activity in the society concerned. The fact remains, however, that some societies stab, others beat, and still others shoot. The African situation, from the tribes represented here, is summed up in Table 9.

Africans are not allowed, under colonial government, to have rifled guns without a license (though some may have clean-bore, muzzle-loading guns without one). The number of small arms or rifled firearms is small in African societies. The rarity is reflected in the fact that firearms as a means of homicide occur only in two tribes—the Tiv and the Nyoro. When accidents are omitted, only one case in each is recorded. Both are atypical. Since firearms are the most commonly used weapons in most Western societies (Philadelphia is atypical of America in this regard), the percentages of killings by means of cutting or striking implements is naturally higher in African societies than in our own. In only two of the societies represented here is there a significant difference between the two methods—again, they are Nyoro and Tiv. Both societies stab. Or, more accurately, both societies, but especially the Nyoro, avoid striking and beating.

These facts, like those of offender-victim relationships, must be explained in terms of the culture of the social groups in which they occur before they can be compared meaningfully.

Another mode of explanation followed by some criminologists has been in terms of motive. Wolfgang traced this

TABLE 9. *Weapons Used in Homicides*

| WEAPON | TIV 87 | GISU 99 | LUO 44 | NYORO 34 | SOGA 100 | LUYIA 114 | ALUR | PHILA-DELPHIA |
|---|---|---|---|---|---|---|---|---|
| **Piercing and cutting** | | | | | | | | |
| Arrows | 30.0 | 2.0 | — | — | — | 1.8 | 0 | |
| Spear | 3.5 | 12.1 | 11.2 | 29.4 | 3.0 | 9.5 | 10.6 | |
| Axe and adze | 5.6 | 1.0 | 4.9 | 5.9 | 5.0 | 3.5 | | |
| Knives (including machete and *panga*) | 33.3 | 23.2 | 38.4 | 26.5 | 22.0 | 26.3 | 23.4 | |
| | 71.4 | 38.3 | 54.5 | 61.8 | 30.0 | 41.1 | 34.0 | 39.0 |
| **Striking** | | | | | | | | |
| Hoe and scythe | — | 4.0 | 0 | — | — | 5.3 | 4.2 | |
| Sticks | 17.2 | 27.3 | 9.8 | 11.8 | 21.0 | 27.2 | } 40.4 | |
| Blows | | 9.1 | 24.5 | — | 3.0 | 12.3 | | |
| Pestles and other household implements | — | 6.1 | — | — | 2.0 | — | 6.4 | |
| | 17.2 | 46.5 | 34.3 | 11.8 | 32.0 | 44.8 | 51.0 | 22.0 |
| Arson | — | — | — | 8.8 | — | 1.8 | — | |
| Firearms | 1.1 | — | — | 2.9 | — | — | — | 33.0 |
| Strangling | — | — | — | 8.8 | 3.0 | — | 4.2 | |
| Misc. or unknown | 10.3 | 15.2 | 11.2 | 5.9 | 35.0 | 12.3 | 10.6 | 6.0 |
| Total | 100% | 100 | 100 | 100 | 100 | 100 | 100 | 100 |

practice in criminology back to Tarde.[10] Several contributors to this book have found motive a useful tool for exposition. However, I have found it useful for comparison only in a rough sort of way, because motive is even more difficult to comprehend cross-culturally than are kinship relationships. In order to illustrate the difficulties involved, I have taken the two contributions to this book which give the fullest analyses in terms of motives, and have compared them, in Table 10, with Wolfgang's analysis of motive for Philadelphia offenders (both Negro and white).

The most obvious fact about Table 10—at least, it was obvious in constructing it—is that the motives assigned by various writers to homicide in various societies are not comparable. To determine whether this lack of comparability is a factor in analysis or one in data, it is essential to look at the method of analysis and the definitions used by the various writers. Wolfgang has had space to be specific in this matter. His statement of the difficulties is worth quoting at length:

The present analysis of motives is necessarily rudimentary and relies upon terminology used by the police to describe those factors which prompt one individual to take the life of another. The Homicide Squad uses the term "motive" in descriptive summaries, but it is well aware of the fact that most underlying "causes" and unconscious motivations usually lie beyond the realm of necessary

TABLE 10.   *Motives for Homicide*

|  | PHILADELPHIA | GISU | SOGA |
|---|---|---|---|
| Altercation of relatively trivial orgin (insult, curse, jostling, etc.) | 36.5 | | |
| Resentment of authority | | 5 | |
| Property rights (including beer distribution) | | 12 | |
| Drunken brawl | | 10 | 12.0 |
| Response to provocation | | 10 | |
| Domestic quarrel | 13.4 | | |
|   Marital disputes | | 10 | 48.0 |
|   Quarrel over bride-wealth | | 2 | |
|   Control of women | | 5 | |
|   Quarrel with in-law | | | 3.0 |
|   Quarrel with agnatic kinsman | | | 4.0 |
| Jealousy | 11.1 | | |
| Altercation over money | 10.3 | | |
| Altercation over land | | 3 | |
| Robbery | 7.9 | | |
|   Killing in connection with another crime | | | 3.0 |
| Revenge | 4.8 | 4 | |
| Accidents | 4.5 | | 8.0 |
|   Intervention in quarrel | | 2 | |
| Self-defense | 1.3 | | |
| Halting a felon | 1.1 | 17 | 15.0 |
| Escaping arrest | 1.0 | | |
| Other and unknown | 8.1 | 19 | 7.0 |
|  | 100% | — | 100% |
|  | (621 cases) | (99 cases) | (100 cases) |

police investigation. The term used in the present analysis refers to the ostensible and police-recorded motive.[11]

The major difficulty lies in Wolfgang's word "ostensible." An "ostensible motive" must be so in terms of some set of cultural valuations. He himself (to give him the benefit of any possible doubt) uses the culture of the members of the Philadelphia Homicide Squad. Therefore the "motive" classification which he gives (and which is duplicated in Table 10) is a part of the ethnographic data of the total situation. Our own contributors, likewise, have been led, in their recording of motive, to use the classifications of the societies concerned insofar as members of those societies explained them or as the contributors from intensive first-hand ethnographic knowledge understood them. Even so, as LaFontaine has pointed out, "a study of individual motive gives only the pattern of precipitating causes."

No better proof of the relativity of "ostensible" motive could be asked than that provided under the listing "domestic quarrel" in Table 10. In American culture, "domestic quarrel" means a quarrel between spouses. In the two African cultures it need not, and the authors have had to make finer subdivisions to accord with the facts of domestic grouping in those societies. In the same way, Wolfgang, who is writing of Americans for Americans, can use the word "altercations" and note that many seem of relatively trivial origin. The reporters of African societies, faced with a translation problem, have had to be more specific.

For a fuller evaluation of "motive" classifications we must be a little more specific about what we mean by "motive." A careful look at the categories that are to be found in Table 10 (all of which are used by one or more of the investigators),[12] shows several uses of the word "motive." Some motives are no more than situations of homicide (domestic quarrel, robbery); others are evaluations made by survivors (jealousy, resentment of authority). A domestic quarrel may be a situation in which homicide recurs, but it is not a "motive" for homicide. Calling it so is to fall into the same sort of logical error that the Fallers report for the Soga— confusion of a relationship with a cause for killing.

The word "motive" has been used with three meanings probably none of which is adequate in the light of dictionary definitions: (1) a psychic state that leads to an act (which MacDougall divided into emotion and intention); (2) an evaluation by survivors of an act of killing (which is, of course, not "motive" at all); and (3) a social situation in which homicide occurs, also not really a "motive." It is the last two of these points that are important here.

Assignment of "motive" by the survivors of a crime or a suicide is relative, without any doubt, to the cultural values; therefore, it varies in greater or less degree from one culture to another. These cultural evaluations of motive, as LaFontaine noted for the Gisu, may be "not entirely irrelevant in deciding the course of events after a murder took place." In the Gisu case, a man's lineage will support him in homicides with some motives, that is, their evaluation of his intentions; it will not support him with others. Evaluations, in this sense, are social facts whatever else they may be—they affect social action. In the three societies dealt with in Table 10, we have sets of social facts as they are perceived and acted upon by Philadelphia policemen and by informants in two African societies. In all these societies, the domestic situation is recognized as touchy, and marital or domestic disputes are recognized as a possible source of homicide. American ideas reflected here are that homicide is a very grave offense and is sometimes—relatively often—mysteriously committed for what appear to be minor motives or none. Furthermore, money is one of the basic values of Philadelphia society, and hence a motive. But altercation over money as a "motive" (incentive) for murder does not occur in the African societies. In Africa, rather, the recognized motives are fear of witches or revenge upon them, and land disputes in areas which are both dependent upon subsistence farming and short of land.

Thus "motive" becomes a social fact when it is made overt by the people of the society concerned, and when their regard for it affects the actions they perform after a homicide. However, studying homicide in terms of "motive" is often only a shorthand for studying social situations in which homicide occurs. Motives need explanation as much as rates among various relationships need it.

It has been the battle cry of anthropologists for over half a century that the procedure of lifting social or cultural facts out of context and comparing them with other facts also lifted out of context is inadmissible procedure. Until now, that battle cry has never been directed toward criminologists, who are still lifting crimes from context by comparing crime rates in general or rates of specific crimes—like homicide—in particular, or occasionally of classifying crimes by "motive."

The differential rates among the sexes are interesting social facts, but they need explaining. The differences in motive assigned by different peoples to homicide are interesting, but they too need explaining. The explanations of these differences and others must be begun by an analysis in terms of basic, functionally defined institutions. The institution comprehends the social relationships and social structures, the culture and the values which are represented in those situations in which homicide is recurrent.

We started this analysis of classification of homicides by pointing out that homicide occurs accidentally in dangerous institutions in some cases, and as an accident intermittently in others; that it may be institutionalized in jural and ritual institutions. In our discussion of culpable homicide we left the institutional frame of reference, and we must now return to it.

The most apparent institution to be involved with homicide —and, as we shall see, with suicide—is the domestic institution. Perhaps the most interesting thing about murder in domestic institutions is that the patterns displayed by men and by women vary comparatively little, whereas they vary almost wholly in nearly all the other institutions. It is nothing new to note that when women kill, they kill "within the family"—usually within the household. Yet, the patterns within the family vary greatly. Who the victim may be, and the means of killing are extremely variable.

First of all, except for the Gisu, killing the husband scarcely occurs in our sample. Rather, in Africa women kill their children, usually in a state of emotional stress following break-up of the family or contravention of important norms. This pattern is found among Tiv and Nyoro, and is almost precisely similar to one presented in a book of case histories by Wertham.[13] These murders of children are often followed by suicide or attempts at it. African women also kill co-wives in some of the tribes recorded here (Nyoro and Luyia). If the term co-wife includes the wives of the husband's close kinsmen, as in most African languages, the Tiv can be added.

When men kill women in domestic institutions, it is overwhelmingly their wives who are their victims—and in extended households this is not a redundant statement as it would be among ourselves. Uxoricide occurs in all our societies—indeed, it probably occurs in *all* societies. The pattern is clearest among the Soga, who have the highest rate, and the Nyoro, where men kill the wives they fear will desert them, thus breaking up the domestic group. In the latter tribe, two-thirds of the female victims of men are deserting wives or long-term mistresses. The Nyoro even extend this pattern to the wife's mother, who is thought to be in league with the absconding wife.

Yet, what appears to be the same pattern in wife-killing can be given vastly different expressions. Among the Luo, for example, uxoricide is not associated particularly with absconding wives, but rather with the disciplining of wives, leading to what are usually considered (at least by the murderous husbands) accidental deaths. In the Luo sample, 10 of 46 cases were of this domestic discipline type. The Luo are unusual in that a woman's brothers may join her husband in administering the discipline. This particular pattern does not occur in homicide cases elsewhere, even in the other East African societies in which bride-wealth is paid in cattle, and where presumably the desire of both husbands and brothers to keep the marriage going is to be found to the same extent.

Among the Soga, the large number of uxoricides (that is, high when compared to total homicides) usually takes place during domestic quarrels, giving still another pattern, though one possibly related to either or both of the above.

In some African groups, men kill men within domestic institutions. This factor is, of course, dependent on the shape and size of the domestic institution. The Tiv are the most pronounced in this regard—there we found men killing their senior kinsmen because they fear they are being bewitched, and their junior kinsmen whom they are bewitching or from whom they fear "counterattack." This pattern was discussed above under jural institutions, because it is undeniably a jural response, and because of the fact that it is likely to occur not only within the domestic group itself but also among kinsmen who live near one another but who do not actually form a single homestead. Tiv do not themselves consider this a domestic matter, but rather one associated with the lineage. This overlapping of the jural and domestic institutions also occurs among the Nyoro—when sorceresses are killed it is usually by a kinsman of their victims, so that the killer's act can sometimes be seen as an act within an anomic household.

One of the most interesting facts is the rarity of patricide. Only among the Luyia has it become a recognizable pattern: there it is usually some form of counterattack, for generally it occurs when the father becomes violent with his grown son. The Gisu show this pattern, but to a much lesser extent—it is, further, usually to the classificatory father, and especially the substitute father, that Gisu react. Father's brothers are more commonly killed in some of our societies than are fathers—the reasoning may be correct that they occupy the disciplinary and authoritarian roles of the father untempered by the kindly, instructive roles of the true father. The Tiv pattern of reaction against witches who are one's agnates can be seen as turning on the father-substitute who is in authority but is without paternal love and the emotional desire to protect.

Matricide is, compared to patricide, almost common insofar as the number of clear-cut cases is concerned. Among Tiv, matricide accounts for 2 of 16 female victims. Both cases showed a context of witchcraft. Among the Gisu, matricide accounted for 4 of 18 female victims, and among the Luyia, for one of 29 female victims.

It would seem, then, that when women kill or when men kill women, the family and household institutions are the ones in which the strain is severe. For women, there tend to be few other relationships in which the strain is sufficient to lead to killing. In our sample, a Gisu woman on one occasion killed a thief (it is rare that women participate quite so actively in this jural institution); there are a couple of examples in which women killed sexual assailants, thus getting into the pattern of killing in connection with a crime. These instances are rare. We can safely say that when women are concerned in homicide, the situation is likely to be domestic.

Aside from domestic institutions, accidents, and killing of witches and thieves in jural institutions, only a single theme occurs in which women are involved: in both Gisu and Tiv there are examples of killing an enemy's daughter, presumably to do him both psychical harm and to deprive him of a source of bride-wealth.

There remain the situations in which only males are involved. The most important factors here are economic and political.

It is, in most parts of Africa, pedantic to separate family institutions from economic institutions. This fact brings the land dispute cases recorded here into a somewhat equivocal position. The Luyia are the most important example because land dispute cases account for almost 10 percent of Luyia killings. The disputes are usually—but not always—between kinsmen. However, they are most often between kinsmen who no longer actually live in the same homestead, and hence they are not domestic in the strict sense of the word. Certainly they occur in terms of economic institutions.

The land-dispute killing occurs in the East African areas of land shortage. It does not occur among the West African Tiv, although land disputes are rife there, and in some areas land is extremely short. Land has, however, become a rallying cry in parts of East Africa, and is one of the major points of strain in the society. This fact emerges clearly not only for the Luyia but for the Gisu as well—and it must be kept in mind that land was one of the ostensible sources of strain that led to Mau Mau.

Aside from the land dispute pattern, the remarkable fact seems to be how *little* homicide occurs in economic institutions, or with an economic motivation. This factor is, of course, partly accounted for by the lack of institutions that are specifically economic—there are few production firms or institutions and only comparatively crude distributional institutions. But so-called "economic motives" are singularly rare in Africa. Undoubtedly this fact is a reflection of another, that is, in a subsistence-dominated economic system, it is not possible for an individual to enjoy the gains of his crimes any more than it is for him to enjoy any other sort of gains. He must share them. In the case of crime, however, his sharing his economic gains would also involve sharing his guilt. The community of sharers seems to act as a sanction against crime—or at least homicide—for gain. One case in Tivland did occur: a foreign trader was murdered for his goods, which were discovered a few days later, distributed among the offenders' kinsmen.

Among the Gisu, 12 per cent of the cases involved "quarrels over property rights other than land, including distribution of beer," and two cases involved sharing of bride-wealth. The latter situation is also equivocal—quarrels over bride-wealth are in a sense domestic, but usually occur between people who are members of different domestic groups. Cases involving quarrels over property that are certainly within domestic institutions or jural institutions can also be found in other tribes. The pattern is not one, however, which is dominant in any of the material.

It would be impossible not to comment here on alcohol as an element in patterns of homicide in African societies, even though its importance seems to be less than is commonly believed, even by Africans. Alur, Luyia and Gisu show "drunken brawl" as a pattern of killing. Southall, LaFontaine and I maintain, however, that this statement usually indicates inadequate reporting or interrogation and hence poor records. Killings that occur at drinking parties are seldom random. Seldom, when the information is complete, is a victim a stranger to his killer. The relationship of killer to victim is too often not given in the record of such cases—we think because the stereotype of killing wantonly in a drunken brawl is so commonly held by European officials that it is deemed sufficient explanation. At least some tribes know this and may take advantage of it. The entire problem of alcohol in Africa and its relation to crime (as well as to many other types of activity) awaits analysis. It would seem, however, to be as a catalytic agent rather than as a cause that alcohol appears in situations of homicide.

What becomes clear from consideration of killings connected with alcohol is that the tensions of one institution may erupt when the members participate in another institution. Killings that occur at beer-drinks among the Luyia and the Gisu tend to be part of a cycle not of beer-drinks, but of domestic or production institutions. The Luyia murders which fall wholly within the institution of the beer-drink are very few. Yet beer-drinks are neighborhood affairs, not domestic affairs. A pattern may, therefore, overlap two institutions: the tensions created in one may erupt in the course of activity in another.

There are, finally, two more patterns which should be mentioned but which seem to be confined to one or two tribes. The Soga seem to be unique in that a "shame" pattern of homicide emerges among them. "Shame" is given by several of our peoples as a recognized motive for suicide, but appears in homicide context in only this instance. The "interference" pattern is to be found among Luyia and, to a lesser degree, among their neighbors, the Gisu. These patterns defy institutional classification, for either "shame" or "interference" may be recognizable in several institutions. The pattern here, like that of the pattern of killing while drunk, forms an example of institutional linkage by common personnel.

It is interesting to compare the patterns we have discovered here with a series of patterns found among executed English murderers between 1949 and 1954.[14] The British sample, including only executed murderers instead of all homicides, would not be strictly comparable to our African samples if statistical means were to be employed or if we were trying to discover all the patterns of homicide in Britain. However, as a source for patterns which do occur, and to underline the narrow range of patterns in Africa, it is useful. In the 85 cases of murder in which offenders were hanged in Britain, two overwhelming patterns emerge, both of which are absent or very rare in Africa. The first of these patterns (25 cases out of 85) involves the murder of a mistress or girl friend. This is very much higher than is wife-murder, though of course our sample here may indicate only that wife murderers are not executed while murderers of mistresses are. The other pattern (16 out of 85) is the murder committed in the course of another crime. This factor occurs in Africa (the Soga material shows 3 out of 100), but it is relatively rare. The English sample also shows an interesting absence of parricide: among those executed there was one case of a man who killed his parents and three cases in which victims were affines. This fact may mean no more than that the English tend to declare anyone who kills a kinsman to be insane—a feature that we have found to be so in the Colonies: killing a kinsman would seem to English colonial judges to be proof par excellence of madness.

We have, throughout this discussion of homicide, emphasized the fact that homicide is a social relationship and that, to be understood, the social relationship between killer and victim must be seen in its institutional setting, with regularities and patterns noted. It would have been equally possible to make this analysis from the standpoint of role: the institutional and societal role of victim or offender or both—to ask what roles in society are homicidogenic. We did not do so because the relationship itself allows a more direct and simple analysis—if there were no other reason, it allows a single classification instead of demanding two, one for offenders and another for victims. . . .

# Murder and
# Other Deviance in
# Ceylon

## ARTHUR LEWIS WOOD

THE SOCIAL dynamics of deviance may be studied by lo-
cating in the social structure positions of relatively high
rates;[1] by identifying the situations experienced as stress;
and by discovering the relevant subjective responses which
facilitate acts of deviance. The approach makes possible an
historical analysis of the emergence of stressful situations
as well as a comparative intra-societal and eventually a cross-
cultural analysis. This conceptualization avoids the attempt
to enumerate the infinite factors present among unique cases,
and leaves largely to the psychologist the differentiation of
deviants and conformists who occupy similar social positions.
The procedure may be used to test empirically the possible
links between objective social conditions—e.g., ecological
and demographic characteristics—and acts of deviance.[2]

It may be assumed that one situation of stress is insecure
status position associated with intense ego involvement. Consequently, the purpose of this paper is to present evidence

REPRINTED with the permission of the author and the publisher from
Arthur Lewis Wood, "A Socio-Structural Analysis of Murder, Suicide
and Economic Crime in Ceylon," *American Sociological Review* (October, 1961), 26:5:744-753.

Paper presented at the American Sociological Association meetings,
New York, August 29, 1960. Space does not allow acknowledgment of
the many Ceylonese who made this study possible, though particular
credit is given to Dr. C. H. S. Jayewardene of the University of Ceylon
for the village interviews. The author held a Fulbright Research ap-
pointment. A grant from the American Philosophical Society made
possible statistical analyses and manuscript preparation, and the complete monograph will be published as one of the Society's forthcoming
*Transactions*.

from Ceylonese data for the hypotheses (1) *Homicide is most frequent in the lowest ranks of an achieved status system, particularly under conditions of subjectively experienced external restraints;* and (2) *Homicide is most frequent among persons alienated, demoralized, and showing reactions of hostility.*

Henry and Short identified low status as one of the conditions of "external restraint" (where "behavior is required to conform to the demands and expectations of other persons") in the explanation of high homicide rates.[3] In the formulation of the first hypothesis above, not *objective* external restraint per se, but conditions *subjectively* defined as undesirably limiting behavior, i.e., stressful or frustrating, are proposed as the basis for high rates of homicide. Thus, a low position in an achieved status system is postulated as more restraining than in an ascribed system. Insecurity of position, status deprivation relative to achievement aspirations, and positions culturally defined as illegitimate are examples of subjectively experienced external restraint. The second hypothesis above states that murderers are characterized by certain attitudes or orientations toward society. It is suggested that these emerge from situations of stress and are necessary for high rates of homicide—the links or intervening variables between social conditions and deviant behavior.[4] It is postulated that offenders against property and suicides also will be found most frequent under conditions of subjectively experienced external restraint, but with a tendency for them, particularly suicides, to be characteristic of higher status positions and of those persons positively oriented toward cultural norms and ethical principles.[5]

## METHODS

In addition to an historical and contemporary study of Sinhalese village life, the sources of empirical data are official government reports, a National Survey, and Village Studies. The National Survey is based on a questionnaire completed by local police officials for 577 persons officially charged with murder or attempted murder and 200 robbers-burglars, 457 homicide and attempted homicide victims, and 86 suicides (a police report is required on the latter) during specified months of 1956 and 1957. Variations in numbers of cases used in the following tables arise from "don't know" answers which were encouraged for the purpose of accuracy, and from statistical controls. Comparisons reported here are consistent among the three ethnic groups (Low-country Sinhalese, Kandyans and Ceylon Tamils), and are based on cases matched by age for males 17 and over. Table and text references to "murderers" also include attempt cases, shown to be similar by separate analysis.

Samples of the Village Studies are based on interviews with males aged 17 and over who had committed "grave" crimes (felonies) against persons (assault) or property during the previous five years (designated "offenders") and a representative sample (every nth case from a special census) of "nonoffenders" residing in the same three villages of the Sinhalese Low-country—total cases 145.[6] Identification of offenders was based on police records, corrected by our judgment of guilt or innocence of these and other persons from evidence provided by local informants. Village Studies were conducted for the ostensible purpose of surveying local conditions for the government and the University of Ceylon; villagers were unaware of the intent of the investigation. Comparisons reported here are consistent for the three villages separately analyzed, and all comparisons are based on cases matched individually by age. Paired sub-samples for offenders against persons-nonoffenders and offenders against property-nonoffenders[7] show only minor differences except where indicated. Reliability of these small samples is contingent on their homogeneity, comparability, and intervillage consistency.

## HISTORICAL PERSPECTIVE

The British extended their control of Ceylon to the less accessible Up-country interior region, formerly known as the Kandyan Kingdom, during the last century, and turned this mountainous region into vast tea plantations. Large sections of the Low-country arable land were subsequently brought under coconut and rubber estates. The impact of this agricultural revolution had far-reaching consequences. From a self-sufficient economy based on paddy cultivation, the country has come to import approximately half of its rice—the major item of food consumption. At one time, two-thirds of the Sinhalese population belonged to the highest Goyigama (cultivator) caste owning family plots of irrigated paddy fields and highland. Large proportions of these high status people were subsequently forced into virtual landlessness— tenancy, fragmentation of holdings, sharing of produce and annual rotation of land among claimants.[8]

Turning the country into the production of commercial agricultural crops forced the development of service industries. From the seat of government in Colombo and its harbor facilities, all forms of modern communication and transportation have been extended to distant sections of the Island. A school system has been established in rural areas, with the consequence that 70 percent of the adult male population are said to be literate. Control of specific diseases and accessibility of medical facilities have decreased the crude death rate to approximately 9. The government administrative machinery extends throughout the Island for purposes of taxation, village development, police protection, courts, public assistance, and other functions of a welfare state.

On a per capita basis, Ceylon is one of the richer Asian countries, although, like other industrially underdeveloped nations, the majority of people are poor by contrast with the small middle and upper classes. Relative to the nation's low rate of economic development and rapid population increase, the Island of nine million people is overpopulated. Acceptance of education as a means of upward mobility into positions of government as well as commercial white-collar and skilled employment has enabled only a few to realize their expectations (see Table 2, section 3). Many village cultivators, members of the Goyigama caste, have had to accept the traditionally degrading status of unskilled laborers, whereas some lower caste persons have achieved high social class positions as indicated by criteria of education, occupation or income.

Direct effects of these historical processes may be seen in the densely populated Sinhalese Low-country villages surrounding Colombo. By contrast, the isolated Kandyan Sinhalese have preserved their traditional way of life, also made possible because non-citizen *Indian* Tamils constitute the labor force on tea estates of this area. *Ceylon* Tamils, citizen residents of the Northern Province, are included in this investigation only for statistical comparisons with Low-country Sinhalese.[9]

## ECOLOGY OF DEVIANCY

Murder is traditionally and legally tabooed in Ceylon although its rate of 4.3 is comparatively high, considerably above the median of 1.7 for 36 countries of the world. The suicide rate of 7.3 is less than the median (8.5).[10] Except for cyclical variations, Ceylon's homicide rate has remained constant since the 1920's, while the incidence of suicide has increased from about 5.[11]

Ecological variations in rates of homicide show that they are not directly related to urbanization and its presumed social disorganization. Whereas homicide rates increase fivefold from the most isolated rural areas of the Kandyan region (1.4) to the hinterland *surrounding* Colombo (6.8), they are lower for Colombo itself (3.7) than for the total Sinhalese area.[12] Suicides contrast with this by their tendency to be more evenly distributed among these regions and by being relatively high in all non-rural areas despite their distance from the metropolitan center (all Sinhalese rural, 6.3; urban, 8.4). If some factors associated with non-rural conditions of living explain the incidence of suicide, an excess of homicides is perhaps a manifestation of the breakdown of traditional rural organization, though actually minimized by urbanization itself. Serious economic crimes, however, increase consistently with urbanization, from a low of 83 in the Kandyan provinces to 142 around Colombo, and to 475 in Colombo itself.

## SOCIAL STATUS OF DEVIANTS

By objective criteria of socio-economic status—title to arable land, occupation, employment for wages, and an English language education—there is a consistent tendency for offenders (cases of assault and economic crime are undifferentiated in these comparisons, except where indicated) to rank lower than nonoffender villagers (Table 1). Knowledge of local conditions makes these data meaningful. About a third of these offenders are cultivators, yet most of them possess far less land (section 1) than the three to four acres assumed necessary to support a family. Almost one-half of them work irregularly as unskilled laborers. Either position is a serious compromise with the traditional high status of the

TABLE 1.  *Percentages of Offenders and Nonoffenders by Status Categories*[a]

| STATUS CATEGORIES | OFFENDERS | NONOFFENDERS |
|---|---|---|
| 1. Title to Land[b] | | |
|     Under 1¾ acres | 71% | 36% |
|     1¾ acres or more | 29 | 64 |
|   Total | 100 | 100 |
|   Number of cases | 17 | 36 |
| 2. Occupation | | |
|     Unskilled and cultivators | 80 | 54 |
|     Semiskilled and higher | 20 | 46 |
|   Total | 100 | 100 |
|   Number of cases | 30 | 63 |
| 3. Employment for Wages | | |
|     Not regularly employed | 85 | 59 |
|     Regularly employed | 15 | 41 |
|   Total | 100 | 100 |
|   Number of cases | 27 | 54 |
| 4. English Language Education | | |
|     None | 93 | 70 |
|     Some English | 7 | 30 |
|   Total | 100 | 100 |
|   Number of cases | 30 | 63 |

[a] From Village Studies. Chi-square for sections: (1) 4.21; (2) 4.81; (3) 4.43; (4) 5.14. In each test, 1 d.f., $P<.05$, with correction for continuity.
[b] Arable land, calculated on proportional shares held in undivided plots. Data not obtained for one village.

Goyigama caste to which most of these villagers belong. Regarding the newer bases for status—regular wage employment and an English language education—these offenders have experienced little success (sections 3, 4).

Not low status per se, but low status subjectively defined as external restraint or severe deprivation is hypothesized as related to high rates of serious crime. A series of tests of this proposition is provided in Table 2. Based on the observation that one's father and family name are important objects of identification in Ceylon, it may be assumed that loss of status vis-à-vis father's position is a serious loss to ego. Thus, in

TABLE 2. *Percentages of Offenders and Nonoffenders by Indices of Self-Evaluation*[a]

| STATUS CATEGORIES | OFFENDER SAMPLE | | NONOFFENDER SAMPLE | |
|---|---|---|---|---|
| **1. Paddy or Highland Owned, by:** | *Fathers* | *Respondents* | *Fathers* | *Respondents* |
| None or only one type | 34% | 72% | 48% | 68% |
| Both types | 66 | 28 | 52 | 32 |
| Total | 100 | 100 | 100 | 100 |
| Number of cases | 29 | 29 | 63 | 63 |
| **2. Occupation, by:** | *Fathers* | *Respondents* | *Fathers* | *Respondents* |
| Unskilled and cultivators | 83 | 80 | 69 | 55 |
| Semiskilled and higher | 17 | 20 | 31 | 45 |
| Total | 100 | 100 | 100 | 100 |
| Number of cases | 30 | 30 | 62 | 62 |
| **3. Career, by:** | *Ambition*[b] | *Position* | *Ambition*[b] | *Position* |
| Unskilled and cultivators | 33 | 80 | 41 | 54 |
| Semiskilled and higher | 67 | 20 | 59 | 46 |
| Total | 100 | 100 | 100 | 100 |
| Number of cases | 30 | 30 | 63 | 63 |

| | Low | High | Low | High |
|---|---|---|---|---|
| **4. Occupation, by Education[b]:** | | | | |
| Unskilled and cultivators | 89 | 67 | 88 | 30 |
| Semiskilled and higher | 11 | 33 | 12 | 70 |
| Total | 100 | 100 | 100 | 100 |
| Number of cases | 18 | 12 | 26 | 37 |
| **5. Career Ambition,[b] by Education[c]:** | | | | |
| Unskilled and cultivators | 39 | 25 | 62 | 27 |
| Semiskilled and higher | 61 | 75 | 38 | 73 |
| Total | 100 | 100 | 100 | 100 |
| Number of cases | 18 | 12 | 26 | 37 |

[a] From Village Studies. Chi-square for sections: (1) 14.27, 3 d.f.; (2) 10.28, 3 d.f.; (3) 16.43, 3 d.f.; (4) 29.82, 3 d.f.; (5) for last two columns alone, 6.15, 1 d.f., with correction for continuity. In each test, $P < .05$. Each section tests differences between two variable in columns against a row variable. If each column variable is tested separately with row variable, all comparisons are not statistically significant.

[b] "Unskilled and cultivators" includes "no ambition."

[c] "Low" is less than fifth standard (about sixth grade) completed; "high" is fifth standard and over.

successive generations offenders are losing status in regard to ownership of highland *and* paddy land (both necessary for a successful farm operation, section 1), and occupational rank (section 2), relative to the changing positions of other villagers.

Status deprivation of these criminals is directly measured by data showing their own expressed career ambitions to be disproportionately higher in relation to achievement than is the case with nonoffenders (Table 2, section 3). Furthermore, if education is pursued for occupational advancement, it can be shown that nonoffenders with "high" educational achievement are twice as often successful occupationally as the corresponding criminals (section 4). Nonoffenders with considerable education not only have frequent occupation success comparable to their career ambitions, but those without the education and low occupational position, had low career ambitions (comparing sections 4 and 5). The opposite tendency exists among offenders: i.e., "high" educational accomplishment does not bring occupational success in spite of high career ambitions. In addition, the occupational failures among criminals with "low" education actually had occupational aspirations about as frequently high as other categories of villagers. Cumulative evidence suggests a self-image of relative failure for the offender group.[13]

Suicides are neither landowners nor regularly employed relative to the comparable group of homicide victims (Table 3, sections 1, 2; giving same conclusions as comparison with homicides).[14] National Survey data show that those committing self-destruction are characteristically persons who have left the occupation of cultivation for the achieved status system, even though subsequent failure has often followed their choice of career. This evidence suggests that suicides also experience external restraint or stress. The fact of their higher occupational position, however, is clear (section 3); and their desire for achieved success is indicated by the large number who pursued a course of English education (section 4).

## SOCIAL ATTITUDES OF DEVIANTS

Data of Table 4 provide evidence for the hypothesis that offenders and nonoffenders manifest differential attitudes or orientations toward society. Alienation of offenders toward

TABLE 3. *Percentages of Suicides and Homicide Victims by Status Categories*[a]

| STATUS CATEGORIES | SUICIDES | HOMICIDE VICTIMS[b] |
|---|---|---|
| 1. Title to Property | | |
|    None | 63% | 53% |
|    Some | 37 | 47 |
|    Total | 100 | 100 |
|    Number of cases | 24 | 121 |
| 2. Employment Status | | |
|    Unemployed | 47 | 18 |
|    Employed (inc. irregularly) | 53 | 82 |
|    Total | 100 | 100 |
|    Number of cases | 32 | 147 |
| 3. Occupation | | |
|    Unskilled and cultivators | 59 | 79 |
|    Semiskilled and higher | 41 | 21 |
|    Total | 100 | 100 |
|    Number of cases | 34 | 139 |
| 4. English Language Education | | |
|    None | 63 | 88 |
|    Some English | 37 | 12 |
|    Total | 100 | 100 |
|    Number of cases | 35 | 130 |

[a] From National Survey. Chi-square for sections: (1) .41; (2) 10.36; (3) 5.00; (4) 11.08. In each test, 1 d.f.; in sections (2), (3), (4) $P<.05$, with correction for continuity.
[b] Reasons for comparing suicides with homicide victims given in footnote 14.

their villages is suggested in answers to "Had you the choice, would you like to go on living in your village"? In their reasons for desiring to leave they complain of oppressive economic conditions or their enemies (section 1). Responses to "Has anyone ever had a rather serious dispute with you"? indicate the proclivity of offenders to become involved in altercations over property or alleged harassment (section 2).

Respondents reply to "What are the worst things a man can do"? by mentioning one of the serious crimes, gambling, or drinking, without differentiating offenders and nonoffenders. With the probe, "Why are these things wrong"? nonoffenders

TABLE 4. *Percentages of Offenders and Nonoffenders by Social Attitudes*[a]

| ATTITUDES | OFFENDERS | NONOFFENDERS |
|---|---|---|
| 1. Remain in Your Village? | | |
| Protests conditions and enemies | 39% | 13% |
| Little or no protest[b] | 61 | 87 |
| Total | 100 | 100 |
| Number of cases | 28 | 63 |
| 2. Bases for Serious Dispute[c] | | |
| Property, harassment | 47 | 8 |
| No disputes | 53 | 92 |
| Total | 100 | 100 |
| Number of cases | 30 | 63 |
| 3. Reasons for Immoral Behavior | | |
| Ethical principle | 33 | 61 |
| Other reasons | 67 | 39 |
| Total | 100 | 100 |
| Number of cases | 30 | 62 |
| 4. Toward Gov't Policies | | |
| "Liberal" | 77 | 52 |
| Neutral or "conservative" | 23 | 48 |
| Total | 100 | 100 |
| Number of cases | 30 | 63 |

[a] From Village Studies. Chi-square for sections: (1) 6.76; (2) 16.45; (3) 5.26; (4) 4.04. In each test, 1 d.f., P<.05, with correction for continuity.
[b] Includes "protests bad people."
[c] Interviewees were asked to describe their serious disputes. Disputes which involved known crimes are excluded in tabulation; if included, offender proportion rises from 47 to 80 per cent.

almost twice as frequently state their reasons in terms of ethical principles: e.g., mention of the Buddhist Five Precepts, "Because of our religion," "It would deprive other people of their rights," "These things cause misery to other people" (Table 4, section 3). Tabulated as "other reasons"—responses often given by offenders—are statements that declare these forms of conduct wrong in terms of self-interest: "One will not gain merit" (a Buddhist reference to the next life), references to legal consequences and "because they are against the law." This evidence suggests that offenders arise from sections of the population where persons have less often internalized the meaning of the Five Precepts such that the norms fail to be applied as guides for social conduct.

Prior to undertaking the Village Studies a new government had been elected to power with policies supporting economic reforms including development of the villages, Sinhalese as the official language, and the Buddhist religion. Reasons for the answers to the query "Is the party in power doing a good job in office"? provided a basis for identifying respondents holding a "liberal" view (favors economic development and opposes harassment by officials), and those more neutral (including reply "too soon to judge," and references to language or religious issue) or "conservative" (opposes economic development or complains of lax law enforcement). The fact that offenders manifest a more "liberal" political orientation (Table 4, section 4) again demonstrates their alienation from the village status quo, their hostility to traditional harassment, and suggests a constructive attitude toward the possibilities for economic improvement. It is significant, however, that most of the contrast between criminals and noncriminals is accounted for by property offenders rather than offenders against persons.[15]

Evidence from the National Survey on "immoral conduct" further differentiates deviant types. Imbibing intoxicating beverages and gambling are generally defined by Ceylonese Buddhism and village custom as immoral behavior; in fact, local option prohibits the sale of alcoholic beverages in most rural areas and gambling dens are proscribed by law. "Rowdyism," translated from the Sinhalese, refers to local bullies, the identification of whom finds wide agreement among villagers as well as local police officials in customary usage. On these three criteria and the record of police reports, arrests or convictions, robbers-burglars are more frequently committed to habitual patterns of "immorality" than homicides (Table 5).[16] Contrasts between suicides and homicide victims show the former to be strongly committed to the moral code, virtually never being designated "rowdy."

## CONCLUSIONS

Ceylon data indicate that a high incidence of assault is a manifestation of persons strongly alienated and demoralized.

TABLE 5.   *Percentages of Murderers, Robbers-Burglars, and Suicides, Homicide Victims by "Immoral Conduct"[a]*

| CONDUCT | MURDERERS[b] | ROBBERS, BURGLARS | SUICIDES | HOMICIDE VICTIMS[c] |
|---|---|---|---|---|
| 1. Uses Alchohol | | | | |
| Yes | 83% | 96% | 36% | 67% |
| No | 17 | 4 | 64 | 33 |
| Total | 100 | 100 | 100 | 100 |
| Number of cases | 273 | 76 | 28 | 111 |
| 2. A Regular Gambler | | | | |
| Yes | 26 | 67 | 12 | 22 |
| No | 74 | 33 | 88 | 78 |
| Total | 100 | 100 | 100 | 100 |
| Number of cases | 206 | 46 | 26 | 93 |
| 3. A "Rowdy" | | | | |
| Yes | 30 | 49 | 3 | 25 |
| No | 70 | 51 | 97 | 75 |
| Total | 100 | 100 | 100 | 100 |
| Number of cases | 264 | 75 | 35 | 127 |
| 4. Police Report, Arrest or Conviction | | | | |
| Yes | 40 | 70 | 14 | 32 |
| No | 60 | 30 | 86 | 68 |
| Total | 100 | 100 | 100 | 100 |
| Number of cases | 272 | 69 | 36 | 125 |

[a] From National Survey. Matching by age is for murderers-robbers, burglars, and separately for suicides-homicide victims. Chi-square is computed for each pair, respectively, for sections: (1) 7.17, 7.71; (2) 26.71, .73, P>.05; (3) 8.54, 7.12; (4) 18.10, 3.70, P>.05. In each test, 1 d.f., P<.05 except where indicated, with correction for continuity.

[b] Includes cases of attempted murder.

[c] Reasons for comparing suicides with homicide victims given in footnote 14.

It is maintained here that this orientation is in turn derivative not of all low status persons, but of those persons who feel their social deprivation, for whom even their modicum of status is being questioned. Alternatively stated, these persons have become committed to an achievement system or this system is being imposed to deny them a formerly ascribed status, i.e., a condition of subjectively experienced external restraint. This can be contrasted with traditional Sinhalese norms which legitimized low status as well as harassment of persons in this position possessing a concomitant submissive and fatalistic personality type.

Indirect evidence presented here supports the conclusion that suicides are strongly committed to the cultural norms. This orientation is functionally compatible with and perhaps derivative of a higher social status and a commitment to the achievement system, for which physical aggression is specifically dysfunctional.[17] Not high status per se, but relatively high status in conjunction with stress from an insecure achieved position is the structural component of a high suicide rate. The Sinhalese upper class apparently manifests infrequent suicide because of its secure ascribed position by virtue of possessing estates.

Because theory has often contrasted homicide with suicide, it is significant that the status of persons committing property crimes is not always differentiated from that of assault cases. The initial postulate regarding property offenders is not well supported. Robbers-burglars, however, are more often unskilled laborers than cultivators; consequently, they less often own land and more often they are unemployed instead of underemployed.[18] They have pursued their education a little further, and above all, these offenders are a product of more urbanized areas: they are deeply involved in a system of achievement. Although property offenders are not differentiated from assault cases by internalization of Buddhist Precepts, the former indicate clearly a permanent commitment to a life of "immoral conduct" and their attitudes toward improvement of village economic conditions show a positive reaction compatible with achievement as opposed to apathy.[19]

Murder and suicide may be legitimately studied from the viewpoint of psychodynamics, although these Ceylon data suggest that the explication of relative rates is to be found in social dynamics and from an historical perspective. Available evidence from child rearing practices, for instance, indicates an insecure Sinhalese personality type.[20] Whether this is related to homicide, however, apparently depends on a low status position and whether this position is undergoing deprivation in contrast with newer conceptions of egalitarianism.

The greatest frequency of homicide in Ceylon lies in the "rurban" villages of the maritime area. This is specifically the area where landlessness, excessive demand for nonagricultural employment, and the nontraditional role of subordinate status for the Goyigama caste have had greatest impact. Our empirical data show that murderers in this area have experienced these changes most keenly and manifest reactions of severe alienation with complaints of harassment.

If the corollary regarding the effect of land scarcity is correct, we would expect to find a larger proportion of Low-country Sinhalese homicides in contrast with other ethnic areas to involve disputes over land, and furthermore, these land disputes should be concentrated among kinsmen (claimants to land are among family members) as well as between persons of whom one or both own some land. These three contrasts are empirically confirmed.[21]

Unlike murder rates, those for suicide are increasing. This trend is historically related to increasing literacy, urbanization, and a larger middle class. Higher status and moral commitment for these persons preclude murder; suicide emerges as a manifestation of increasing numbers of persons in an insecure achieved status.

Whether trends, rural-urban areas, or characteristics of individual cases are compared, there is basis for concluding that increasing participation in an achievement as opposed to an ascribed status system is a necessary precondition for increasing rates of specified forms of deviance. The relationships, however, depend on the proportion of persons in the various status positions of the population and the stresses and strains that are subjectively experienced. Conceptually, it appears that stresses of a status position induce varying orientations to society (subcultural norms as intervening variables) which in turn facilitate or inhibit certain types of deviance. Differential rates of homicide and suicide are the direct effects of variations in these normative orientations.

# PART V

# Suggested Theoretical Propositions

# Status and the
# Relational System

ANDREW F. HENRY and
JAMES F. SHORT, JR.

## DATA

LET US assume that white persons are of higher status than
Negroes, that residents of the highly industrial North are of
higher status than residents of the economically depressed
South, and that males as a gross category rank higher in the
American status hierarchy than females, and let us test the
hypothesis that homicide rates are higher in the low status
categories and lower in the high status categories.

Cause of death by homicide statistics provide our most
reliable comparison of homicide rates of whites and Negroes.[1]
There were approximately ten times as many deaths of
Negroes by homicide in the United States in 1940 as deaths
of white persons by homicide. The rate for "all other races"
in the United States in 1940 was 33.3 per 100,000. The rate
for white persons was only 3.1 per 100,000. We have presented data elsewhere indicating that the overwhelming
majority of murders are committed by members of the same
race as the person murdered.

These data show a very much higher homicide rate for
the low status Negro category as compared with the rate for
higher status whites. The higher homicide rate of Negroes
does not appear to be merely a reflection of higher Negro
crime rates in general, since Negro rates of homicide and

---

assault are even higher in relation to white rates for these crimes than are rates for other crimes. Sutherland indicates that,

While 3.1 times as many Negroes as white persons, per 100,000 population, were arrested in 1940 for all types of crimes, 8.6 times as many were arrested for assault, 7.2 times as many for homicide, 4.7 times as many for robbery, 4.2 times as many for larceny, 3.4 times as many for burglary, and 3.0 times as many for rape.[2]

It has long been noted by criminologists that crimes of violence against the person are especially present in the Southern part of this country.[3] Thus, a compilation of "Urban Crime Rates, 1951, by Geographic Divisions and States" reveals the following facts with reference to murder and aggravated assault:[4]

TABLE 1.   *Urban Rates of Murder and Aggravated Assault, by Geographic Divisions of the United States, 1951*

| GEOGRAPHIC DIVISION | MURDER RATE | AGGRAVATED ASSAULT RATE |
|---|---|---|
| East South Central | 12.45 | 102.6 |
| South Atlantic | 10.30 | 214.9 |
| West South Central | 9.11 | 75.9 |
| East North Central | 4.33 | 66.4 |
| Pacific | 3.21 | 49.7 |
| West North Central | 3.05 | 52.3 |
| Mountain | 2.76 | 36.3 |
| Middle Atlantic | 2.56 | 34.9 |
| New England | 1.24 | 12.1 |

This regional variation in rates of crimes of violence against the person has usually been explained in terms of the traditions of feuding and lynching in the South and in terms of the large number of Negroes in that section of the country.[5] Regarding the latter point, however, we note with Sutherland that "homicides, at least, cannot be explained so simply, for the death rate by homicide for white persons in the South is approximately five times as high as in New England. . . ."[6] Negro homicide rates tend also to be lower in the North than in the South.

Table 2 brings together data on white and Negro homicide

rates for such states as had Negro and white homicide victims, and stable rates, for the year 1940. These states are
grouped according to the broad North-South distinction.

The median of white homicide death rates, from Table 2,
is 5.0, the rate of South Carolina and Virginia, two Southern
states. All eight Northern states fall below this median, while
eight Southern states out of eleven are above it and only one
below it. Three of the Border states, including Washington,
D. C., are above the median, and three below it.

The median of Negro homicide death rates is 33.5, the rate
of Indiana, a Northern state. Five out of eight Northern states
fall below this median, only two above it. Five out of eleven
Southern states are above the median. Of the Border states,
all commonly associated with "the South," only Maryland is
below the median.

The regional variation in crimes of violence against the
person conforms with our hypothesis that low status groups
have higher homicide rates than higher status groups. The
economically depressed South reacts to poverty and a generally lower socio-economic status with higher homicide rates
than the highly industrialized states of the North.

Porterfield has recently noted that "in Southern cities, with
some exceptions, crime rates are higher and suicide rates
lower than in non-Southern cities paired with the former.
Since the latter tend to be relatively high in socio-economic
status and the former relatively low, it turns out that higher
suicide rates appear in cities with higher, not the lower
status."[7] Uniform Crime Reports indicate, however, that the
Southern states do not have the highest rates in the country
for crimes against property, indicating that the North-South
differential is accounted for primarily by crimes against persons.[8] Porterfield's conclusion is of particular interest to our
theory. He finds that "areas with high suicide and low crime
rates are high in social status . . . ," and "areas of low suicide
and high crime rates have low scores for social status. . . ."[9]

The following table of death rates from suicide and homicide reveals the tremendous contrast in these rates between
the states comprising the East South Central and the South
Atlantic states, the two highest divisions with respect to
murder and aggravated assault in Table 1, and the states in
the New England and Middle Atlantic divisions, which had
the lowest rates of murder and aggravated assault.

TABLE 2.  *Number of Deaths from Homicide per 100,000 Population, by State and Race, 1940[a]*

| STATES | RACE | |
| --- | --- | --- |
| | WHITE | ALL OTHER |
| **North** | | |
| California | 3.9 | 24.8 |
| Illinois | 2.6 | 42.5 |
| Indiana | 2.2 | 33.5 |
| Michigan | 1.9 | 28.6 |
| New Jersey | 1.6 | 15.3 |
| New York | 2.0 | 20.2 |
| Ohio | 2.6 | 43.4 |
| Pennsylvania | 1.9 | 22.2 |
| **South** | | |
| Alabama | 6.9 | 34.4 |
| Arkansas | 5.1 | 24.6 |
| Florida | 7.5 | 59.4 |
| Georgia | 5.6 | 47.1 |
| Louisiana | 5.5 | 23.6 |
| Mississippi | 5.7 | 28.7 |
| North Carolina | 4.0 | 28.3 |
| South Carolina | 5.0 | 24.0 |
| Tennessee | 7.1 | 61.5 |
| Texas | 5.3 | 35.4 |
| Virginia | 5.0 | 27.2 |
| **Border** | | |
| Kentucky | 10.4 | 61.6 |
| Maryland | 2.8 | 32.4 |
| Missouri | 2.9 | 42.4 |
| Oklahoma[b] | 3.2 | 35.3 |
| Washington, D. C.[c] | 5.3 | 35.0 |
| West Virginia[d] | 5.4 | 54.3 |

[a] SOURCE: United States Department of Commerce, Bureau of the Census, *Vital Statistics Rates in the United States, 1900–1940,* (Washington: Government Printing Office, 1943), adapted from Table 20.
[b] Indian territory at the time of the Civil War, controlled by the Confederacy.
[c] Though the Northern capital during the Civil War, traditionally considered a "Southern" area.
[d] Broke off from Virginia during the Civil War.

TABLE 3.　*Number of Deaths from Suicide and Homicide per 100,000 Population, for Selected States, 1940[a]*

| STATES | SUICIDE DEATH RATES | HOMICIDE DEATH RATES |
|---|---|---|
| New England | | |
| Connecticut | 17.9 | 1.8 |
| Maine | 15.7 | 1.5 |
| Massachusetts | 13.3 | 1.5 |
| New Hampshire | 16.3 | 1.4 |
| Rhode Island | 12.6 | 1.4 |
| Vermont | 16.7 | 0.8 |
| Middle Atlantic | | |
| New Jersey | 16.4 | 2.3 |
| New York | 16.7 | 2.8 |
| Pennsylvania | 12.9 | 2.9 |
| South Atlantic | | |
| Delaware | 14.3 | 4.5 |
| Florida | 15.0 | 21.6 |
| Georgia | 9.1 | 20.0 |
| Maryland | 16.3 | 7.7 |
| North Carolina | 8.1 | 10.8 |
| South Carolina | 6.3 | 13.2 |
| Virginia | 14.9 | 10.5 |
| West Virginia | 10.3 | 8.4 |
| East South Central | | |
| Alabama | 8.3 | 16.4 |
| Kentucky | 10.1 | 14.3 |
| Mississippi | 6.4 | 17.0 |
| Tennesse | 8.8 | 16.6 |

[a] SOURCE: United States Department of Commerce, Bureau of the Census, *Vital Statistics Rates in the United States, 1900–1940,* (Washington: Government Printing Office, 1943), adapted from Table 21.

As we move from North to South in the United States, the probability of suicide decreases as the probability of homicide increases. At the same time, the proportion of Negroes in the total population is increasing with an associated strengthening of the rigidity of color caste. But the fact that rates of homicide remain higher in the economically depressed South than in the higher status North when the effect of race is held constant provides additional verification for our hypothesis that homicide is negatively related to position in the status hierarchy.

The relation between homicide and sex provides the third test of our hypothesis that homicide is inversely related to status. We would predict that homicide rates would be higher for females, the lower status category, than for males.

The facts contradict this prediction. In 1950, according to the Uniform Crime Reports, 5,482 males were arrested for the offense of criminal homicide. Only 854 females were arrested for the same offense in 1950. The same pattern holds up when we examine the distribution of arrests for assault by sex. Over 53,000 males were arrested for this offense as compared with about 6,300 females.[10] Over 7 times as many males as females were arrested for homicide and over 8 times as many males were arrested for assault. The male-female differential is somewhat greater for assault than for homicide.

With very few exceptions, such as homicide of persons under 1 year of age—committed almost exclusively by women—males commit more of all types of crimes than females. But an interesting and important difference between the sexes appears when we examine the number of homicides as a proportion of all crimes committed by each of the sex categories. In 1940, 8.4 per cent of all females committed to state and federal prisons or reformatories were committed for the offense of homicide. Only 4.2 per cent of all males committed were committed for the offense of homicide.[11] This ratio of approximately two to one is maintained over a number of years.[12]

There are two additional factors which may be introduced in an attempt to rationalize this contradiction. We have already noted that the homicide rate among Negroes, our low status category, is about ten times as great as the homicide rate among white persons. Since Negroes make up a disproportionate share of the total number of homicides, the status differentiation between males and females is worth examining. [In a previous chapter] we presented the finding that the suicide rate of Negro females correlated more highly with the business cycle than the suicide rate of Negro males. Since this finding represented the single exception to data showing consistently higher correlations for males than for females, we suggested that it was congruent with the observations of a number of writers that females in the Negro community tend to enjoy a prestige position equal to, if not exceeding that of males.

It is interesting that the same interpretation can be applied in the present contradiction. If it is true that the prestige position of the Negro female is higher, on the average, than the prestige position of the Negro male, we would predict from our hypothesis that the Negro female would have a lower homicide rate than the Negro male.

Data are not available adequately to test this formulation. If it is correct, however, further research should show that the ratio of male to female homicide among Negroes is higher than the ratio of male to female homicide among whites.

One additional "extenuating" factor may be introduced in the interpretation of the contradictory finding with respect to sex. Cultural definitions about the external expression of aggression differ by sex. The culturally-prescribed passivity for females contrasts sharply with the masculine premium on aggressiveness and physical strength.

We had assumed [in a previous chapter] that persons beyond the age of 65 years were of lower status than persons in the younger age categories and were forced to reject the hypothesis that the age category with the highest status would have the highest rate.

We are similarly forced to reject the parallel hypothesis positing higher homicide rates in the older, lower status age categories. Data collected by Frankel are presented in Table 4.[13]

Additional data are presented in Table 5 in the form of a rough index of homicide and aggravated assault by age groups in the United States.[14]

Beginning with the age group, 20–24, the relation between age and these crimes of violence against the person is clearly negative. Homicide is concentrated in the younger age groupings and is virtually non-existent beyond the age of 65.

In two of our four tests the hypothesis that homicide varies inversely with status is confirmed. In the case of sex, the hypothesis is not confirmed. We have offered several speculative rationalizations of this negative case but are unable to demonstrate them with the data available. The denial of the hypothesis when tested on sex is weakened, however, by three facts: (1) the proportion of all female criminals sent to

TABLE 4.   *Per Cent of Homicides Committed in New Jersey,*
*by Age, Nativity, and Race, 1925–34*

| AGE GROUP | TOTAL | NATIVE BORN WHITE | FOREIGN BORN | NEGRO |
|---|---|---|---|---|
| All Ages | 100 | 100 | 100 | 100 |
| Under 20 Years | 7.9 | 13.1 | 3.4 | 8.1 |
| 20–24 | 18.9 | 25.6 | 14.9 | 16.8 |
| 25–29 | 19.8 | 23.8 | 17.8 | 18.2 |
| 30–34 | 17.5 | 12.8 | 19.3 | 20.2 |
| 35–39 | 12.9 | 8.7 | 15.1 | 14.5 |
| 40–44 | 8.5 | 4.7 | 11.0 | 9.4 |
| 45–49 | 5.5 | 4.4 | 6.5 | 5.4 |
| 50–54 | 4.1 | 1.6 | 5.2 | 5.4 |
| 55–59 | 2.3 | 2.5 | 3.1 | 1.0 |
| 60–64 | 1.7 | 2.2 | 2.4 | 0.3 |
| 65 and over | 0.9 | 0.6 | 1.3 | 0.7 |

prison who are committed for the crime of homicide is twice
as high as the proportion of all male criminals sent to prison
who are committed for the crime of homicide. (2) Since a
disproportionate number of homicides are committed by
Negroes, and since the status position of the Negro female

TABLE 5.   *Homicides and Aggravated Assaults per 100,000*
*Population in the United States, by Age, 1950[a]*

| AGE GROUP | HOMICIDE RATE | AGGRAVATED ASSAULT RATE |
|---|---|---|
| All Ages | 4.20 | 39.48 |
| 15–19 | 4.84 | 39.47 |
| 20–24 | 10.27 | 101.95 |
| 25–29 | 9.84 | 99.17 |
| 30–34 | 8.14 | 83.59 |
| 35–39 | 7.16 | 67.94 |
| 40–44 | 5.84 | 54.41 |
| 45–49 | 4.78 | 40.62 |
| 50 and over | 1.91 | 14.40 |

[a] SOURCES:   for computing rates, United States Bureau of Commerce, Bu-
reau of the Census, *1950 Census of Population—Advanced Reports,* Series
PC-14, No. 5, October 31, 1952; and Federal Bureau of Investigation,
*Uniform Crime Reports for the United States and its Possessions,* Vol. XXI,
No. 2 (Washington: Government Printing Office, 1950).

equals and perhaps is higher than the status position of the Negro male, the finding that males commit more homicide than females becomes less damaging to our hypothesis. (3) The American culture pattern denies external expression of aggression to females while sanctioning it for males. Aggressive behavior is defined as a masculine trait. Docility and passivity are the prescribed feminine characteristics.[15]

Let us delay our interpretation of the negative relation between homicide and age until we have examined two additional sociological correlates of homicide, urbanism and urban ecological distributions.

Crime rates in general are positively associated with urbanism,[16] and it is often assumed that homicide is similarly related. Conclusive evidence is lacking, but several studies have been made.

Frankel comments that his findings, in New Jersey, do not confirm the higher urban homicide rates which are generally assumed to exist. By dividing New Jersey counties according to degree of urbanization, he provides us with an interesting rural-urban comparison (Table 6).

TABLE 6. *Degree of Urbanization and Homicide in New Jersey, 1925–34*[a]

| DEGREE OF URBANIZATION | AVERAGE ANNUAL RATE OF HOMICIDE PER 100,000 POPULATION 1925–34 | AVERAGE ANNUAL RATE OF COMMITMENT FOR HOMICIDE PER 100,000 POPULATION 1925–34 |
|---|---|---|
| Densely Urban Counties | 4.29 | 2.69 |
| Urban Counties | 5.13 | 3.43 |
| Semi-Rural Counties | 4.41 | 3.35 |
| Rural Counties | 4.70 | 4.08 |
| Total | 4.49 | 3.00 |

[a] SOURCE: Emil Frankel, "One Thousand Murderers," *Journal of Criminal Law and Criminology*, XXIX (January-February, 1939), pp. 672–88.

These data indicate a negative, rather than a positive, association between urbanism and homicide. "Densely Urban Counties" have the lowest average annual rate of homicide per 100,000 population and the lowest rate of commitment for homicide for the period examined. "Urban Counties" have the highest homicide rate, but "Rural Counties" have the highest rate of commitment for this offense. The greater differential between homicide rate and rate of commitment for homicide which is found in urban counties may be due to a higher proportion of murders committed by professional or organized crime. Such murders more often go unsolved than do murders committed by "legitimate" persons.

Vold quotes F.B.I. data indicating that the percentage of all rural crime comprising offenses against the person is higher than the percentage of all urban crime consisting of these types of offenses.[17] He cites Minnesota data, for which he claims greater reliability than F.B.I. data, indicating equal rates per 100,000 population of murder and non-negligent manslaughter for both rural and urban populations of Minnesota.[18] Vold concurs with Sorokin and Zimmerman that the data "seem to indicate a tendency to higher rural rates in offenses against the person, such as homicides, infanticides, and grave assaults."[19]

We had interpreted the relation between suicide and urbanism in Chapter V [not reprinted here] as a function of differences in the degree of familial and community control over behavior in urban and rural areas. This led us to relate theoretically the positive association between suicide and urbanism and the association between suicide and marital status under the more general relationship between suicide and the strength of the relational system.

It is unfortunate that data on homicide by marital status are so limited in view of the interesting reversal in the relation of urbanism to suicide and homicide. The positive association between urbanism and suicide was interpreted as one of three demonstrations of the negative relation between suicide and strength of the relational system. The negative association between urbanism and homicide suggests, by the same logic, the existence of a positive relation between homicide and strength of the relational system.

This suggestion is strengthened by the decrease in homicide with age. In Chapter V we formulated the hypothesis that the strength of the relational system decreases with age to account tentatively for the positive association between suicide and age. Once again, the relation of age with suicide and homicide is reversed. Suicide varies positively and homicide varies inversely with age.

If our hypothesis that the strength of the relational system decreases with age proves to be correct, it follows that the inverse relation between homicide and age may be viewed as a second instance[20] of the positive association between homicide and strength of the relational system. If involvement in meaningful relationships with other persons proves to be at a maximum in the age groupings under 45 years and at a minimum in the categories beyond age 65, both postulates of a positive relation of homicide with strength of the relational system and a negative relation of suicide with strength of the relational system would receive strong confirmation.

If the negative relationship of homicide, and the positive relationship of suicide with urbanism reflect the positive association of homicide and the negative association of suicide with the strength of the relational system, we would predict that homicide would be lowest in the same central disorganized areas of cities where suicide is at its highest. Research forces us to reject this hypothesis. Instead of being low, homicide is in fact concentrated in these areas characterized by extremes of "urbanism." Let us summarize briefly the data on the ecological distribution of homicide.

The ecology of homicide has been investigated by Schmid and others, and has been found to follow the pattern typical of many other indices of social and personal disorganization. Schmid summarizes his findings as follows:

First, about 25 per cent of the homicides were concentrated in a district less than ten blocks long and four blocks wide; with a population of 6,863 people, of whom less than 20 per cent are females, precincts Nos. 214, 215, 216, and 217, which constitute the large part of this district and 40 homicidal crimes, or relative to 100,000 of population, 58.0. Secondly, there is a fairly large percentage, about 20 in number, in the business district. Thirdly, computing the homicide rate of the residential sections north of Lake Union and the Lake Washington Canal with a population of 81,000 people, of whom over 50 per cent are females, and 12 homicidal deaths during decennium, 1914 to 1923 inclusive, we have the very low figure of 1.5 per 100,000 of population. Fourthly, in the industrial and residential sections in the southern part of Seattle there are about 52 homicides, which may well be considered disproportionate.[21]

More recently, Harlan has found the distribution of homicides in Birmingham to follow a similar pattern,[22] as has Lottier for the Detroit region.[23]

In spite of the general negative correlation between homicide and urbanism, more homicides are committed in the disorganized sectors of cities characterized by high residential mobility, anonymity, and extremes of "urbanism" than in the better integrated residential sections of cities. This contradiction was not present in our analysis of suicide. Studies of suicide indicated that suicide was rare in rural areas and reached its height in the central disorganized sections of cities.

The available data permit no more than the most speculative attempts to resolve this contradiction. Our other data suggested that the homicide rate would be low among persons freed from the restraints of neighborhood, family and community.

This contradiction points up sharply the difficulties in the use of ecological correlation. While the "central disorganized sectors of cities" include within them areas of "homeless men" and rooming house districts, they also include ethnic colonies composed of the more recent immigrants, Negro districts and the locus of operations of the underworld. And it is clearly impossible to determine from which one of these component sections is derived the population which accounts for the spatial correlates of suicide and homicide.

From the general negative correlation between homicide and status position, we would expect the low status ethnic and Negro inhabitants of these areas to raise the homicide rate. From the suggested relation between homicide and strength of the relational system, we would expect the "homeless men" and "anonymous" residents of rooming houses in these areas to lower the homicide rate.

Data are not presently available to permit untangling of the interrelationships among these variables in the central disorganized sectors of cities. But our formulation would lead to the suggestion that those groupings accounting for the high suicide rate in "central disorganized" areas would be sharply differentiated from those categories accounting for the high homicide rate in these same areas.

While we are unable to separate the effects of status and strength of relational system in these areas as they effect the rate of suicide and homicide, we are able to suggest tentatively that the operation of "organized crime" within these sectors would constitute an additional factor operating to raise the homicide rate. The volume of homicide generated by organized crime is difficult to measure and undoubtedly fluctuates with the intensity of gang warfare. Numerous writers have pointed out the rigidity and integration of the underworld culture. With its own set of values, techniques and tight social organization, the underworld society maintains exceedingly strong control over its members as a condition for survival in opposition to the legitimate world of law and order.[24]

Furthermore, one of the tools of the underworld is homicide. Murder of the stool pigeon is evidence of the seriousness with which violation of the social code is taken. The underworld culture sanctions and encourages the use of violence against legitimate society. Data are not available indicating the extent to which murders as part of the routine business of the underworld account for the high rates of homicide in disorganized areas. We suggest the hypothesis, however, that the high homicide rate may be accounted for in part by the maneuvers of organized crime, a highly integrated community operating within the anonymity of these disorganized areas.

The violent and murderous tendencies in the underworld culture, viewed in terms of our general theoretical formulation, provide support for the hypothesis that the external expression of aggression varies positively with the strength of external restraint. The underworld, viewed as a system, is subjected to constant pressure and restraint by legitimate society. The fact that the strong external restraints are associated with crimes of violence by the group subjected to the restraint provides a test of the hypothesis when applied at the system level.

## INTERPRETATION

Our examination of the relation between homicide and social control has been hampered by lack of data in many crucial areas. But using the research available, we have tried to test two hypotheses suggested by the material on suicide presented in Chapter V. Neither of these hypotheses has been tested adequately, but in both cases, the available data tend to confirm rather than to deny them.

The first hypothesis states a negative relation between status and homicide. The hypothesis held up when tested on race and by region, comparing rates in the industrial North and the economically depressed South, with race held constant. The homicide rate among Negroes, the low status category, is some ten times as high as the homicide rate among white persons, the higher status category.

Data by sex and age deny the hypothesis. Since males commit more of all crimes than females, and since cultural definitions about external expression of aggression differ radically by sex, the finding that females commit more homicide relative to other types of crime than males weakens this negative case. The positive association between status by sex and homicide is further weakened by the fact that the status differential between Negro males and females (the race committing a disproportionate number of homicides) is slight. In fact certain writers suggest that the status of the lower class Negro female may be higher than that of the Negro male. As in the case of suicide, the relation with status by age contradicts the hypothesis.

The second hypothesis states a positive relation between homicide and the degree of involvement in social cathectic relationships with other persons. If this hypothesis is correct, the homicide rate among the married should exceed the rate among the single, the widowed or the divorced. Durkheim's data do in fact indicate that "while family life has a moderating effect upon suicide, it rather stimulates murder."[25] Adequate test of this hypothesis for the United States would provide an important link in the test of our formulation. The available data, unfortunately, group together the sizable widowed and divorced categories and fail to discriminate between those who become "single," widowed or even "divorced" by murdering the spouse and those who belong to these categories because they either have never married or were legitimately widowed or divorced. If adequate test in the United States should confirm Durkheim's finding, it would provide striking support for the proposition that suicide varies negatively and homicide positively with the strength of the relational system.

The higher homicide rates found in rural as compared with urban areas support this proposition. In areas of extreme urbanism—the disorganized central sectors of large cities—the homicide rate is relatively high whereas the hypothesis predicts that it would be relatively low. Further, this finding is inconsistent with data showing a general negative association between homicide and urbanism. Evidence is inadequate to assess the relative importance of the presence in disorganized areas of low status ethnic and Negro categories which might be expected to have high rates of homicide. The presence of organized crime in these areas may account in part for the high rate of homicide since (a) murder is an approved tool of gang warfare and (b) aggressive behavior in response to the external restraints imposed on the underworld by legitimate society would be predicted by our formulation.

Homicide was found to be concentrated in the younger age categories. This is the reverse of the relation between age and suicide, with the highest rates of suicide centered in the older age groupings. In Chapter V we had suggested the hypothesis that the strength of the relational system decreases with increasing age. It is worthy of note that if further research should confirm this hypothesis, it would at the same time support our postulation of a negative association between suicide and strength of the relational system and of a positive association between homicide and strength of the relational system.

The data of this Chapter provide a very tentative confirmation of our two hypotheses, that homicide varies negatively with status and positively with strength of the relational system. The variables of status and degree of involvement in meaningful relationships have been related conceptually to the strength of external restraints over behavior.

Low status persons are required to conform to the demands and expectations of others by virtue of their low status. We have labeled the type of external restraint varying with status position as "vertical" restraint over behavior or restraint imposed by persons or groups higher in the status system. The strength of vertical external restraint decreases with increasing status. Our data showing a negative relation between homicide and status position lead us to the postulate that homicide varies positively with the strength of vertical external restraint.

Persons with strong relational systems are required to conform to the demands and expectations of others as a condition of the maintenance of these relationships. Persons involved in minimal relationships with other persons are subject to fewer demands and expectations simply by virtue of the slight degree of involvement. We have labeled the type of external restraint varying with the strength of the relational system as "horizontal" restraint over behavior, or restraint imposed by other parties to the relationship. The strength of horizontal external restraint increases as the strength of the relational system increases.

Our data very tentatively indicating a positive association between homicide and strength of the relational system lead us to the postulate that homicide varies positively with the strength of horizontal external restraint. Test of the hypotheses (1) that homicide rates are higher for the married than for the non-married, and (2) that the strength of the relational system decreases with age will provide either effectice confirmation or effective denial of this postulate. . . .

# Subculture of Violence—
# A Socio-Psychological
# Theory

## MARVIN E. WOLFGANG
## and FRANCO FERRACUTI

## PROBLEMS OF INTERPRETIVE ANALYSIS

ONE OF THE most socially visible deviations from our conduct norms is the taking of human life by intentional murder or by voluntary manslaughter.[1] Like all human behavior, this kind of deviation must be viewed in terms of the cultural context from which it springs. De Champneuf,[2] Guerry,[3] Quetelet[4] early in the nineteenth century, and Durkheim[5] later, led the way toward emphasizing the necessity to examine *physique sociale*, or social phenomena characterized by "externality," if the scientist is to understand or interpret crime, suicide, prostitution, and other deviant behavior. Without promulgating a sociological fatalism, analysis of broad macroscopic correlates in this way may obscure the dynamic elements of the phenomenon and result in the ecological fallacy to which Selvin[6] refers. Yet, because of wide individual variations, the clinical, idiosyncratic approach does not necessarily aid in arriving at Weber's *Verstehen*, or meaningful adequate understanding of regularities, uniformities, or patterns of interaction. And it is this kind of understanding

REPRINTED with the permission of the authors and the publisher from Marvin E. Wolfgang and Franco Ferracuti, "Subculture of Violence: An Interpretive Analysis of Homicide," *International Annals of Criminology* (1962, 1er Semestre), 1-9.

Paper presented at the 1960 Annual Meeting of the American Sociological Association, New York, August 29-31, 1960.

we seek when we examine either deviation from, or conformity to, the normative structure.[7]

Confronted with descriptive and test statistics, with validated hypotheses and some confirmed replications of propositions regarding patterns in criminal homicide reported in recent research,[8] interpretive analysis is now required. A criminological contribution to such an analysis must seek to examine the value system, or conduct norms, of those segments of the community that contribute most disproportionately to the incidence of this form of violent deviation from the legal norms. In *Suicide*,[9] Durkheim's emphasis on "anomie" and the "degree of integration" of the group to which the individual belongs, and in *Culture Conflict and Crime*[10] Sellin's discussion of conduct norms, conflict of norms, and the "resistance potential" of norms, provide probably the most fruitful direction of analysis for theoretical interpretation of deviation that takes the form of homicide.

There are two common inherent dangers in interpretive analysis: (A) the danger of going beyond the confines of empirical data collected in response to some stated hypothesis;[11] and (B) the danger of interpretation that produces generalizations emerging inductively from the data and that results in tautologous reasoning.[12] Relative to the first type of danger, the social scientist incurs the risk of "impressionistic," "speculative" thinking, or of using previous peripheral research and trying to link them to his own data by theoretical ties that often result in knotted confusion calling for further research. Relative to the second danger, the limitations and problems of tautologies are too well known to elaborate. We are suggesting that these two approaches to interpretation be combined in small degrees that do not compound the fallacies or dangers of both, but that unite the benefits of each. Let us see how and where this leads us with respect to an interpretive analysis of criminal homicide as a form of extreme deviation. We shall try to stay within the limits imposed by the empirical social facts, yet not become lost in speculative reasoning that combines accumulated, but unrelated, previously known facts for which there is no empirically supportive link.

There are also two basic kinds of criminal homicide: (A) premeditated, felonious, intentional murder;[13] (B) slaying in the heat of passion, or killing as a result of intent to do harm but without intent to kill.[14] A slaying committed by one recognized as psychotic, legally insane, or by a psychiatrically designated abnormal subject involves clinical deviates who are generally not held responsible for their behavior, and who, therefore, are not considered culpable. We are eliminating these cases from our present discussion.

Probably less than 5 per cent of all known homicides are premeditated, planned intentional killings, and the individuals who commit them are most likely to be episodic offenders who have never had prior contact with the criminal law. Because they are rare crimes often planned by rationally functioning individuals perhaps they are more likely to remain undetected. We believe that a type of analysis different from that presented here might be applicable to these cases.[15]

## EMERGENT THEORY OF A SUBCULTURE OF VIOLENCE

Our major concern is with the bulk of homicide (about 90 per cent of the Philadelphia cases)—the passion crimes, the violent slayings that are not premeditated or psychotic manifestations. Like Cohen[16] who was concerned principally with most delinquency that arises from the "working class" ethic, so we are focusing on the preponderant kind of homicide.

These related to frustration-aggression, general ecologic correlates, and anomie are not entirely satisfactory in explaining patterns in criminal homicide. The causal nexus between frustration and aggression that ends in homicide has not been specified and the different reactions to frustration of human subjects have not been accounted for. Ecology performs a valuable service but only inferentially points to the importance of the normative structure. Anomie, whether defined as the absence of norms (which is doubtful conceptualism), the conflict of norms (either normative goals or means),[17] or the redefinition by Powell as "meaningless,"[18] does not coincide with empirical evidence on homicide. The concept of anomie would have to postulate that those individuals with a "marginal man" status, who harbor psychic anomie that reflects (or causes) social anomie, have the highest rates of homicide. Data reject this contention. Anomie as culture conflict, or conflict of norms, suggests that there is one segment (the prevailing middle-class value system) of a given culture whose value system is the antithesis of, or in conflict with, another smaller segment of the same culture. This conceptualism of anomie is a useful tool for referring to subculture as ideal types, or mental constructs. But to transfer this normative conflict approach from the social to the individual level, theoretically making the individual a repository of culture conflict, again does not conform to the patterns of known psychological and sociological data. Such an approach would be forced to hypothesize that socially mobile individuals and families would be most frequently involved in homicide, or that persons moving from a formerly embraced subvalue system to the predominant communal value system would commit this form of violent deviation in greatest numbers. Not only is there logical inconsistency in this position, but there are no homicide data that show high rates among persons manifesting higher social aspirations in terms of occupational or other forms of mobility.

That there is a conflict of value systems we agree: that is, there is a conflict between a prevailing culture value and some subcultural entity. But commission of homicide among those actors from the subculture at variance with the prevailing culture cannot be explained in terms of frustration due to failure to attain normative goals of the latter, in terms of inability to succeed with normative procedures (means) for attaining those goals, nor in terms of an individual psychological condition of anomie. There is a preponderance of homicide, or highest rates of homicide, among a relatively homogeneous subcultural group in any large urban community. The value system of this group, we are contending, constitutes a *subculture of violence*. One of us has only briefly alluded to this concept in *Patterns in Criminal Homicide*.[19] If there exists a subculture of violence (and we shall attempt to show that empirical data indicate its existence), then we must further propose that the greater the degree of integration of the individual into this subculture the higher the likelihood that his behavior will often be violent; or, we may assert that there is a direct relationship between rates of homicide and the degree of integration of the subculture of violence to which the individual belongs.[20]

The Philadelphia homicide data indicate significantly[21] high rates among certain socially meaningful groups: males (10.2), nonwhites (24.6), and the age group 20–24 (12.6).

Moreover, over 90 per cent of all offenders are from the lower socio-economic classes. Similar figures can be found for other societies in many countries. Inductive reasoning emerging out of these data suggests that because some groups have significantly higher rates of homicide than do others, the existence of a subculture of violence must be significantly more obvious among the former. For example, Negroes, as a socially visible (if not genetically identifiable) ethnic group have significantly higher rates of homicide than do whites. When we approach a variety of social variables in terms of increasing specificity of the homogeneity, we find that the rate of homicide rises in certain race-sex-age-specific groups; and this fact in turn suggests an equivalent rise in the value of violence found in the subculture from which these groups emerge. The single race-sex-age group with the highest rate of homicide is among Negro males aged 20–24, whose rate is 92.5 compared to 24.6 for all Negroes and 1.8 for all whites. We suggest that by identification of groups with the highest rates of homicide we shall find the most intense degree of a subculture of violence; and having focused on this group we shall subsequently be required to examine the value system of this subculture, the importance of human life in the scale of values, the kinds of expected reactions to certain types of stimuli, the perceptual differences in the evaluation of the stimuli, the general personality structure, etc. In the original study it has been pointed out that:

. . . the significance of a jostle, a slightly derogatory remark, or the appearance of a weapon in the hands of an adversary are stimuli differentially perceived and interpreted by Negroes and whites, males and females. Social expectations of response in particular types of social interaction result in differential "definitions of the situation." A male is usually expected to defend the name and honor of his mother, the virtue of womanhood . . . and to accept no derogation about his race (even from a member of his own race), his age, or his masculinity. Quick resort to physical combat as a measure of daring, courage, or defense of status appears to be a cultural expression, especially for lower socio-economic class males of both races. When such a culture norm response is elicited from an individual engaged in social interplay with others who harbor the same response mechanism, physical assaults, altercations, and violent domestic quarrels that result in homicide are likely to be common. The upper-middle and upper social class value system defines and codifies behavorial norms into legal rules that often transcend subcultural mores, and considers many of the social and personal stimuli that evoke a combative reaction in the lower classes as "trivial." Thus, there exists a cultural antipathy between many folk rationalizations of the lower class, and of males of both races, on the one hand, and the middle-class legal norms under which they live, on the other.[23]

We cannot "prove" the existence of a subculture of violence save by examination of the social groups and of the individuals that experience highest rates of violent manifestations. This need not be, of course, confined to the study of one national or ethnic group. On the contrary, the existence of a subculture of violence could perhaps receive even non-cultural confirmation. We have used criminal homicide as the most acute and highly reportable example of this type of "proof," limiting our analysis, at this stage, to the sociological data. Some circularity of thought is here employed for purposes of maintaining logical consistency, because we are using homicide rates to specify our dependent factor (homicide), and also to infer our independent factor(s), the existence of a subculture of violence. Highest rates of rape, aggravated assaults, persistency in arrests for assaults (recidivism) among these same groups with high rates of homicide are, however, empirical addenda to the contention of a subculture of violence. Residential propinquity of these same groups reenforces the socio-psychological impact of integration of this subculture, and Sutherland's thesis of "differential association,"[24] or a psychological reformulation of the same theory in terms of learning process could be effectively employed to describe more fully this impact in its intensity, duration, repetition frequency. The more thoroughly integrated the individual is into this subculture, the more intensely he embraces its proscriptions of behavior, its conduct norms and integrates them in his personality structure. Thus, ready access to weapons may become essential for protection against others in this milieu who respond in similarly violent ways, and the carrying of knives or other protective devices becomes a common symbol of willingness to participate in and to expect violence, and to be ready for its retaliation. The degree of integration may be measured partly by resort to public records of contact with the law—the codified norms on the opposite end of a continuum from violence to nonviolence. Thus, the higher arrest rate among the groups that form the subculture of violence, particularly high rates of assault crimes and high rates of recidivism for assault crimes, indicate allegiance to the values of violence.

Thus, overt physical violence becomes a common sub-culturally expected response to certain stimuli. However, it is not merely rigid conformity to the demands and expectations of other persons, as Henry and Short[25] suggest, that results in the high possibility of homicide. Considerable conformity of middle-class families to the value system of their social group is a widely discussed contemporary topic. Our concern is with the value of violence that is an integral component of the subculture which experiences high rates of homicide. It is the conformity to this value, as a result of its integration in the personality structure of the subject, and not rigid conformity per se to the expectations of others, that gives important meaning to the subculture of violence.

If violence is a common subcultural response to certain stimuli, there must exist penalties for deviation from *this* norm. The comparatively non-violent individual may be ostracized,[26] but if social interaction must occur because of residential propinquity, he is most likely to be treated with disdain or indifference. One previously considered a member of the ingroup who has rebelled or retreated from the subculture is now an outgroup member, a possible threat, and one to avoid. Alienation or avoidance takes him out of the normal reach of most homicide attacks that are highly personalized offenses occurring with greatest frequency among friends, relatives, and associates. If social interaction continues, however, the deviant from the subculture who fails to respond to a potentially violent situation may find himself a victim of an adversary who conforms to the violence value.

It is not farfetched to suggest that a whole culture may accept the violence value, demand or encourage adherence to it, and penalize deviation. During periods of war the whole nation accepts the principle of violence against the enemy. The non-violent citizen turned soldier adopts the value as an intimately internalized re-enforcement for his rationalization to kill. This is, of course, selective killing of an enemy, and in this respect is different from most homicide. But criminal homicide is also "selective," not discriminate slaying. There is abundant literature showing the intra-group nature of the homicide drama. And as in combat on the front lines where the "it-was-either-him-or-me" situation arises, there are similar attitudes and reactions among participants in homicide. The original study on the Philadelphia subjects found that 65 per cent of the offenders and 47 per cent of the victims had a previous police record of arrest. Here, then, is a situation not unlike that of individual combat which two individuals committed to the value of violence come together, and in which chance often dictates the identity of the slayer and of the slain. On the other hand, the peaceful non-combatant in both sets of circumstances is penalized because of the allelomimetic behavior of the group supporting violence by his being ostracized as an outgroup member and is segregated (imprisoned, in wartime, as a conscientious objector). If he continues to be involved in social interaction (in the public street or on the front line of combat) with the culture of violence, he may fall victim to the shot or stab from one who embraces the value of violence.

The internal need for aggression and the readiness for the use of violence of the individual who belongs to a subculture of violence must find their psychological foundation in personality traits and in attitudes which can, through careful studies, be assessed in a way leading to a differential psychology of these subjects. Psychological tests have been repeatedly employed to study the differential characteristics of criminals and, if the theoretical frame of reference of acceptance of a subculture of violence is used, it will be possible to sharpen their discriminatory power. The fact that a subject belongs to a specific subculture (in our case, a deviant one), defined by the ready use of violence, will, among other consequences, cause the subject to adopt a differential perception of the environment and of its stimuli. The variations in the surrounding world, the continuous challenges and daily frustrations which are faced and solved by the adaptive mechanism of the individual, have a greater chance of being perceived and reacted upon, in a subculture of violence, as menacing, aggressive stimuli, which calls for immediate defense and counter-aggression. This hypothesis lends itself to objective study through appropriate psychological methodologies. The work of Stagner[27] on industrial conflict exemplifies a similar approach in a different field. This perceptual approach is of great importance in view of the studies on the physiology of aggression, which seem to prove, in all cases, the need of outside stimulation in order to elicit aggressive behavior.[28]

The individual, clinical approach to the study of criminals, as proposed by Di Tullio,[29] may, through inclusive and prolonged examination of single offenders belonging to a subculture of violence, enlarge the nosography of this group, at the same time establishing a sharper differentiation between its components and the psychopathological cases. For this latter group, the subcultural factors related to violence and aggression may also play a determining role in the type of psychopathological symptoms and in the canalizations of abnormal reactions towards criminal behavior.

## SUMMARY AND CONCLUSION

This paper has briefly outlined a theory of the subculture of violence as an interpretive analysis of empirical data that describe a recognized form of social deviation—namely, criminal homicide. The deviation is from an accepted, prevailing legal and communal norm that places high value on human life and non-violent behavior. The presence in society of a subculture of violence has been subsumed from the significantly high rates of homicide among particular groups. The concomitance of meaningfully related variables to this subculture strengthens the contention of its existence. The more integrated this subculture is, the more deeply internalized in the individual is the value of violence. Hence, an expected pattern of violent action and reaction often makes non-violence, in specifically defined situations, a form of deviation from the subculture and results in the ban of penalties similar in type, if not in specific form, to those found in penalties attached to deviation from the larger societal norms.

We have not attempted to explain the cause of the subculture of violence. Such an endeavor undoubtedly involves analysis of social class and race relations that would include residential, occupational, and other social forms of discrimination and cultural isolation as important factors. Some consideration of role theory, reference groups, and particularly child-rearing practices that employ physical punishment and promote early overt aggressive patterns[30] would aid the search for causal factors and remedial methods. At this point

we are suggesting that further probing analysis of the identified subculture of violence as a meaningful concept in understanding homicide and other assaultive crimes would be most
productive if it focused on the creation and description of the
value system of this subculture.

Dispersion of the group that shares the subcultural violence value should weaken the value. Through wider economic
opportunities, freedom of residential mobility, etc., integration of the group members into the larger society and its
predominant value system should function to destroy or at
least to mitigate the subculture of violence. In the correctional
environment, the treatment program, especially when using
individual or group psychotherapy, should try to counterbalance or to eliminate the allegiance of the subject to the
subculture of violence and his differential perspective of the
world.[31]

# Notes

# CRIMINAL HOMICIDE AND THE SUBCULTURE OF VIOLENCE

*Marvin E. Wolfgang*

1. Howard Harlan, "Five Hundred Homicides," *Journal of Criminal Law and Criminology* (1950), 40:736-752.

2. Marvin E. Wolfgang, *Patterns in Criminal Homicide*, Philadelphia: University of Pennsylvania Press, 1958.

3. J. L. Gillin, *The Wisconsin Prisoner*, Madison: University of Wisconsin Press, 1946.

4. This generalization about age and homicide appears in almost every sociological study. For example, see the following:

   Ralph S. Banay, "A Study of 22 Men Convicted of Murder in the First Degree," *Journal of Criminal Law and Criminology* (July, 1943), 34:106-111, p. 110.

   R. C. Bensing and O. J. Schroeder, *Homicide in an Urban Community*, Springfield, Ill.: Charles C Thomas, 1960.

   H. C. Brearley, *Homicide in the United States*, Chapel Hill: University of North Carolina Press, 1932, pp. 78-79.

   J. Cassidy, "Personality Study of 200 Murderers," *Journal of Criminal Psychopathology* (1941), 2:296-304, p. 297.

   J. V. De Porte and E. Parkhurst, "Homicide in New York State. A Statistical Study of the Victims and Criminals in 37 Counties in 1921-30," *Human Biology* (1935), 7:47-73, p. 57.

   L. I. Dublin and Bessie Bunzel, "Thou Shalt Not Kill: A Study of Homicide in the United States," *Survey Graphic* (March, 1935), 24:127-131, p. 128.

   Evelyn Gibson and S. Klein, *Murder*, London: H. M. Stationery Office, 1961, pp. 24-27.

   Andrew F. Henry and James F. Short, Jr., *Suicide and Homicide*, Glencoe, Ill.: The Free Press, 1954, pp. 88-89.

   Frederick L. Hoffman, *The Homicide Problem*, Newark, N.J.: The Prudential Press, 1925, p. 23.

   J. J. Kilpatrick, "Murder in the Deep South," *Survey Graphic* (October, 1943), 32:395-397, p. 396.

   Stuart Palmer, *A Study of Murder*, New York: Thomas Y. Crowell Co., 1960.

   Otto Pollak, *The Criminality of Women*, Philadelphia: University of Pennsylvania Press, 1950, p. 156.

   *Royal Commission on Capital Punishment, 1949-1953 Report*, London: H. M. Stationery Office, 1953, pp. 308-309.

   Saverio Siciliano, "Risultati preliminari di un'indagine sull' omicidio in Danimarca," *La Scuola Positiva* (1961), 4:718-729, p. 723.

   Hans von Hentig, *Crime: Causes and Conditions*, New York: McGraw-Hill, 1947, p. 115.

   Terence Morris and Louis Blom-Cooper, "Murder in Microcosm," *The Observer* (1961), pp. 3-26.

5. There is no need to document this generalization about sex and homicide. Every study known reports this fact.

6. Veli Verkko, *Homicides and Suicides in Finland and Their Dependence on National Character*, Copenhagen: G. E. C. Gads Forlag, 1951, pp. 51-57. For further comments on Verkko's "static and dynamic laws" relative to sex and homicide, see Wolfgang, *Patterns in Criminal Homicide*, pp. 61-64.

7. There are some exceptions, of course, to this generalization, but the fact that children under 14 who kill constitute a statistical deviancy from the mean, median and mode renders them more vulnerable to the social machinery that requires their being examined for biopsychological and psychiatric abnormalities.

8. Enrico Morselli, *Il suicidio*, Milano: Dumolard, 1879.

9. Verkko, *Homicides and Suicides in Finland and Their Dependence on National Character*, Chapter XV, pp. 145-162.

10. Henry and Short, *Suicide and Homicide*. For further discussion of these twin phenomena, major sources include Emile Durkheim, *Suicide*, Glencoe, Ill.: The Free Press, 1951; Enrico Ferri, *L'Omicidio*, Torino: Fratelli Bocca, 1895; and Enrico Altavilla, *Il Suicidio*, Napoli: Alberto Morano, 1932.

11. Wolfgang, *Patterns in Criminal Homicide*, pp. 36-39.

12. A bibliographical compilation and discussion of these self-reporting studies appears in Robert H. Hardt and George E. Bodine, *Development of Self-Report Instruments in Delinquency Research*, Syracuse, N.Y.: Youth Development Center, Syracuse University, 1965. Another recent listing with additional data appears in James F. Short, Jr., and Fred L. Strodtbeck, *Group Process and Gang Delinquency*, Chicago, Ill.: University of Chicago Press, 1965.

13. Nils Christie, Johs. Andenaes, and Sigurd Skirbekk, "A Study of Self-Reported Crime," in *Scandinavian Studies in Criminology*, Vol. I, London: Tavistock, 1965, pp. 86-116.

14. Kerstin Elmhorn, "Study in Self-Reported Delinquency among School Children in Stockholm," *Scandinavian Studies in Criminology*, Vol. I, London: Tavistock, 1965, pp. 117-146.

15. Enrico Ferri, *L'Omicidio*, pp. 712-719.

16. Brearley, *Homicide in the United States*, pp. 43-45, relative to education.

17. Bensing and Schroeder, *Homicide in an Urban Community*, pp. 119-157.

18. Kaare Svalastoga, "Homicide and Social Contact in Denmark," *American Journal of Sociology* (1956), 62:37-41.

19. Terence Morris and Louis Blom-Cooper, *A Calendar of Murder*, London: Michael Joseph, Ltd., 1963.

20. Verkko, *Homicides and Suicides in Finland and Their Dependence on National Character*.

21. C. H. S. Jayewardene, "Criminal Homicide. A Study in Culture Conflict," Ph.D. Thesis, University of Pennsylvania, 1960; "Criminal Cultures and Subcultures," *The Probation and Child Care Journal* (June, 1963), 2:1-5; "Criminal Homicide in Ceylon," *The Probation and Child Care Journal* (January, 1964), 3:15-30. Cf. Herbert Bloch, "Research Report on Homicide, Attempted Homicide and Crimes of Violence," *Colombo, Ceylon Police Report,* 1960; Edwin D. Driver, "Interaction and Criminal Homicide in India," *Social Forces* (1961), 40:153-158.

22. Arthur Wood, "A Socio-Structural Analysis of Murder, Suicide, and Economic Crime in Ceylon," *American Sociological Review* (1961), 26:744-753; *Crime and Aggression in Changing Ceylon,* Transactions of the American Philosophical Society, New Series, Vol. 51, Part 8, December, 1961. For an earlier study in Ceylon, see J. H. Straus and M. A. Straus, "Suicide, Homicide and Social Structure in Ceylon," *American Journal of Sociology* (1953), 58:461-469.

23. Miguel E. Bustamante and Miguel Angel Bravo, "Epidemiologia del homicidio en Mexico," *Higiene* (1957), 9:21-33. Also, Paul Friedrick, "Assumptions Underlying Tarascan Political Homicide," *Psychiatry* (1962), 25:315-327.

24. A. M. Lamont, "Forensic Psychiatric Practice in South African Mental Hospital," *South Africa Medical Journal* (1961), 35:833-837.

25. Aldo Franchini and Francesco Introna, *Delinquenza minorile,* Padova: Cedman, 1961, pp. 611-618.

26. Homicide death rates for countries reporting to the United Nations appear in order from highest to lowest as follows:

| RATE | COUNTRY | YEAR |
|------|---------|------|
| 34.0 | Colombia | 1960 |
| 31.1 | Mexico | 1958 |
| 28.8 | Nicaragua | 1959 |
| 21.2 | South Africa | 1959 |
| 10.8 | Burma | 1959 |
| 9.9 | Aden Colony | 1956 |
| 9.8 | Guatemala | 1960 |
| 6.1 | Turkey | 1959 |
| 5.9 | Panama | 1960 |
| 5.3 | Puerto Rico | 1959 |
| 5.3 | St. Vincent | 1955 |
| 4.9 | Chile | 1957 |
| 4.6 | Uruguay | 1955 |
| 4.6 | Trinidad/Tobago | 1960 |
| 4.5 | United States | 1960 |
| 4.4 | Nigeria | 1960 |
| 4.3 | Ceylon | 1959 |
| 3.9 | Dominican Republic | 1955 |
| 3.2 | Costa Rica | 1960 |

| RATE | COUNTRY | YEAR |
|------|---------|------|
| 3.0 | Channel Islands | 1959 |
| 3.0 | Reunion | 1956 |
| 2.9 | Finland | 1960 |
| 2.7 | Bulgaria | 1960 |
| 2.6 | North Borneo | 1960 |
| 2.5 | Barbados | 1960 |
| 2.3 | United Arab Republic | 1958 |
| 2.2 | Peru | 1959 |
| 2.1 | Poland | 1959 |
| 1.9 | Japan | 1960 |
| 1.8 | Fed. Rep. of Germany–West Berlin | 1959 |
| 1.8 | Singapore | 1960 |
| 1.7 | France | 1960 |
| 1.6 | Hungary | 1960 |
| 1.5 | Australia | 1960 |
| 1.5 | Greece | 1960 |
| 1.4 | Canada | 1960 |
| 1.4 | Italy | 1959 |
| 1.2 | Austria | 1960 |
| 1.2 | Jordan | 1960 |
| 1.1 | New Zealand | 1960 |
| 1.0 | Hong Kong | 1960 |
| 0.9 | Mauritius ex. dep. | 1960 |
| 0.9 | Northern Ireland | 1960 |
| 0.9 | Portugal | 1960 |
| 0.9 | Switzerland | 1959 |
| 0.8 | Spain | 1959 |
| 0.7 | Belgium | 1959 |
| 0.7 | Ryukyu Islands | 1960 |
| 0.7 | Scotland | 1960 |
| 0.7 | Sweden | 1959 |
| 0.6 | England/Wales | 1960 |
| 0.6 | Iceland | 1959 |
| 0.6 | Luxembourg | 1960 |
| 0.6 | Sarawak | 1958 |
| 0.5 | Cape Verde Islands | 1959 |
| 0.5 | Denmark | 1959 |
| 0.5 | Norway | 1959 |
| 0.4 | British Guiana | 1958 |
| 0.3 | Malta/Gozo | 1960 |
| 0.3 | Netherlands | 1960 |
| 0.2 | Ireland | 1960 |

Item BE50–E964, E965, E980–E999, from *Demographic Yearbook,* Thirteenth Issue, New York: United Nations Publication, 1961, pp. 398–471.

27. Donald R. Cressey, *Other People's Money,* Glencoe, Ill.: The Free Press, 1953.

28. Robert K. Merton, *Social Theory and Social Structure,* rev. ed., Glencoe, Ill.: The Free Press, 1957, esp. Chapters 4 and 5.

29. Richard Cloward and Lloyd Ohlin, *Delinquency and Opportunity,* Glencoe, Ill.: The Free Press, 1960.

30. Marvin E. Wolfgang, *Crime and Race: Conceptions and Misconceptions,* New York: Institute of Human Relations Press, 1964, p. 31.

31. See *ibid.* both for a critique of general crime statistics by race and for a selected bibliography on criminal homicide by race.

32. Most of the studies previously cited have references to one or more of these items. Some additional studies arranged chronologically that may be consulted and that contain similar findings for specific variables are:

Albert W. Stearns, "Homicide in Massachusetts," *The American Journal of Psychiatry* (1925), 4:725-749.

Calvin F. Schmid, "Study of Homicides in Seattle," *Social Forces* (1926), 4:745-756.

A. Raven, "A Theory of Murder," *American Sociological Review* (1930), 22:108-118.

K. E. Barnhart, "A Study of Homicide in the United States," *Social Science* (1932), 7:141-159.

L. I. Dublin and Bessie Bunzel, "Thou Shalt Not Kill: A Study of Homicide in the United States," *Survey Graphic* (1935), 24:127-131.

Emil Frankel, "One Thousand Murderers," *Journal of Criminal Law and Criminology* (1939), 29:672-688.

Lewis Lawes, *Meet the Murderer,* New York: Harper & Row, 1940.

I. A. Bery and Vernon Fox, "Factors in Homicides Committed by 200 Males," *Journal of Social Psychology* (1947), 26:109-119.

Hans von Hentig, *The Criminal and His Victim,* New Haven: Yale University Press, 1948.

Harold Garfinkel, "Research Note on Inter- and Intra-Racial Homicides," *Social Forces* (1949), 27:369-381.

Howard Harlan, "Five Hundred Homicides," *Journal of Criminal Law and Criminology* (1950), 40:736-752.

Viscount Templewood, *The Shadow of the Gallows,* London: Victor Gollancz, Ltd., 1951.

Austin L. Porterfield, "Indices of Suicide and Homicide by States and Cities: Some Southern–Non-Southern Contrasts with Implications for Research," *The American Sociological Review* (1952), 57:331-338.

Henry Allen Bullock, "Urban Homicide in Theory and Fact," *Journal of Criminal Law, Criminology and Police Science* (1955), 45:565-575.

Albert Morris, *Homicide: An Approach to the Problem of Crime,* Boston: Boston University Press, 1955.

John Macdonald, *The Murderer and His Victim,* Springfield, Ill.: Charles C Thomas, 1961.

John M. Macdonald, "The Threat to Kill," *The American Journal of Psychiatry* (1963), 120:125-130.

33. For an especially keen and concise analysis of some theories about homicides, see Frank E. Hartung, *Crime, Law and Society*, Detroit: Wayne State University Press, 1965, see especially pp. 136-153 and the footnote references to this section. It should be noted that Hartung accepts the validity of the concept, subculture of violence (*ibid.*, p. 147).

That many of the social variables found to be associated with homicide are also characteristic of the offense, offenders, and victims of other assaultive crimes may be confirmed in Richard A. Peterson, David J. Pittman, Patricia O'Neal, "Stabilities in Deviance: A Study of Assaultive and Non-Assaultive Offenders," *Journal of Criminal Law, Criminology and Police Science* (1962), 53:44-48; and in David Pittman and William Handy, "Patterns in Aggravated Assault," *Journal of Criminal Law, Criminology and Police Science* (1964), 55:462-470.

Pittman and Handy conclude: "This comparison of findings concerning acts of homicide and aggravated assault indicates that the pattern for the two crimes is quite similar. Both acts, of course, are reflections of population subgroupings which tend to externalize their aggression when confronted with conflict situations" (*ibid.*, p. 470).

34. An effort was made to deal with this problem analytically in Marvin E. Wolfgang and Rolf Strohm, "The Relationship Between Alcohol and Criminal Homicide," *Quarterly Journal of Studies on Alocohol* (1956), 17:411-425.

35. For interesting comparisons between homicide in Western studies and homicide in several African tribes, see the excerpts in this volume from Paul Bohannan, ed., *African Homicide and Suicide*, Princeton, N. J.: Princeton University Press, 1960.

## A SOCIOLOGICAL ANALYSIS OF CRIMINAL HOMICIDE

### Marvin E. Wolfgang

1. Marvin E. Wolfgang, *Patterns in Criminal Homicide*, Philadelphia, Pennsylvania: University of Pennsylvania Press, 1958, pp. 413.

2. Manfred S. Guttmacher, *The Mind of the Murderer*, New York, N. Y.: Farrar, Strauss and Cudahy, 1960.

3. Stuart Palmer, *A Study of Murder*, New York, N. Y.: Thomas Y. Crowell, 1960.

4. Paul Bohannan (ed.), *African Homicide and Suicide*, Princeton, N. J.: Princeton University Press, 1960.

5. The advantages of police statistics and limitations of other sources of data for criminal homicide research have been discussed in: Thorsten Sellin, "The Basis of a Crime Index," *Journal of Criminal Law and Criminology*, (September, 1931), 22:335-356; T. Sellin, *Crime and the Depression*, New York: Social Science Research Council Memorandum, 1937, chapter 4; T. Sellin, "The Measurement of Criminality in Geographic Areas," *Proceedings of the American Philosophical Society* (April 1953), 97:163-167. For addi-

tional references, see the author's *Patterns in Criminal Homicide*, p. 12, n. 1.

6. It is obvious to any student in the field that there are many criminal offenses committed that are never reported or recorded by the public authorities. This generalization is applicable to criminal homicide as it is to other offenses. But a theoretical analysis of the social visibility of crime, or the varying degrees of high and low reportability of specific offenses, leads us to suggest that there is a relatively low ratio between offenses committed and those known to the police in cases of criminal homicide.

7. For the most part, the statistical tests involved use of the nonparametric technique of Chi-square $(X^2)$ with corrections for continuity and a probability level of $(P)$ less than .05.

8. Some recent analysis of this hypothesis has been made for Ceylon. See Cleobis Jayewardene, "Criminal Homicide: A Study in Culture Conflict," Ph.D. thesis, University of Pennsylvania, 1960.

9. Problems of analyzing the presence of alcohol in the victim and in the offender were particularly trying. In addition to Chapter 8 in the book, the reader is referred to the author's paper (with R. Strohm) for discussion of these problems in "The Relationship Between Alcohol and Criminal Homicide," *Quarterly Journal of Studies in Alcohol* (September 1956), 17:411-425.

10. See also the author's analysis of "Husband-Wife Homicides," *The Journal of Social Therapy* (1956), 2:263-271.

11. For more detailed treatment of this concept of victim-precipitation, which is increasingly becoming an important element in theoretical discussions of the poorly designated term, "victimology," see Chapter 14 in the book as well as "Victim-Precipitated Criminal Homicide," *Journal of Criminal Law, Criminology and Police Science*, (June 1957), 48:1-11.

12. "Suicide by Means of Victim-Precipitated Homicide," *Journal of Clinical and Experimental Psychopathology* (Oct.-Dec. 1959), 20:335-349.

13. John M. MacDonald, *The Murderer and His Victim*, Springfield, Ill.: Charles C Thomas, 1961.

14. In addition to Chapter 15 in the book, see also the author's "An Analysis of Homicide-Suicide," *Journal of Clinical and Experimental Psychopathology* (July-Sept. 1958), 19:208-218.

15. Cf. Edward Green, "An Analysis of the Sentencing Practices of Criminal Court Judges in Philadelphia," Ph.D. thesis, University of Pennsylvania, 1959.

16. Albert Morris, *Homicide: An Approach to the Problem of Crime*, Boston: Boston University Press, 1955.

17. The most recent theoretical statement about criminal homicide, based on data from the Philadelphia study, has been made by the author with the collaboration of Professor Ferracuti in "Subculture of Violence: An Interpretive Analysis of Homicide," paper presented before the Annual Meeting of the American Sociological

Association, Section on The Sociology of Deviation, Marshall Clinard, chairman, New York, N.Y., August 29-31, 1960.

18. Wolfgang, *Patterns in Criminal Homicide*, pp. 188-189.

## HOMICIDE IN ENGLAND

### Terence Morris and Louis Blom-Cooper

1. Criminal Statistics, 1961.

2. In the United States, for example, the rate for 1958 was 47 per million of the population.

3. The square root of the mean of the squares of the deviations of each yearly rate from their arithmetic mean.

4. 1949-53, Appendix 3, Table 1, paragraph 298.

5. *Murder*, p. 2.

6. Marvin Wolfgang. *Patterns in Criminal Homicide*, 1958.

7. *Murder*, op. cit., p. 18 passim.

8. Ibid.

9. Quoted by the Gowers Commission. Report, p. 330.

10. "The number of murders for robbery or financial gain rose from 6 a year to 12 a year after the Homicide Act, in spite of the fact that murder in the course of furtherance of theft is capital." *Murder*, op. cit. p. 41.

11. This should not, however, obscure the fact that 64 per cent of *all* murderers still have no criminal record.

## STATIC AND DYNAMIC "LAWS" OF SEX HOMICIDE

### Veli Verkko

1. In Finland, the parallism between the incidence of larcenies and burglaries and the price of grain (rye) terminated later than in other countries from which information is available, viz. not until 1898, whereas in Sweden it occurred in the 1850's. See Verkko, Veli: Kongruensen mellan rägpriset och antalet tjuvnadsbrott samt den tidigare kriminalstatistiken i Finland (The Congruence between the price of rye and the number of larcenies, and earlier criminal statistics of Finland). Nordisk Tidskrift for Strafferet 1946, p. 199 et seq.

2. The victims of infanticide are included in these figures but as their numbers, e.g. 1917–1924, fluctuated between 1 and 5 only, they do not affect the picture to any noticeable extent.

3. Both the static and the dynamic law are probably also applicable to assault and battery leading to grievous bodily harm.

4. Verkko, Veli: Biologisluontoisten tekijäin vaikutuksesta henki- ja pahoinpitelyrikollisuuteen (On the Influence of Factors of Biolog-

ical Character on Frequency of Crimes against Life, and of Assault and Battery). A statistico-criminological investigation, Helsinki 1933, p. 58.

## INTER- AND INTRA-RACIAL HOMICIDES

### *Harold Garfinkel*

1. The fact that many instances of homicide involved more than one defendant and/or victim raised certain questions about the arrangement of the data for analysis. If instances of homicide were taken, there were 673 cases. If all defendants were taken, 821 cases were available. To have used all instances as 100 percent would have entailed the use of a summary card to represent those cases where more than one defendant and/or more than one victim were involved. There were 101 such instances involving 247 defendants. The principal difficulty of following such a procedure was encountered in the problem of determining which sentence to use to represent the case. This difficulty might have been overcome by allowing the principal defendant to represent the case. The shortcomings of this procedure lay in the fact that an important intent of the study, namely, to discern differentials in the treatment of Negro and white defendants would have been lost. This was especially true in the cases involving Negroes versus whites, where, contrary to what might popularly be assumed, the sentences were not "all of a piece" but indicated by their disparity that the various offenders in a given instance had been clearly marked off from each other in the course of trial. To have used the "principal" defendant would have resulted in a picture distorted in the direction of severity of treatment given to Negroes.

Because there was only one instance in which white and Negro victims were involved—the other instances involving victims who were homogeneous as to race—the procedure was adopted of using the term case or offender to mean a defendant considered by the courts as implicated in the slaying of a given race of victim. No more cases were defined for a given multiple instance than the number of defendants.

The table [on p. 292] shows the distribution of offenders or cases by the simple or complex character of the instance. The following symbols have been used: "N" means Negro; "W" means white; "M" means male; "F" means female; "=" means versus, or considered as the slayer of; "D" means defendant; "V" means victim; "s" means a single person, D or V, involved with no other; "m" means a single person, D or V, involved with others.

2. For purposes of economy of presentation and clarity of expression the terms N=W, W=W, N=N, and W=N will be used throughout the remainder of the paper to mean, respectively, Negro versus white, white versus white, Negro versus Negro, and white versus Negro. "M" and "F" as modifiers mean respectively male and female; i.e. MN=FW means male Negro offender versus female white victim.

3. By "indictment" we mean the offense as it is defined by the Grand

|                                              | ALL | N = W | W = W | N = N | W = N |
|----------------------------------------------|-----|-------|-------|-------|-------|
| All cases                                    | 821 | 51    | 165   | 581   | 24    |
| Simple: Homogeneous as to race of D and/or V |     |       |       |       |       |
| sD = sV                                       | 574 | 21    | 99    | 441   | 13    |
| mD = sV                                       | 214 | 25    | 51    | 130   | 8     |
| sD = mV                                       | 17  | 0     | 8     | 9     | 0     |
| mD = mV                                       | 4   | 0     | 4     | 0     | 0     |
| Complex: Races of D's and/or V's were mixed  |     |       |       |       |       |
| 1 MW and 2 MN—1 MW                            | 3   | 2     | 1     | —     | —     |
| 1 MW and 1 MN—1 FW                            | 2   | 1     | 1     | —     | —     |
| 1 MW and 1 MN—1 MN                            | 2   | —     | —     | 1     | 1     |
| 1 MW and 2 MN—1 MW                            | 3   | 2     | 1     | —     | —     |
| 2 MW—2 MW and 2 MN                            | 2   | —     | —     | —     | 2a    |

a Represented as W = N because of the circumstances of the case.

Jury in its "True Bill." After the indictment has been rendered, the case is turned over to the county solicitor who is the county's prosecuting attorney. On the basis of his examination of the case he may recommend that the indictment be changed so that the offense as it is presented in court may be legally defined differently than the definition proposed by the Grand Jury. It may be that the defendant enters a plea of some kind. In any case, the term, "charge" refers to the offense as it was defined at the time that the court considered the case. Conviction refers to the offense as it was defined in the court's final judgment of the case.

4. For economy of presentation the expressions 1° and 2° are used to mean respectively "first degree murder" and "second degree murder."

5. After examining a case the solicitor may decide that an indictment of 1° is not suitable while at the same time ambiguities about the case, or legal strategies make a flat charge of 2° or manslaughter inadvisable. He may then enter the charge of "second degree murder or manslaughter as the evidence permits."

6. Under the provisions of North Carolina statutes, death is a mandatory sentence for convictions of first degree murder, while life imprisonment is mandatory for convictions of accessory before the fact. Hence it is possible to consider these two as extremes of punishment and lump them together, thus resulting in a "U" shaped distribution for N = W.

7. The relation between the offender as an object of social treatment and the way in which the object is attended to is intended here in the sense of the relation between object and "attitude" as it is described in the phenomenological researches of Edmund Husserl,

Aron Gurwitsch, Alfred Schuetz, Dorian Cairns, and others. For further elaboration the reader is referred to the following writings: Edmund Husserl, *Ideas: General Introduction to Pure Phenomenology*, translated by W. R. Boyce Gibson (New York: The Macmillan Company, 1931), pp. 212-281; Alfred Schuetz, *On Multiple Realities*, Philosophy and Phenomenological Research, v. 5, no. 4 (June, 1945), pp. 533-575.

## THE VICTIM'S CONTRIBUTION

### *Terence Morris and Louis Blom-Cooper*

1. The tremendous physical resistance of some victims of rape may indeed provoke the additional force which brings about their death. Such instances were not uncommon in wartime: see, for example, the cases of William Collins (21), a merchant seaman hanged at Durham in 1942 for the murder of a young W.A.A.F.; Charles Raymond (23), a Canadian soldier hanged at Wandsworth in 1943, who mortally injured a 22 year-old W.A.A.F. while raping her; Terence Casey (22), a private soldier, also hanged at Wandsworth in the same year for strangling a woman of 45 while attempting rape; Ernest Kempt (24), a gunner, hanged at Wandsworth in 1944 after raping a W.A.A.F. of 21; John Davidson (18), a private soldier, hanged at Walton in 1944 for strangling a woman of 27 during attempted rape; and Horace Gordon (28), a Canadian private, hanged at Wandsworth in 1945 for stabbing a girl of 18 during rape. All, except Gordon, killed by the use of bodily force during the sexual act.

2. He may use only such force as is necessary for him to exercise his legal rights. See Hodgson (1959).

3. From *Modern Love*, XLIII.

## VICTIM-PRECIPITATED CRIMINAL HOMICIDE

### *Marvin E. Wolfgang*

1. Hans von Hentig, *The Criminal and His Victim*, New Haven: Yale University Press, 1948, pp. 383-385.

2. Gabriel Tarde, *Penal Philosophy*, Boston: Little, Brown, and Company, 1912, p. 466.

3. Thomas De Quincey, *On Murder Considered as One of the Fine Arts, The Arts of Cheating, Swindling, and Murder*, Edward Bulwer-Lytton, and Douglas Jerrold, and Thomas De Quincey, New York: The Arnold Co., 1925, p. 153.

4. Baron Raffaele Garofalo, *Criminology*, Boston: Little, Brown, and Company, 1914, p. 373.

5. For an excellent discussion of the rule of provocation, from which these four requirements are taken, see: Rollin M. Perkins, "The Law of Homicide," *Jour. of Crim. Law and Criminol.*, (March-April, 1946), 36:412-427; and Herbert Wechsler and Jerome Michael, "A

Rationale of the Law of Homicide" *Columbia Law Review* (May, December, 1937), 37:701-761, 1261-1325, esp. pp. 1280-1282. A general review of the rule of provocation, both in this country and abroad, may be found in *The Royal Commission on Capital Punishment, 1949-1952 Report.* Appendix II, pp. 453-458.

6. *Ibid.,* p. 425. The term "cause" is here used in a legal and not a psychological sense.

7. In order to facilitate reading of the following sections, the *victim-precipitated* cases are referred to simply as VP cases or VP homicides. Those homicides in which the victim was not a direct precipitator are referred to as non-VP cases.

8. Of 588 victims, 228, or 39 percent, were stabbed; 194, or 33 percent, were shot; 128, or 22 percent were beaten; and 38, or 6 percent, were killed by other methods.

9. Only 550 victim-offender relationships are identified since 38 of the 588 criminal homicides are classified as unsolved, or those in which the perpetrator is unknown.

10. The diagonal line represents "killed by." Thus, Negro male/Negro male means a Negro male killed by a Negro male; the victim precedes the offender.

11. Austin L. Porterfield, and Robert H. Talbert, *Mid-Century Crime in Our Culture: Personality and Crime in the Cultural Patterns of American States,* Fort Worth: Leo Potishman Foundation, 1954, pp. 47-48.

12. Von Hentig, *op. cit.,* p. 383.

## JUSTIFIABLE HOMICIDE BY POLICE OFFICERS
### *Gerald D. Robin*

1. Rollin M. Perkins, "The Law of Homicide," *Journal of Criminal Law and Criminology,* 36 (6) (March-April, 1946), 392-97; and Melvin F. Wingersky, *A Treatise on the Law of Crimes* (Chicago: Callaghan & Co., 1958), 414-16. The common law distinction between justifiable and excusable homicide has been abandoned in many jurisdictions, all killings which are not criminal being considered as justifiable homicides.

2. For the country, excluding accidental homicides, police slayings of criminals from 1952 through 1955 constituted 3.2% of all homicides. The causes of death on which this calculation is based include: late effect of injury purposely inflicted by another person (not in war); nonaccidental poisoning; assault by firearms and explosives; assault by cutting and piercing instruments; assaults by other means; injury by intervention of police; and execution. The annual contribution of police slayings (injury by intervention of police) to these seven types of intentional violent deaths was 3.2% in 1952, 3.3% in 1953, 3.2% in 1954, and 3.1% in 1955. Calculated from: *Vital Statistics—Special Reports,* "Mortality from Each Cause: United States 1952-54," National Office of Vital Sta-

tistics, Federal Security Agency, *44* (1) February 29, 1956, p. 31. The 1955 percentage was calculated from Vol. 46, No. 1, November 6, 1956, pp. 31-2. Of 662 homicides occurring in the urban area of Greater Cleveland, Cuyahoga County, Ohio, between January 1, 1947 and December 31, 1953, 35, or 5.4% were justifiable police homicides. Robert C. Bensing and Oliver Schroeder, Jr., *Homicide in an Urban Community* (Springfield: Charles C Thomas, 1960), 1, 80. From 1948 to 1952 the Philadelphia Police Department listed 627 homicides, 14, or 2.2% of which were justifiable killings. Marvin E. Wolfgang, *Patterns in Criminal Homicide* (Philadelphia: University of Pennsylvania Press, 1958), 24. Of 739 homicides committed during 1921 and 1922 in Atlanta, Birmingham, Memphis, and New Orleans, 42, or 5.7% of the victims were shot while resisting arrest. J. J. Durrett and W. G. Stromquist, "Preventing Violent Death," *Survey*, 54 (8) (July 15, 1925), 437.

3. Of the 1438 homicides committed in Cook County, Illinois, in 1926 and 1927, 223 (15.5%) were non-criminal. These 223 non-criminal killings include 89 police slayings of criminals. It is likely that a good number of the remaining non-criminal homicides are excusable, although they are identified as justifiable. *Illinois Crime Survey* (Chicago: Blakely Printing Co., 1929), 601. In Washington, D. C., for the period 1914–1918 justifiable and excusable homicides comprised 32% of the total, 26.6% of homicides committed in Detroit in 1920, and 31.5% of those in Chicago in 1920. H. C. Brearley, *Homicide in the United States* (Chapel Hill: University of North Carolina Press, 1932), 63.

4. During this period there was a single case of the slaying of a criminal by a private citizen. A young colored man attempted to rape Barbara Willis. She screamed and her husband came to her assistance. The husband, Jerry, struck the offender in the jaw, causing him to fall down a flight of steps. Jerry then took the man back to his apartment where he continued beating him. The offender died a few days later from head injuries.

5. Since the majority of crimes committed by the V-O's were Part I offenses, it could be argued that the calculation of the Negro's contribution to the arrest picture should be restricted to Part I offenses. Such a computation reveals that 37.5% of persons arrested for Part I offenses between 1950 and 1960 were Negroes. *Uniform Crime Reports*, Federal Bureau of Investigation, United States Department of Justice, Washington, D.C., 21 (2) 1950 and 1960.

6. In 28 of the 32 cases the offenders were shot immediately following the commission of their crimes, in the course of the commission of their crimes, or in the pursuit process. In these 28 cases, therefore, there was a very brief and unbroken chain from the commission of the crime until the fatal shooting. In the remaining 4 cases the instant offenses had been committed at least a day before they were shot; however, in each of these 4 cases the offenders forcefully resisted arrest when they were approached by the officers.

7. Marvin E. Wolfgang, *Patterns in Criminal Homicide* (Philadelphia: University of Pennsylvania Press, 1958), 106–10; and Robert C. Bensing and Oliver Schroeder, *Homicide in an Urban Community* (Springfield: Charles C Thomas, 1960), 11.

8. Sylvester B. Sadler, *Criminal and Penal Procedure in Pennsylvania* (Rochester: The Lawyers' Co-Operative Publishing Co., 1903), 145.

9. Clarence Alexander, *The Law of Arrest in Criminal and Other Proceedings* (Buffalo: Dennis & Co., 1949), 488.

10. Maurice H. Brown and Ronald A. Anderson and Leonard Sarner, *Review Series Pennsylvania Law* (Philadelphia: Maurice H. Brown Law Institute, 1956), 12. A reasonable mistake may be used as a defense where death is caused in the attempt to prevent what appears to be the commission of an atrocious felony.

11. Melvin F. Wingersky, *A Treatise on the Law of Crimes*, (Chicago: Callaghan and Co.), 1958, 420. The courts have held that "life may be taken, if necessary, in effecting an arrest for a misdemeanor, or in order to prevent the escape of a person who is in custody for a misdemeanor (State v. Phillips, 119 Iowa 652, 94 N. W. 229, 67 L. R. A. 292 [1903]; State v. Garrett, 60 N. C. 144, 84 Am. Dec. 359 [1863]. The better opinion, however, is to the contrary (Handley v. State, 96 Ala. 48, 11 So. 322, 38 Am. St. Rep. 81; State v. Smith, 101 N. W. 110 [Iowa 1904]; Stephens v. Com., 20 Ky. L. Rep. 544, 47 S. W. 229)" and numerous other cases.

12. Aggravated assault and battery is defined as a misdemeanor in Pennsylvania. See Purdon's Pennsylvania Statutes Annotated, Title 18: Crimes and Offenses, section 4709, headed Aggravated Assault and Battery.

13. The seventeen cities contacted were: Miami, Dallas, Washington, D. C., Kansas City, Mo., Baltimore, Md., Chicago, Cincinnati, Seattle, Boston, Columbus, Los Angeles, New York, Pittsburgh, Akron, Buffalo, St. Paul, Milwaukee. The information requested from each was the number of justifiable police homicides in their city from 1950 through 1960, the race and age of each decedent, and whether the decedent had a previous criminal record.

14. The number of officers responsible for taking the lives of the criminals among the cities contacted by letter was not known. However, in the Philadelphia data there were 1.3 officers for each decedent. The number of decedents in each of the nine cities surveyed was multiplied by 1.3 to approximate the number of officers responsible for the killings.

15. The number of officers contributing to the death of criminals for the nation as a whole was determined as stated above.

16. This figure includes all deaths of police personnel as long as the employee was killed while performing official police duties. Therefore the rate of officers killed by criminals would be less—and perhaps considerably so—than 31.7 per 100,000 police department personnel. FBI Director J. Edgar Hoover announced that of the 71

law enforcement officers who met violent deaths in the line of duty in 1961, 34 died as a result of injuries sustained from accidents, most of which were traffic mishaps. *The Police Chief*, 29 (6) (June, 1962) 46.

17. It is recognized that certain classes of police officers are exposed to greater danger than others. However, it is equally true that for selected subclasses of other occupational groups the risk of death in the course of work is also greater.

## THE THREAT TO KILL
### *John M. Macdonald*

1. K. Svalastoga, *Am. J. Sociol.* 62:37, 1956.
2. J. M. Macdonald, *The Murderer and His Victim*, Springfield: C. C Thomas, 1961.

## THE NORMAL AND THE SOCIOPATHIC MURDERER
### *Manfred Guttmacher*

1. Paul Reiwald, *Society and its Criminals*, International University Press, New York, 1950, 107.

2. Criminal responsibility and the legal criteria for the establishment of irresponsibility on psychiatric grounds has been discussed by each of the previous Isaac Ray lecturers and the reader is referred to their published lectures for a full consideration of the subject. The excellent lectures of Professor Henry Weihofen, *The Urge to Punish*, Farrar, Straus and Cudahy, New York, 1956, are almost entirely concerned with it.

   The Durham Rule originated in Judge David Baselon's decision for the U. S. Court of Appeals of the District of Columbia on July 1, 1954, in the appeal of Monte Durham from a burglary conviction. It states in essence that if a defendant is suffering from a mental disease or defect and the alleged criminal act is adjudged to be a product of it, he is not guilty and should be committed to a psychiatric institution rather than to a penal institution. New Hampshire is the only state that had had previously a similar rule of responsibility. The M'Naghten Rule, which forms the chief basis of the rules for all of the other states and for the other Federal jurisdictions, was enunciated in the House of Lords in 1843, when the Learned Law of Judges answered questions propounded to them, growing out of the acquittal of Daniel M'Naghten of a murder charge because of insanity. The chief element of the M'Naghten Rule is the so-called right and wrong test: was the accused so mentally disordered "as not to know the nature and quality of the act he was doing, or if he did know it, that he did not know he was doing what was wrong?"

   On June 19, 1957, the General Assembly of the State of Vermont enacted a statute providing for a new test of insanity in criminal cases. It is essentially the statute which has been adopted by the

American Law Institute, in its proposed Model Penal Code. (Tentative Draft No. 4, paragraph 401) The Vermont statute states: (a) A person is not responsible for criminal conduct if at the time of such conduct as a result of mental disease or defect he lacks adequate capacity either to appreciate the criminality of his conduct or to conform his conduct to the requirement of law. (b) The terms "mental disease or defect" do not include an abnormality manifested only by repeated criminal or otherwise anti-social conduct. The terms "mental disease or defect" shall include congenital and traumatic conditions as well as disease. (Vermont Public Acts, 1957, No. 228.)

Similar legislation is being introduced in New York, Maryland, and other states.

3. Isaac Ray, *Treatise on the Medical Jurisprudence of Insanity*, 5th ed., Little Brown and Company, Boston, 1871, 289.

4. *The 1959 World Almanac* states that there were 15,980 suicides and 8,500 murders in the United States in 1957.

5. Glanville Williams, *The Sanctity of Life and the Criminal Law*, Knopf, New York, 1957, 272, and Grünhut, Max, "Murder and the Death Penalty in England," *The Annals*, 284, 1952, 158.

6. Andrew F. Henry, and James F. Short, Jr., *Suicide and Homicide*, Free Press, Glencoe, Illinois, 1954. The inverse relationship between suicide and homicide was found by Guerry in his study of mortality statistics of the French provinces from 1825 to 1830 and published in his *Essai sur la Statistique morale de la France* in 1833.

7. Twentieth Annual Report of the Department of Post Mortem Examiners of the State of Maryland. Negligence deaths from motor vehicles are not included in any of these statistics.

8. Marvin E. Wolfgang, *Patterns in Criminal Homicide*, University of Pennsylvania, Philadelphia, 1958, 272.

9. H. C. Brearley, "The Negro and Homicide," *Social Forces* 9, 1930, 247.

10. Marvin E. Wolfgang, *op. cit.*, 44.

11. Andrew F. Henry, *op. cit.*

12. Louis I. Dublin, and Bessie Bunzel, *To Be or Not to Be*, Harrison Smith and Robert Haas, New York, 1933, 381.

13. Nineteenth Annual Report of the Department of Post Mortem Examiners of State of Maryland, 1957.

14. Benjamin Malzberg, Statistical Data for the Study of Mental Disease Among Negroes in New York State, Albany, 1955, and "Mental Disease Among Negroes: An Analysis of First Admissions in New York State, 1959–51," *Mental Hygiene*, XLIII, 1959, 422.

15. Quoted in John M. Macdonald, *Psychiatry and the Criminal*, Charles C Thomas, Springfield, 1958.

16. Gregory Zilboorg, *The Psychology of the Criminal Act and Punishment*, Harcourt, Brace and Company, New York, 1954, 52.

17. Paul Schilder, "The Attitude of Murderers Toward Death," *Abnormal and Social Psyhology*, 31, 1936, 348.

18. Sheldon Glueck, and Eleanor Glueck, *Unravelling Juvenile Delinquency*, The Commonwealth Fund, New York, 1950, 162.

## THE MURDERER IN THE MENTAL INSTITUTION

*Bernard A. Cruvant and Francis N. Waldrop*

1. Saint Elizabeths Hospital is a mental institution of more than 7,000 beds, now a bureau in the Federal Security Agency. It was established by Act of Congress in 1855 under the name of The Government Hospital for the Insane. The name was changed to Saint Elizabeths Hospital by Congress in 1916. Its purpose, in the words of Dorothea Lynde Dix, who wrote the bill, was to provide "the most humane care and enlightened curative treatment of the insane of the Army and Navy of the United States and of the District of Columbia." Primarily, the hospital provides services for the District of Columbia in lieu of a "state" mental hospital. In addition, during the period of this study, patients were admitted from the entire United States and its territories, and included insane nationals abroad, insane Indian wards of the federal government, persons from the armed services, the Merchant Marine, federal prisons, and federal enclaves, and individuals accused of crimes on the high seas.

2. B. A. Cruvant, "Maximum Security and the Therapeutic Millieu," *Mental Hospitals*, June, 1952.

## PSYCHIATRIC STUDY OF A MASS MURDERER

*James A. V. Galvin and John M. Macdonald*

1. John Gilbert Graham was executed in the gas chamber of the Colorado State Penitentiary.

## THE SUDDEN MURDERER

*Joseph W. Lamberti, Nathan Blackman, and James M. A. Weiss*

1. N. Blackman, "Medical Responsibility for Juvenile Delinquency." *Postgraduate Medicine* 10:499, 1951.

2. N. Blackman, "The Effects of Group Psychotherapeutic Techniques on Community Attitudes Toward Social Maladjustment." *Jour. of Social Therapy*, 3:1957.

3. N. Blackman, "The Emotionally Shut-In Family." *Missouri Medicine* 51:102, 1954.

4. N. Black~nan, T. T. Flynn, T. P. Melican, J. G. Napoli and J. M. A. Weiss, "The Social Maladjustment Unit: A Community-Wide Approach to the Problem of Delinquent Behavior." *Amer. Jour. of Psychiatry*, 114:536, 1957.

5. D. E. Bowlus and A. M. Shotwell, "A Rorschach Study of Psychopathic Delinquency." *Amer. Jour. of Mental Defic.*, 52:23, 1947.

6. H. Cleckley, *The Mask of Sanity* (Third Edition). St. Louis: C. V. Mosby Co., 1955.

7. Committee on Nomenclature and Statistics of the American Psychiatric Association. *Diagnostic and Statistical Manual: Mental Disorders.* Washington, D.C.: The American Psychiatric Association, 1952.

8. M. A. Guttmacher, "Diagnosis and Etiology of Psychopathic Personalities." *Proc. Amer. Psychopathic Assoc.*, 1951 (p. 139).

9. B. Karpman, "Conscience in the Psychopath." *Amer. Jour. of Orthopsych.*, 18:455, 1948.

10. B. Karpman and others: "The Psychopathic Delinquent Child." *Amer. Jour. of Orthopsych.* 20:223, 1950.

11. S. Maughs, "The Psychopathic Personality—Review of the Literature." In: *Progress in Neurology and Psychiatry* (Volume XI). New York: Grune and Stratton, 1956.

12. A. H. Smykal and F. C. Thorne, "Etiological Studies of Psychopathic Personality." *Jour. of Clin. Psychol.*, 7:229, 1951.

13. R. Spitz, in: "Roundtable on the Psychopathic Delinquent Child." *Amer. Jour. of Orthopsych.*, Vol. 20, 1950.

14. J. M. A. Weiss, T. T. Flynn, R. E. Jones, T. P. Melican, J. G. Napoli, G. A. Ulett and N. Blackman, "The Social Maladjustment Study Unit: An Experiment in Community Mental Health Education." *Amer. Jour. of Public Health*, 47:1513, 1957.

# SUICIDE IN MURDERERS

## T. L. Dorpat

1. T. L. Dorpat and H. S. Ripley, *Compr. Psych.* 1:349-359, 1960.

2. M. E. Wolfgang, et. al., *J. Crim. Law, Criminol. & Police Sci.*, 53: 301–311, 1962.

3. M. S. Guttmacher, *The Mind of the Murderer*, Farrar, Straus & Cudahy, New York, 1960.

4. M. E. Wolfgang, *J. Clin. Exp. Psychopath.*, 19:208, 1958.

5. L. T. Dublin & B. Bunzel, *Survey Graphic*, 24:127, 1935.

6. G. McDermoid & E. G. Winkler, *J. Clin. Psychopath.*, 11:93–146, 1950.

7. A. I. Rabin, *Am. J. Orthopsych.*, 16:516–524, 1946.

8. R. Cavan, *Suicide*, University of Chicago Press, Chicago, 1928, pp. 254–262.

9. B. M. Cormier, *Corrective Psych. & J. Social Therapy*, V. 8, 1962.

10. A. H. Schmale, *Psychosom. Med.*, 20:259-277, 1958.

11. T. L. Dorpat & H. S. Ripley, "Object Loss and Suicide Behavior," in preparation.

12. E. R. Geleerd, *Psychoanal. Stud. Child*, 11:336, 1956.

13. F. Jones, "On Dying Together with Special Reference to Heinrich von Kleist's Suicide," in *Essays in Applied Psycho-Analysis*, The Hogarth Press, London, 1951. Vol. 1, pp. 9–15.

14. F. Jones, "An Unusual Case of Dying Together," in *Essays in Applied Psychoanalysis*, The Hogarth Press, London, 1951. Vol. II, pp. 16–21.

## PATTERNS OF HOMICIDE AMONG TRIBAL SOCIETIES IN AFRICA
### Paul Bohannan

1. Details of this case are to be found in Aidan W. Southall, *Alur Society*, Cambridge, pp. 198–199.

2. Southall, *op. cit.*, pp. 142–143.

3. Marvin E. Wolfgang, *Patterns in Criminal Homicide*, Philadelphia, University of Pennsylvania Press, 1958, pp. 218, 246.

4. *Ibid.*, pp. 46 ff.

5. Otto Pollak, *The Criminality of Women*, Philadelphia, University of Pennsylvania Press, 1950, p. 81.

6. *Ibid.*, pp. 16–19.

7. Veli Verkko, *Homicides and Suicides in Finland and their Dependence on National Character*, København, 1951, especially pp. 51–55.

8. Wolfgang, *op. cit.*, pp. 61–64.

9. Kaare Svalastoga, "Homicide and Social Contact in Denmark," *American Journal of Sociology*, LXII, No. 1, pp. 37–41.

10. Wolfgang, *op. cit.*, p. 185.

11. *Ibid.*, p. 187.

12. I have for the two African societies, combined thieves, adulterers, and sorcerers, and put them under Wolfgang's heading "halting a felon."

13. Frederick Wertham, *A Show of Violence*, Garden City, pp. 25 ff.

14. Vigil, "Patterns of Murder," a pamphlet published by the *Observer*, London, 1956.

## MURDER AND OTHER DEVIANCE IN CEYLON
### Arthur Lewis Wood

1. Robert K. Merton has said, ". . . the comparison of rates of deviance is of course at the core of any theory of anomie and deviant behavior": "Social Conformity, Deviation, and Opportunity Struc-

tures: A Comment on the Contributions of Dubin and Cloward,"
*American Sociological Review,* 24 (April, 1959), p. 187.

2. See other suggestions for relating objective conditions and psychic
processes in the analysis of deviance: David J. Bordua, "Delin-
quency Theory and Research in the United States: Major Trends
Since 1930," Department of Sociology, University of Michigan, n.d.:
Albert K. Cohen, *Delinquent Boys, The Culture of the Gang,* Glen-
coe, Illinois: The Free Press, 1955; Gwynn Nettler, "Antisocial
Sentiment and Criminality," *American Sociological Review,* 24
(April, 1959), pp. 202–208; and Dorothy L. Meier and Wendell
Bell, "Anomia and Differential Access to the Achievement of Life
Goals," *ibid.,* pp. 189–202.

3. Andrew F. Henry and James F. Short, Jr., *Suicide and Homicide:
Sociological and Psychological Aspects of Aggression,* Glencoe, Illinois: The Free Press, 1954. Quotation from page 17. "External
restraints" on all positions of low status were assumed to legitimize
both directly and psychologically other-oriented aggression in the
form of homicide. Their formulation, incorrectly predicted that low
status positions of females and of the aged in American culture
would manifest high homicide rates. The present explanation better
accounts for these and similar facts regarding suicide.

4. Thus, it is hypothesized that weak internalization of cultural norms,
not objective "external restraint," legitimizes physical aggression.
Emile Durkheim assumed absence of the "moral constitution" of a
population in his explanation of "altruistic" and "anomic" types
of homicide: Cf. *Suicide: A Study in Sociology,* Glencoe, Illinois.:
The Free Press, 1951, pp. 356–357. This formulation is compatible
with the common assessment of weak superego formation among
murderers.

5. Henry and Short explained the positive association between suicide
and high status by the absence of "external restraint" for legitimiz-
ing other-oriented aggression, with the consequent turning inward
of aggression. We suggest that higher status positions in professional, business, and bureaucratic systems are often subject to "the
demands and expectations of other persons" (objective "external
restraint"), and that expectations vis-à-vis low status persons are
often permissive. Empirically, suicide does not always increase
with status: Cf. Elwin H. Powell, "Occupation, Status, and Suicide," *American Sociological Review,* 23 (April, 1958), pp. 131–139.
Parenthetically, other-oriented aggression in the form of economic
and social sanctions and insults *is* manifested by higher status
persons; only physical aggression is minimized. Furthermore, the
psychoanalytic literature is far from unanimous in asserting that
suicide is always a symptom of self-aggression; some types are
believed to be a reaction of utter dejection, hopelessness: Cf. Edwin
S. Shneidman and Norman L. Farberow, *Clues to Suicide,* New
York: McGraw-Hill, 1957, Ch. 2. Consequently, our formulation is
that relatively high status persons subjectively experiencing external restraint or stressful situations—neither their high status
nor the absence of (objective) "external restraint" per se—is the

basis for frequent suicides. Homicide and suicide are differentiated by the subcultural normative systems of different status positions. Further speculation suggests that a weakening of norms that taboo physical assault takes place in stressful low status positions because such aggression does not seriously endanger loss of status and other types of aggression are ineffective. Conversely, physical aggression in higher status positions is dysfunctional on both counts.

6. Two additional adjacent hamlets are included with their respective villages. Two villages were selected for their high official crime rates and one for its low rate.

7. These terms are used in tables and text to distinguish them from references to samples of National Survey. "Assault" includes murder and its attempt, hurt by knife and grievous hurt—all similar to murder cases. Property offenses include "grave" crimes of theft, robbery and burglary.

8. The University of Ceylon, *The Disintegrating Village, Report of a Socio-Economic Survey*, Colombo: The Ceylon University Press Board, 1957.

9. Indian Tamils, numbering one million and the small numbers of other ethnic peoples of Ceylon are excluded from consideration here.

10. All rates in this paper are based on 100,000 population; those above are averages for five years, 1951–1955, as reported from vital statistics, recorded in the *Demographic Yearbook* of the United Nations for appropriate years. Medians are based on the 36 countries for which data are available for at least two of five years. Ceylon data are from the *Report of the Registrar-General of Ceylon on Vital Statistics* for appropriate years.

11. From 1880 to 1920 official data show that both homicide and suicide rates increased regularly, some of which is undoubtedly the effect of better reporting. Since then, there is evidence that variations in rates are not mere artifacts of enumeration: (1) Data from the same collection agency (vital statistics of the Registrar-General) show the trend in suicides to increase while for homicides it remains constant; (2) Cyclical rather than trend varitions become clear after 1920; (3) Current ecological variations are distinctly different for homicides and suicides; (4) Colombo homicide rates are relatively low, precisely the area where reporting is presumably most complete; (5) Current homicide data reported by different agencies—Police Service and Registrar-General —are very similar; (6) In the isolated Kandyan rural areas where underreporting should be greatest and where reported deaths from homicide are infrequent, the crude death rate is highest; (7) Since suicide and not homicide tends to be an urban phenomenon, it is reasonable to find an upward trend only for suicides. Unlike findings for some other countries, homicides in Ceylon apparently are inversely correlated with economic conditions, while suicides are almost unrelated to cyclical variations—data to be analyzed in subsequent publications.

12. Three-year average rates, 1954–1956, based on vital statistics by place of residence. These findings are obscured by using nation-wide categories rural-urban and using data by place of death. Consequently, above conclusions differ from those reported by Jacqueline H. and Murray A. Straus, "Suicide, Homicide, and Social Structure in Ceylon," *American Journal of Sociology*, 58 (March, 1953), Table 3, p. 465. Average rates of economic offenses presented below are based on crimes reported to police, five years, 1951–1955; a similar distribution obtains for place of residence of accused persons.

13. Preliminary evidence not presented here supports the conclusion that homicides by lower caste persons increase when the caste system is weakened.

14. Suicide data is from the National Survey for which no nonoffender sample is available. It was assumed that a comparison of suicides with homicide victims is more conservative than with a lower status criminal group; and since the initial age distributions of the two former groups were more comparable, matching of suicides and homicide victims by age eliminated fewer cases of the already small sample of suicides. Subsequently, it was discovered that identical conclusions are obtained by comparing suicides with homicides because the latter are similar to their victims.

15. A "liberal" position is taken by 92 per cent of offenders against property and only 67 per cent of offenders against persons.

16. Percentage frequencies of paired samples of suicides and homicide victims cannot be compared with paired murderers and robbers-burglars in Table 5 (see Table footnote). It may be argued that the police attributed "immoral conduct" to criminals because of their crimes or that they were charged with crime because of their known "immoral conduct." With some caution, however, the reliability of these data may be accepted for the following reasons: (1) Police officials were asked by their Inspector-General to report only substantiated information, with the consequence that these data had more "not known" answers recorded than other data of the questionnaire; (2) Local police officials who reported these data are well acquainted with the people of their districts and with the reliability of those from whom they obtained information; (3) Villages are sufficiently small to enable the conduct of their inhabitants, e.g., drinking and gambling, to be known by everyone; (4) All data of the National Survey that were comparable with those of the Village Studies produced similar conclusions; (5) The frequency of "immoral conduct" of homicides is similar to that of their victims (not significantly more as might be expected), and less than for robbers-burglars (contrary to the relative strength of sanctions toward these categories of crime); (6) Charges against these criminals had to be supported in court by the Police.

17. If a type of subjective orientation is essential for the explication of suicide rates, objective criteria of status integration as developed by Jack P. Gibbs and Walter T. Martin will fail to predict accurately: see "A Theory of Status Integration and Its Relation-

ship to Suicide," *American Sociological Review*, 23 (April, 1958), pp. 140–147.

18. From National Survey, Chi-square tests: title to no property, robbers-burglars 70 and murderers 51 per cent ($N=70$, 259, $\chi^2=7.01$, $P<.05$); unemployed, robbers-burglars 36 and murderers 17 per cent ($N=88$, 295, $\chi^2=14.69$, $P.<.05$); computations by 1 d.f. and correction for continuity.

19. Persons in positions of low status and stress do not always have homicidal reactions. The contrasting deviant behavior of assault (including murder) and property offenses is then accounted for by the intervening variable of strong achievement orientation of those in the latter category. A forthcoming publication presents data to show that this variable, in turn, often is a manifestation of different "opportunity structures." Cf. Richard A. Cloward, "Illegitimate Means, Anomie, and Deviant Behavior," *American Sociological Review*, 24 (April, 1959), pp. 164–176.

20. Murray A. Straus, "Childhood Experience and Emotional Security in the Context of Sinhalese Social Organization," *Social Forces*, 33 (December, 1954), pp. 152–160.

21. Chi-square tests for Low-country vs. Kandyan and Ceylon Tamil, respectively, for the three comparisons, among all murder cases: (1) land disputes 23 vs. 12 per cent ($N=181$, 93, $\chi^2=4.00$, 1 d.f., $P<.05$); (2) land disputes among kin 35 and nonkin 18 per cent vs. 14 and 9 per cent ($N=51$, 114 vs. 29, 55, $\chi^2=13.04$, 3 d.f., $P<.05$); (3) land disputes where assailant or victim own land 35 and neither own 13 per cent vs. 12 and 14 per cent ($N=84$, 38 vs. 51, 21, combining "own" and "neither own" for Kandyan and Ceylon Tamil, $\chi^2=13.12$, 2 d.f., $P<.05$).

## STATUS AND THE RELATIONAL SYSTEM

*Andrew F. Henry and James F. Short, Jr.*

1. There is some justification of the use of mortality statistics to index the relative incidence of homicide committed by Negroes and whites.

2. Edwin H. Sutherland, *Principles of Criminology* (Chicago: J. B. Lippincott Company, 1947), p. 120.

3. For a recent documentation of regional variations of capital crimes in the United States, see George B. Vold, "Extent and Trend of Capital Crimes in the United States," *The Annals of the American Academy of Political and Social Science*, Vol. 284 (November, 1952), pp. 1–7.

4. Adapted from U. S. Federal Bureau of Investigation, *Uniform Crime Reports for the United States and its Possessions*, Vol. XXII, No. 2 (1951) (Washington: Government Printing Office, 1952), Table 31.

5. Cf. Harry Elmer Barnes and Negley K. Teeters, *New Horizons in Criminology* (New York: Prentice-Hall, Inc., 1951), p. 128; and

Walter C. Reckless, *The Crime Problem* (New York: Appleton-Century Crofts, Inc., 1950), p. 95.

6. Sutherland, *op. cit.*, pp. 134–135.

7. Austin L. Porterfield, "Suicide and Crime in the Social Structure of an Urban Setting: Fort Worth, 1930–1950," *American Sociological Review*, XVII (June, 1952), p. 341. Alpert has used life insurance statistics of suicide and homicide rates among Ordinary and Industrial policy holders to indicate the same relationship. See Harry Alpert, "Suicides and Homicides," *American Sociological Review*, XV (October, 1950), p. 673.

8. *Uniform Crime Reports, op. cit., passim.*

9. Porterfield, *op. cit.*, p. 344 f. Recent research by Miller and Swanson bears upon Porterfield's findings. In their studies of adolescent boys in the Detroit public schools they find that the "general defensive distortions" of lower income and occupation level children are "extrapunitive," while these distortions of middle level children are "intrapunitive." See Daniel R. Miller and Guy E. Swanson, "Studies Relating Mechanisms of Defense to Levels of Income and Occupation," paper read at the annual meeting of the American Sociological Society, Berkeley, California, August 31, 1953.

10. See *Uniform Crime Reports, op. cit.*, Vol. XXI, No. 2, p. 107.

11. U. S. Bureau of the Census, *Prisoners in State and Federal Prisons and Reformatories* (Washington: Government Printing Office, 1940).

12. The proportion of men and women who are committed to prison for any given offense may of course be a function of fluctuations in other offenses. The consistency of the ratios obtained suggests that this is not true in the case under consideration. Failure to detect women in other offenses, e.g., shoplifting, may also lead to a spuriously high proportion of women offenders being imprisoned for homicide. But this may also be true of men. Regarding the incidence of homicide among women, Pollak presents evidence from the United States and from other countries pointing up the fact that "the woman who kills uses poison more often than other means" and that "they also use it more frequently than men." See Otto Pollak, *The Criminality of Women* (Philadelphia: University of Pennsylvania Press, 1950), pp. 16-19, *et passim*. Pollak stresses the fact that the use of poison as a means for perpetrating homicide, taken together with the social roles played by women in society, provides additional evidence of the greater concealment of female homicide. That is, such roles as housewife and mother, nurse, servant, and secretary, lend themselves to secrecy in the performance of many crimes, perhaps especially to homicide by way of poison.

13. Emil Frankel, "One Thousand Murders," *Journal of Criminal Law and Criminology*, XXIX (January-February, 1939), p. 684.

14. These data are not as reliable as we would wish, since the population base is the entire United States and the homicide and aggravated assault data are for only those jurisdictions reporting to the Federal Bureau of Investigation. The error introduced, how-

ever, may be assumed to be distributed randomly over the eight age groups.

15. The difference by sex in the direction of expression of aggression may also be related to psychological factors arising from dependency of children of both sexes primarily upon the mother in the early years of life. In particular, see Talcott Parsons, "The Social Structure of the Family," *The Family: Its Function and Destiny.* Ruth N. Anshen (New York: Harper and Brothers, 1949), pp. 186-88.

16. *Uniform Crime Reports, op. cit., passim.*

17. George B. Vold, "Crime in City and Country Areas," *The Annals of the American Academy of Political and Social Science,* CCXVII (September, 1941), pp. 38-45.

18. *Ibid.,* p. 41. The average rate was 1.4 per 100,000 population for the three year period, 1936–38.

19. P. A. Sorokin, C. C. Zimmerman, and C. J. Galpin, *A Systematic Source Book in Rural Sociology* (Minneapolis: University of Minnesota Press, 1930), II, pp. 266-86.

20. The negative relation tentatively established between homicide and urbanism is the first instance.

21. Calvin F. Schmid, "A Study of Homicides in Seattle, 1914 to 1924." *Social Forces,* IV (June, 1946), p. 749.

22. Howard Harlan, "Five Hundred Homicides," *The Journal of Criminal Law and Criminology,* XL (March-April, 1950), pp. 737-52.

23. Stuart Lottier, "Distribution of Criminal Offenses in Metropolitan Regions," *Journal of Criminal Law and Criminology,* XXIX (May-June, 1938), pp. 37-50.

24. A number of descriptions of underworld culture have been published. With particular reference to attitudes toward violence, see Barnes and Teeters, *op. cit.,* pp. 30 ff; also Danny Ahern, *How to Commit a Murder* (New York: Washburn Press, 1930); and B. B. Turkus and Sid Feder, *Murder, Inc.* (New York: Farrar, Straus, and Young, 1951).

25. Emile Durkheim, *Suicide,* trans. John A. Spaulding and George Simpson (Glencoe, Illinois: The Free Press, 1951), p. 354.

## SUBCULTURE OF VIOLENCE—
## A SOCIO-PSYCHOLOGICAL THEORY
*Marvin E. Wolfgang and Franco Ferracuti*

1. Marshall B. Clinard, *Sociology of Deviant Behavior,* New York: Rinehart & Company, 1958, p. 210; see also pp. 23-24.

2. For an interesting account of the contribution of M. de Guerry de Champneuf, see M. C. Elmer, "Century-Old Ecological Studies in France," *American Journal of Sociology,* 39 (July, 1933), pp. 63-70.

3. A.-M. Guerry, *Essai sur la Statistique morale de la France,* Paris, 1833.

4. A. Quetelet, *Sur l'Homme et le développement de ses facultés; essai de physique sociale,* Paris: Bachelier, 1835. For excellent summarization and interpretation of the influence of Quetelet, Guerry, and others during the early nineteenth century, see Alfred Lindesmith and Yale Levin, "The Lombrosian Myth in Criminology," *American Journal of Sociology,* 42, (March, 1937), pp. 653-671.

5. Emile Durkheim, *Suicide,* Glencoe, Illinois: The Free Press, 1951.

6. Hanan C. Selvin, "Durkheim's *Suicide* and Problems of Empirical Research," *American Journal of Sociology,* 63 (May 1958), pp. 607-619.

7. As described, for example, in Talcott Parsons, *The Social System,* Glencoe, Illinois: The Free Press, 1951, pp. 41-42.

8. Marvin E. Wolfgang, *Patterns in Criminal Homicide,* Philadelphia: University of Pennsylvania Press, 1958.

9. Durkheim, *op. cit.*

10. Thorsten Sellin, *Culture Conflict and Crime,* New York: Social Science Research Council Bulletin 41, 1938.

11. See C. Wright Mills' discussion of "grand theory," Chapter 2 in *The Sociological Imagination,* New York: Oxford University Press, 1959.

12. Critics of Freudian psychology are quick to point to this danger in that theoretical system. See Robert G. Caldwell's succinct analysis in *Criminology,* New York: The Ronald Press Co., 1956, p. 190.

13. William F. Hoffman, *Pennsylvania Criminal Law and Criminal Procedure,* 4th ed., Wynnewood, Pennsylvania: Wm. F. Hoffman, 1952, p. 121.

14. *Ibid.,* p. 112.

15. It may be profitable to study "middle class" murder—the episodic, planned, rational murder—from the same perspective that Cressey uses in examining embezzlement (Donald Cressey, *Other People's Money,* Glencoe, Illinois: The Free Press, 1953). Paraphrasing Cressey's final revised postulate and applying it to "middle class" murder, we might say: These persons conceive of themselves as having a problem which is non-shareable, are aware that this problem can be secretly resolved by violation of the middle-class norms, and are able to apply to their own conduct in that situation rationalizations which enable them to adjust their conceptions of themselves as law-abiding persons with their conceptions of themselves as slayers.

16. Albert K. Cohen, *Delinquent Boys,* Glencoe, Illinois: The Free Press, 1955.

17. Robert K. Merton, *Social Theory and Social Structure,* rev. ed., Glencoe, Illinois: The Free Press, pp. 131-194.

18. Elwin H. Powell, "Occupation, Status, and Suicide: Toward a Redefinition of Anomie," *American Sociological Review,* 23 (April, 1958), pp. 131-139.

19. Wolfgang, *op. cit.,* pp. 328-331.

20. This is different from the strength of the relational system discussed by Henry and Short in their provocative analysis (Andrew F. Henry and James F. Short, Jr., *Suicide and Homicide*, Glencoe, Illinois: The Free Press, 1954, pp. 16-18, 91-92, 124-125). Relative to the Henry and Short suggestion, see Wolfgang, *op. cit.*, pp. 278-279. The attempt of Gibbs and Martin to measure Durkheim's reference to "degree of integration" is a competent analysis of the problem. A subculture of violence integrated around a given value item or value system may require quite different indices of integration than those to which these authors refer (Jack P. Gibbs and Walter T. Martin, "A Theory of Status Integration and Its Relationship to Suicide," *American Sociological Review*, 23 (April, 1958), pp. 140-147.

21. In the original study "significant" refers to test statistics, usually non-parametric, with confidence limits at .05, or in some cases, .01.

22. Wolfgang, *op. cit.*, pp. 65-78 comparing race-sex-age-specific rates, the higher rate amount Negro males is obvious. For ages 20-24: Negro males (92.5); Negro females (12.4); white males (8.2); white females (1.2).

23. *Ibid.*, pp. 188-189.

24. Edwin H. Sutherland and Donald Cressey, *Principles of Criminology*, 5th ed., Philadelphia: Lippincott Co., 1955, pp. 74-81.

25. Henry and Short, *op. cit.*, p. 102. On this same point of conformity, see the statement of Jackson Toby, "Social Disorganization and Stake in Conformity: Complementary Factors in the Predatory Behavior of Hoodlums," *Journal of Criminal Law, Criminology and Police Science*, 48 (May-June, 1957), pp. 12-17.

26. Withdrawal from the group may be the deviant's own design and desire, or by response to the reaction of the group. Cf. Robert A. Dentler and Kai T. Erickson, "The Functions of Deviance in Groups," *Social Problems*, 7 (Fall, 1959), pp. 98-107.

27. Ross Stagner, *Psychology of Industrial Conflict*, New York: Wiley, 1956.

28. John Paul Scott, *Aggression*, Chicago: The University of Chicago Press, 1958, pp. 44-64.

29. B. Di Tullio, *Principi di Criminologia Clinica e Psichiatria Forense*, Roma: Ist. di Medicina Sociale, 1960.

30. Martin Gold, "Suicide, Homicide and the Socialization of Aggression," *American Journal of Sociology*, 63 (May, 1958), pp. 651-661. See also, Albert K. Cohen and James F. Short, Jr., "Research in Delinquent Subcultures," *The Journal of Social Issues*, 14 (1958), pp. 20-37.

31. See for a comprehensive discussion of perceptual factors in personality structure and in treatment: Robert R. Blake and G. V. Ramsey (eds.), *Perception: An Approach to Personality*, New York: Ronald Press, 1951. Also: Ross Stagner, "Le teorie della personalità," *Rassegna di Psicologia Generale e Clinica*, 2 (1957), pp. 34-48.

# INDEX